Judaism: The Classical Statement

Chicago Studies in the History of Judaism

EDITED BY

Jacob Neusner

Judaism

The Classical Statement

The Evidence of the Bavli

Jacob Neusner

The University of Chicago Press

Chicago and London

Para 37.00 9/9/86

The University of Chicago Press, Chicago 60637
The University of Chicago Press, Ltd., London

95 94 93 92 91 90 89 88 87 86   5 4 3 2 1

Library of Congress Cataloging-in-Publication Data

Neusner, Jacob, 1932–
Judaism: the classical statement.

(Chicago studies in the history of Judaism)
Bibliography / by Joseph M. Davis: p.
Includes index.
1. Talmud—Criticism, Redaction.   I. Title.
II. Series.
BM503.6.N48   1986   296.1'2506   85-28875
ISBN 0-226-57620-5

JACOB NEUSNER is University Professor and Ungerleider Distinguished Scholar of Judaic Studies at Brown University. In addition to editing and translating the 35-volume series *The Talmud of the Land of Israel,* he is the author of many books, including *Judaism: The Evidence of the Mishnah, Judaism in Society: The Evidence of the Yerushalmi,* and *Judaism and Scripture: The Evidence of Leviticus Rabbah,* all published by the University of Chicago Press.

For
CONRAD CHERRY
Director of Scholars Press

A token of thanks to the friend
of all who work hard and in good faith

A tribute to the servant of scholarship and learning
in the American humanities

A token of recognition of loyalty, respect, and
unfailing commitment

What tribute can we pay to this
splendid and dedicated man?
For his life and work
pay a tribute to all of us,
whom he serves.

Contents

Preface

The Babylonian Talmud, the last document of Judaism in its formative age—the late antiquity of the first seven centuries A.D.—defined from then to the present the classical system of Judaism. It mediated to the medieval and modern West the worldview and way of life of Israel's philosophical sages of the antique world. This book addresses two questions: first, the overall points of interest and emphasis of the text viewed whole and as a literary problem, with stress on redaction and recurrent rhetoric, and second, the testimony of the text's blatant redactional character as to the worldview of its framers—authors of the summa of Judaism. Dealing only with the literary-redactional matter, I answer the question of why the Bavli served to define Judaism from its time to ours.

Produced circa A.D. 600, the Babylonian Talmud, a systematic commentary on an earlier law code, the Mishnah, of circa A.D. 200, fills nearly five thousand pages with terse, highly stylized rhetoric. The document is important because it forms the authoritative statement of the Judaism that took shape in late antiquity and predominated until modern times. But it is interesting for a quite different reason, one relevant to people with slight interest in Judaism in particular. The Babylonian Talmud provides us with a sizable example of how a community of intellectuals (sages) with a continuous past of half a millennium proposed to say everything they wished to say about every subject, and to do so while talking about something that, to begin with, they themselves had not produced. For the document at hand tells us that through commentary on things past, a generation of intellectuals shaped a long future.

The Babylonian Talmud is interesting for a second reason as well. It presents us with a problem of how to speak intelligibly and cogently about the social vision of a massive, arcane text. That is, in the Bavli we face a problem of social description, analysis, and interpretation of a preoccupied and inner-facing document. I focus upon a literary problem of some complexity, but I mean to move from text to context, teasing out of the threads of text the warp and woof of a social fabric in which the threads are joined. If, along these

xi

same' lines, the classical writings of the church fathers had reached us in homogeneous form, adhering to a single rhetoric and making intelligible statements in accord with a single logic of discourse about matters of slight concrete substance, the cultural problem would be parallel. How so? Before us we have in a single statement what the ultimate authors claim a long line of authorities, over hundreds of years and living in two different empires, Rome and Iran, wished to say, all together and all at once. Let me offer yet another analogy. If some university faculty proposed to write what all of the Supreme Courts from John Jay and John Marshall to our own day had to say about not only the Constitution but also the Magna Charta and, also, in their commentary on that old document, said whatever they wished to say about the character of American civilization, its goals and its values, and if, furthermore, the American people were to spread over the face of the civilized world and govern their lives in accord with the unitary and homogeneous message of the (then long-ago) faculty and Courts, we should have a cultural event of the compelling curiosity and exceptional interest of the one at hand. Here the message of a long prior age is in a single moment organized and restated for long ages to come. Not many documents of antiquity or any other age accomplished so critical a social and cultural mission. But the Bavli did.

How, then, the sages at hand did their work is for us to discover. My interest is in a very specific problem of the larger task of the social and cultural reading of a literary monument. The problem is somewhat technical and requires a sequence of probes, recorded in charts throughout the book. But the inquiry bears broad interest as well as implications for a variety of long-standing issues. Let me explain.

The Bavli is an exceedingly complex document. Normally people read it in such a way as to underline its fissiparous character. They contemplate phrases and words, reaching upward to entire sentences. Then they stop. So among the generality of talmudists and pious students, the Bavli expresses brief and episodic messages. Because they find little evidence of order and organization in the text, so they frame the problematic of the text in small-scale terms—philology on the one side and exegesis of phrases on the other. Complementing that approach, they absorb the Bavli into a framework encompassing the entirety of rabbinic writings of late antiquity and the definitive Middle Ages. They leap from small detail to great construct, ignoring the middle ranges of text and context. Everything regarded as authoritative addresses common problems of law and theology, viewed out of social context and perceived ahistorically. So the canon of Judaism, ancient, medieval, and even modern, first is dissected into its constituent words and phrases—even sentences. Then it is reassembled in universal categories of law and theology, each with its definitive classifications. For this larger purpose, the exegetical approach, treating all words and phrases as part of a larger conversation on perennial issues, works well. By obliterating the lines of structure imposed by the covers and bindings of books, treating everything as part of one thing, the lawyers and theologians impose other, to them self-evidently valid lines of structure. Within such a framework, asking about the Bavli in particular produces uncomprehending silence. The Bavli does not exist in particular, only as part of a larger and eternal conversation. That conversation leaps over centuries, ignoring the limits of time and location, seeking truth—torah in the mythic language of the system—wherever and whenever it is to be found. That same ahistorical and anti-contextual approach to the hermeneutics of Judaism in its canon of course characterizes modern and contemporary scholars who pursue philological and text-critical questions. The received method endures for them.

In my view the various documents of the canon of Judaism produced in late antiquity demand a different hermeneutic altogether—one that is secular at its foundation. For it is a hermeneutic shaped to teach us how to read the texts at hand in the way in which we read any other text bearing cultural and social insight. Let me spell out what I think is at issue. The three key words of the inherited hermeneutic are *continuity, uniqueness,* and *survival.* Scholars view the texts as continuous with one another. They seek what is unique in the system formed by the texts as a whole. With the answer, the unique, they propose to explain the survival of Israel, the Jewish people. The principal slogan of the proposed hermeneutic, by contrast, invokes the words *description, analysis,* and *interpretation.* I am trying to learn how to describe the constituents of the canon, viewed individually, each in its distinctive context. I wish to discover appropriate analytical tools, questions to lead me from description of one text to comparison and contrast between two or more texts of the canon. Only at the end do I address the question of interpretation of how all of the texts of the canon at hand flow together into a single statement, a "Judaism."

Within the inherited hermeneutic the existence of the group defines the principal concern, an inner-facing one, hence the emphasis on uniqueness in quest of explanation of survival. Within the proposed hermeneutic, by contrast, the existence of the group does not frame the issue. It is taken for granted. The problematic emerges from without. What I want to know is not how and why the group survived. I want to know how to describe the society and culture contained within, taken as a given, an enduring worldview and way of life, expressed by the artifacts in hand. The texts therefore are to be viewed one by one, each in context, then all together and all at once.

Since I begin with a question bearing no meaning for earlier approaches to the text at hand, the generative problematic of this book and of the six prior books of which it forms the conclusion will require different exercises from those with which people are familiar. They will yield different results. The question at hand addresses the Bavli in particular: How shall I describe the document as a whole? How shall I interpret, as artifacts of a textual community, the literary formalities of the Bavli's structure and redaction? The answer derives from a study of relationships. How so? When I turned to a colleague whose field is remote from mine with the question, "What have you always wanted to know about the Bavli but have been afraid to ask?" he responded without a moment of hesitation, "How it relates to the Yerushalmi." Since, while following scholarship in a number of areas, this colleague works in modern and contemporary Christian and Jewish thought, he provided me with exactly the perspective that I required. I see analogy to portray relationship.

The Bavli did not emerge alone and all by itself. It flowed from three or four centuries of continuous tradition, beginning with the Mishnah and passing through a sequence of documents devoted to the exegesis of the Mishnah. We cannot pretend that, wholly on its own, the Bavli came to expression and realization. Then we must find out in what ways the Bavli relates to what had gone before. That question will strike scholars familiar with the literature as entirely routine. For more than a hundred years work on the way in which the authors of one document state a position of their own on detailed materials received and revised from an earlier one has gone forward. But I do not know any inquiry into how one document, viewed whole and complete, relates to those that came before. Comparing merely the contents of one with the contents of the other, after all, hardly will have surprised the long centuries of exegetes of a harmonious Judaism, a system expressed everywhere and equally in all of the documents of the canon. So to ask why and how the Bavli relates to the Yerushalmi in detail will not prove alien. But the question about comparing one whole to another whole—that is quite another matter.

Why the Yerushalmi in particular? The answer derives from two distinct facts.

First, the authors of both the Yerushalmi and the Bavli organize their materials around the exegesis of the Mishnah. The materials they produced, moreover, fall into essentially the same taxonomic framework. Accordingly, out of all of the documents of the canon of Judaism of late antiquity, the Yerushalmi and the Bavli stand closest to the source on which both comment and also to one another.

Second, when I investigated the formation of critical ideas in the symbolic and mythic structure of the Judaism presented by the canon as a whole, I repeatedly reached a single conclusion. Whatever data we find in the many other components of the canon as a whole—one group of facts here, another sort of emphasis there—nearly all of the data of a given symbol or myth find a place in the two Talmuds and nowhere else.

So the Yerushalmi and the Bavli both stand together and also take up a position separate from the remainder of the canon. They therefore form a subdivision of the canon as a whole. How do they compare to one another? As we shall see, the Bavli tended to give a fuller and more characteristic statement of matters than did the Yerushalmi. The Bavli comes last in time and also—it would appear—draws together a substantial proportion of the data expressed in a variety of prior compositions.

So to define the Bavli, to begin with, we have to compare and contrast the Bavli to that one prior composition to which it stands closest in doctrine and in form, the one that it is most like. Finding out, then, how the Bavli is like and unlike the Yerushalmi, we may undertake a judgment on what defines the Bavli. What makes the Bavli the Bavli, therefore, is the subject of this book. And, from that judgment, I frame a theory of why the Bavli made all the difference, standing as it does as the ultimate authority of Judaism.

I claimed that the results of the literary problem would prove illuminating for inquiry into society and culture. I have now to explain why I think so. After all, who apart from a talmudist of a rather distinctive sort—my sort—cares how the Bavli compares to the Yerushalmi? From no one else does the issue compel sustained attention. The answer lies in the capacity to generalize out of details a judgment on a broad issue of culture, exemplified in the small problem at hand. That broad issue for me emerges from what also interested the earlier scholars of the literature at hand: continuity and survival. But the issue here is secular. How do the components of the canon as a whole form a continuity? Why did this document in particular survive as epigone for the whole? The answers to these questions describe and promise insight for the study of other canonical religions, other documents that attained the status of a summa. The Judaism represented by the Bavli lasted for an exceptionally long time and flourishes today. The document before us persisted as the authoritative statement of that Judaism from some point after its composition to our own day. Within the method of the intellectuals who created the document, therefore, lies the secret to how people may speak once for all time.

The Bavli stands square in the middle of a path of transmission that stretches back to the Mishnah, so the authors received a great deal. The Bavli takes up a position at the center of the tradition to follow, so the authors authoritatively handed on to a welcoming future exactly what they chose. How many documents out of a long-ago age sustain such a description and claim? The writings of Plato, the New Testament and the fathers of Christianity, some classics of drama and poetry, but not much else. And within the corpus of the successful writers of antiquity, remote and late alike, I think we may claim that the authors of the Bavli in many ways present a document that is, for good and for ill, unique.

That is why asking about the literary traits of their composition and relating their work to what had gone before should yield more than routine insight into the persistence of culture in the material form of literature. When we ask, in broad terms, about the interplay of literature and society, when we speak of the sociology of learning and recognize, as we do, the power of intellectuals to make and reshape culture, and when we ask why one set of ideas endures and expands and another desiccates, we can do worse than to turn for answers and insight to the example of the Bavli.

But then we have to wait patiently for the answers, given in the idiom of the Bavli and in the context of its own facts. That is what, in this book, I ask the reader to do. In all, I propose to move from text, viewed as example, to context, seen as indicative. To state matters most simply, the issue is partly inquiry into the cultural meanings of rhetoric viewed broadly, partly analysis of the implications of the logic of composition and redaction. What I mean to say, in this inquiry into redactional choice and logic, is how I think the framers of the text thought they put things together into a comprehensive, intelligible statement. *How* they said what they said, that is, their formalized compositions, seen particularly as solutions to redactional problems in the organization of learning, must guide me to understand why they thought another mind (theirs, ours) could grasp and find persuasive *what* they said. In these approaches to the text, we find our route outward from the text. That leads us, clearly, to context, so I claim.

The question therefore is inductive: what do these particular traits of literary mind tell us about the worldview of people who talked this way and put their thoughts together into the logical and topical framework at hand? In moving from the text to the imagination contained and conveyed within its redactional traits, I seek the context that they envisaged. I want to recover that world they imagined they saw but we know that they constructed. And, to move rapidly to the end, out of that context within their minds, I want, as I said, to tease out strands and threads joined to a yet broader fabric of faith and culture, a matrix that imparted life and sense to the sages at hand, yet to which they, for their part, never gave articulated expression.

To whom then do I hope to speak in this book? I like to think that anyone who wants to know how a religious culture framed by intellectuals expresses its system and addresses its society will find my book interesting despite its technicality and attention to detail. Why so? Because we who work to describe, analyze, and interpret the world of late antiquity seek to uncover the roots of Western civilization, the sources of that sense of proportion and self-evidence shared from then to nearly now. Ancient Israel, Rome, and Greece speak to us through the voices of Christianity, Judaism, Islam, philosophy, politics of late antiquity, even out of the institutions of law and civilization and the continuous traditions of learning shaped in that brief moment, twilight of the ancient, dawn of the medieval and the modern. Here is a test case, a glimpse into how a small group of sages defined the life of an entire nation, one that would endure in this very vision of theirs. I certainly wish, therefore, to speak to as broad an audience of students and scholars as I can. I think that for much too long Western intellectuals have been denied access to the vast and enormous record of mind represented by the rabbinic canon in general and the two Talmuds in particular. So I write because I want everybody to read what the documents have to say and what I have to say about them.

At many points in the exercises that follow, I refer to texts not contained within the pages of this book. Ordinarily, I prefer to supply everything the reader needs to follow an argument. But here I should have to reprint my English translations of three Mishnah tractates as they occur in both the Yerushalmi and the Bavli. The consequent book would be too big and ungainly to use conveniently. Readers may refer to the translations, which contain all of the divisions and analyses important for the argument of this book, in my *Talmud of the Land of Israel: A Preliminary Translation and Explanation* (Chicago, 1982ff.), volume 17, *Sukkah;* volume 27, *Sotah;* and volume 30, *Sanhedrin;* and my *Talmud of Babylonia: An American Translation* (Chico, 1984–85), volume 6, *Sukkah;* volume 17, *Sotah;* and volume 23, *Sanhedrin.* My hope is that my references to texts not reproduced here will not render the book at hand incomprehensible. These references to facts I believe I have established elsewhere always address questions of this book alone and should serve the purposes of the argument I mean to unfold here. But I recognize the problem and express the hope that the reader will find this book's proposition and argument accessible and clear.

Introduction

The Formation of Judaism in Its Canon

Autonomy, Connection, Continuity

From today's perspective the entire canon of Judaism—"the one whole Torah of Moses, our rabbi"—equally and at every point testifies to the entirety of Judaism. Why so? Because all documents in the end form components of a single system, in its own language, the Torah. Each makes its contribution to the whole. If, therefore, we wish to know what Judaism or, more accurately, the Torah, teaches on any subject, we are able to draw freely on sayings relevant to that subject wherever they occur in the entire canon of Judaism. Guided only by the taste and judgment of the great sages of the Torah as they have addressed the question at hand, we thereby describe Judaism. Composites of sayings drawn from diverse books in no way violate the frontiers and boundaries that distinguish one part of the canon from some other part of the same canon. Why not? It is because, viewed as serving the Torah, which is a single and continuous revelation, frontiers and boundaries stand only at the outer limits of the whole. They demarcate inside from outside—that alone. Within, as the saying has it, "There is neither earlier nor later," that is to say, temporal considerations do not apply. But if temporal distinctions make no difference, no others do either. Accordingly, as Judaism comes to informed expression in the Judaic pulpit, in the Judaic classroom, above all in the lives and hearts and minds of Jews loyal to Judaism, each part of the canon of Judaism speaks equally authoritatively. All parts, all together, present us with one harmonious worldview and way of life, one Torah (Judaism) for all Israel. That view of "the Torah," that is to say, of the canon of Judaism, characterizes every organized movement within Judaism as we now know it, whether Reform or Orthodox, whether Reconstructionist or Conservative, whether in the "Exile" (diaspora) or in the State of Israel. How so? Among circles of Judaism indifferent to considerations of time and place, anachronism and context, every document, whenever brought to closure, testifies equally to that single system. For those circles Judaism emerges at a single moment ("Sinai"), but comes to expression in diverse times and places, so any composition that falls into the category of Torah serves, without further differentiation, to tell us about the substance of Judaism, its theology and law.

An important qualification, however, has now to make its mark. Among those circles of Judaism to whom historical facts make a difference, for example, Orthodoxy in the West, Reconstructionist, Conservative, and Reform Judaism and the like, considerations of what is completed earlier as against what comes to closure only later on, for instance, in the second century as against the eighteenth century, do make some difference. Earlier documents provide more compelling and authoritative evidence than later ones. But even in the view of this other sector of Judaism, all documents, if not everywhere equally authoritative, still form part of a continuous whole. While the former position enjoys the label, among its supporters, of "authentic" and "true," and among its detractors, of "uncritical," and while the latter position calls itself "critical" and "historical" and, by its enemies, is called "fraudulent" and "heretical," the distinction between the two positions makes no material difference. Why not? Because both circles stand upon one premise. All hold as self-evident that the numerous components of the canon of Judaism form a continuity, beginning, middle, and end. That is why considerations of priority of closure, should these considerations find their way into discourse at all, change little and affect nothing. Torah is Torah, early, middle, and late. And so it is—except from the perspective of one outside the magic circle of the faith. Here we ask exactly how various documents became Torah, what each document added to the whole, in what ways the several documents related to one another and to the larger system, and, in all, reverting to mythic language, what makes Torah Torah.

For a person engaged in such an inquiry into the formation of Judaism studied through the analysis of the literary evidence of the canon, documents stand in three relationships to one another and to the system of which they form part, that is, to Judaism, as a whole. And the specification of these relationships constitutes the principal premise of all that follows, since to begin with the relationships derive not inductively from the documents at hand but from the mind of the one who turns to analyze the documents. So I cannot claim to approach matters inductively.

Each document, as a matter of theory, is to be seen all by itself, that is, as autonomous of all others.

Each document, again as a matter of theory, is to be examined for its relationships with other documents universally regarded as falling into the same classification, as Torah.

And, finally, each document is to be allowed to take its place as part of the undifferentiated aggregation of documents that, all together, constitute the canon of Judaism, that is to say, Torah.

Simple logic makes self-evident the proposition that, if a document comes down to us within its own framework, as a complete book with a beginning, middle, and end, in preserving that book the canon presents us with a document on its own and not solely as part of a larger composition or construct. So we too see the document as it reaches us, that is, as autonomous. If, second, a document contains materials shared verbatim or in substantial content with other documents of its classification, or if one document refers to the contents of other documents, then the several documents that clearly wish to engage in conversation with one another have to address one another. That is to say, we have to seek for the marks of connectedness and ask for the meaning of those connections. Finally, since, as I said at the outset, the community of the faithful of Judaism, in all of the contemporary expressions of Judaism, concur that all documents held to be authoritative constitute one whole, seamless Torah, that is, a complete and exhaustive statement of God's will for Israel and humanity, we take as our further task the description of the whole out of the undifferentiated testimony of all of its parts, viewed, as is clear, as equally authoritative for the composition of the whole: one, continuous system. And in taking up such a question, we address a problem not of theology alone, though it derives from theological conviction, but one of description, analysis, and interpretation of an entirely historical order.

In this way we may hope to trace the literary evidence—which is the only evidence we have—for the formation of Judaism. By seeing the several components of the canon of Judaism in sequence, first one by one, then one after the other, and finally all together all at once, we may trace the literary side of the history of Judaism. We may see how a document came into being on its own, in its context (so far as we may posit the character of that context). We interpret the document at its site. Moreover, all documents of the rabbinic canon except for the Hebrew Scriptures relate to prior ones, on the one side, and all, especially the Scriptures, stand before those to follow, on the other. The Mishnah normally is understood to rest upon the written Torah and, later in its history in Judaism, came to be called the oral Torah. So even the Mishnah stands not distinct and autonomous but contingent and dependent. The two Talmuds rest upon the Mishnah (a statement we shall later see as somewhat simple), and the several compilations of exegeses of Scripture (called "midrashim") rest upon Scripture. So, in all, like the bones of the body, each book is connected to others, with Scripture and the Mishnah the backbone. All together they form a whole, a frame that transcends the parts and imparts meaning and harmony to them.

The bones of the body develop more or less in shared stages, however, while the documents of the Torah—the canon of Judaism—developed in a sequence that is mostly clear. First came Scripture, then the Mishnah, then the Talmud of the Land of Israel and earlier compilations of biblical exegeses, then the Talmud of Babylonia and the later compilations of biblical exegeses. So is the sequence of the important texts. In that sequence we shall find whatever evidence of growth, development, and change we shall ever have to tell us the history of Judaism. To complete the matter, so far as we can relate growth, development, and change in the history of Judaism, traced through the formation and character of its canon, to the growth, development, and change in the history of the Jewish people, we shall also claim not only to describe and analyze but also to explain the history of the formation of Judaism. That is to say, we may frame theories not only on the formative history of the worldview and way of life we call Judaism but on the reasons that the history went the route it took, rather than some other route. How so? We may ask why people thought what they thought and did what they did rather than thinking other thoughts and doing other things. When we can relate the ideas people held and the way they lived their lives to the context in which they found themselves, we shall have reached that level of interpretation at which present and past come together in the setting of shared human existence: the meeting of text and context. But we stand at a distance from that elusive goal. So let us begin.

The Bavli in Its Canonical Context

Let me make these general remarks more concrete. The framers of the Babylonian Talmud present us with an encyclopaedia encompassing a great part of what we find in texts produced before their time. But they put together whatever materials they chose in a way that was distinctive to themselves. Their encyclopaedia of Judaism—for that is what it was—in retrospect appears to be the last and fullest statement of the Judaic component of classical antiquity. Within a century of the Bavli's closure in circa A.D. 500, the Islamic world would bring to an end the late antique world in which Judaism, like Christianity, had taken shape. So though no one could have known it, it was a serendipitous moment for the creation of an encyclopaedia of pretty much everything worth knowing about anything. And that is what the sages at hand accomplished. Thus, as I have explained, the rhetoric, logic of composition, and topical program of their encyclopaedia define the points of interest in not only the text they made but in their authorship as well.

So that is the arena of our inquiry. The matter of context keeps us within the bounds of the text, though drawing us closer to the outer limits. By describing the text, we gain access to a set of traits of mind and culture. In the inquiry into context we attempt to generalize from mental traits to social ones, to analyze the social vision (not the reality envisaged, of that we have no evidence outside the text at hand) conveyed within the utensils of intellect and imagination. Then, as I said, we look backward to earlier texts, already analyzed by this writer along the lines under description here. These have ultimately to be interpreted and set into comparison and contrast with the last of the sequence of the Judaic canon, the Talmud at hand. But this book deals only with the description of the Bavli in its canonical setting.

Having completed equivalent description of the Mishnah, circa A.D. 200, the first document of this kind of Judaism; of Pirqe Abot, circa A.D. 250; of the Tosefta, a complement to the Mishnah of the Talmud of the Land of Israel, circa A.D. 400; of the first of the two Talmuds, and one of the earliest great compilations of scriptural exegeses, Genesis Rabbah and Leviticus Rabbah, circa A.D. 400 and 450, respectively; as well as fairly substantial work on another of those compilations, Sifra, circa A.D. 300–350, I turn to the last major document of Judaism in its formative age. My intent, beyond the present study, is to point toward the history of the formation of Judaism, as a reading of each of the documents of the formative period apart from, and in comparison and contrast to, all of the others, allows us to see points of continuous unfolding and marks of change and development. But, as is clear, the final work of describing, analysing, and interpreting a single document has to reach full conclusion. God will decide what comes next.

The Results of Completed Research

In the earlier projects I worked along simple lines. First, I translated the text at hand, in some cases (Tosefta, Sifra, and the Talmud of the Land of Israel) for the first time into English, in others (the Mishnah, Leviticus Rabbah, and the Bavli) for the second. This book in particular rests upon the translation of 10% of the Bavli that I have completed in *Talmud of Babylonia: An American Translation* covering tractates *Berakhot, Sukkah, Sotah, Sanhedrin,* and *Arakhin.* The sample at hand suffices because of the rhetorical and redactional uniformity of the Talmud of Babylonia. The work of translation allowed me to confront the several successive texts, down to Bavli, in exquisite detail, if not invariably with definitive philological results. Then, in each case, I composed a history of the ideas of the text, and this in two aspects. First, I said what I thought those ideas amounted to as a complete and entire statement. Is there a viewpoint in the text at hand and, if so, on what subject and with what contents? Second, I specified, so far as I could, where and how the viewpoint at hand took shape, for whom the text speaks in particular.

In some documents, the Mishnah being the main one, I could say which ideas came first, which later, and even propose to correlate the unfolding of sets of ideas with definitive historical events of the day. In others, the Talmud of the Land of Israel being the best example, I was able to specify the relationship of the end product to the age in which it came to closure, although I could not isolate prior layers of discourse. That I take to be the ultimate outcome of the Babylonian Talmud project too, but it is too soon to say.

In some documents I emphasized the inner structure—the relationship of one document in the formative Judaism at hand to some other. For example, I systematically related paragraphs of the Tosefta to those of the Mishnah. For another example, through a simple taxonomy I compared the work of Mishnah exegesis, in the Talmud of the Land of Israel, to the work of Scripture exegesis, in the work on Genesis Rabbah accomplished at much the same time. In other instances I stressed the issue of logical discourse in relationship to the exegetical mode of rhetoric at hand. For example, the work on Leviticus Rabbah stressed the relationship of the logic of public and intelligible discourse to the formal and topical mode of expression at hand. So I wanted to know how people could express their own ideas by attaching them to biblical verses. I further asked in what ways they proposed to demonstrate the truth of their allegations in relationship to the ways philosophical truth was expressed. All of this of course has carried me on a journey across a rather substantial territory of writings. I stress, then, that my goal of describing the whole of the formative literature of Judaism dictates this next and, in the present phase of my scholarly life, final project, on the Talmud of Babylonia. What lies beyond falls outside the bounds of this statement, but I know exactly where I am going.

Since, as I said, the project at hand follows the earlier pattern—translation, then literary study, finally cultural analysis in terms of some large issue—I should specify one example of the repeated sequence. For this purpose I call attention to *Talmud of the Land of Israel* (Chicago, 1982ff.), in which I translated the text (twenty-five of the thirty-four volumes of translation are mine, and all are done; my students are nearly done with the rest). Then I did my literary exercises in volume 35, *Introduction: Taxonomy*. Finally I proposed the cultural inquiry in *Judaism in Society: The Evidence of the Yerushalmi* (a Hebrew name for the document at hand). Again, in *History of the Mishnaic Law of Purities* (22 vols.), *Holy Things* (6 vols.), *Women* (5 vols.), *Appointed Times* (5 vols.) and *Damages* (5 vols.) I translated and explained the Mishnah and the Tosefta for five of the six divisions. My graduate students did the other one. In each of those projects I then went on to the literary and historical work, that is, *Purities*, volumes 21 and 22; *Appointed Times*, volume 5; *Women*, volume 5; *Damages*, volume 5; and *Holy Things*, volume 6. At the end came the large-scale synthetic work of cultural description and analysis, *Judaism: The Evidence of the Mishnah*. In that book I identified what I conceived to be the principal points of stress and tension in the Mishnah and asked why the Israelite sages of the second century A.D. turned out to select those same points of insistence that had proved so important to priestly writers in the Old Testament books, for example, Leviticus and Numbers.

This inquiry, following along the questions framed for us by Max Weber, shaped the work on *Judaism: The Evidence of the Mishnah*. I could give examples from the other projects, but I believe the point is not obscure, and hence, the context and purpose of the project at hand should be clear as well. Essentially I am asking two questions which are one: Why did the system of Judaism as defined by the rabbis of late antiquity work when it worked? Why did it prove irrelevant or lose the power to persuade when it did? To answer these questions, I have to know the social world in which the several components of the canon came into being and persuaded the Jews, first, to see the world as the sages (rabbis) saw it; second, to live their lives as the sages taught them to; and third, to shape and define the life of their social group (nation) within the way of life and world view of the sages, represented by the canon of Judaism as we have it. In all this, the point of climax, as is now clear, is the Talmud of Babylonia.

The Work at Hand

In this book I conduct redactional probes on the basis of a sample of the Yerushalmi and the Bavli consisting of three tractates—Sukkah, Sotah, and Sanhedrin. I compare the Yerushalmi's and the Bavli's treatment of the Mishnah tractates just now specified, in the claim that my sample—in the range of 10% of the whole of each of the Talmuds—provides a statistically ample representation of the whole. Given the uniformity in composition and redaction of the two Talmuds, respectively, I believe my judgment to be sound, indeed, probably conservative. The tractates I have chosen are, in length, short, medium, and long. The first is mainly devoted to legal problems, the second both to legal and theological ones, and the third presents a sizable discussion of theological issues. The three critical areas of Mishnaic discourse—the calendar, the family, the institutions of the community—are represented. These are the topics that would undergo development for many centuries after the closure of the Bavli, while others would not. While the Yerushalmi treats the Mishnah's division on agricultural taboos and the Bavli does not, and the Bavli provides extensive discussion of the Mishnah's description of the everyday conduct of the cult and the Yerushalmi does not, with regard to the three divisions represented by the tractates I have chosen, the Talmuds concur on the need for detailed exegesis of the Mishnah's tractates. This explains the choice of tractates and my claim that they represent much beyond themselves.

My tables and charts rest upon my prior analytical division of the tractates. In my translation of the Yerushalmi, I contributed the notion that we deal not with long and undifferentiated columns of type but with cogent compositions, discourses with a beginning, middle, and end. These I call "units of discourse." All of the specifications of such units of discourse refer back to my translation, the first such analytical presentation of the Yerushalmi in any language, including the original. There I made possible explicit and specific reference to a given passage and claimed to define the limits of discourse within which said passage finds its context and meaning. In my translation of the Bavli for the tractates at hand, I have the advantage of excellent translations, produced by Soncino Press, London, in which long columns are divided, normally quite properly, into paragraphs. But the paragraphs are not numbered, the components of the paragraphs not indicated. More critical, the beginnings and middles and ends of sustained discourse, covering numerous paragraphs, are not then given boundaries. In my translation of the tractates at hand I imposed my own definition of the limits of sustained discourse, as I saw them. In that way, for both Talmuds, I made possible the conduct of the sorts of analytical inquiries and comparisons worked out in this book.

Let me now turn to the procedure and argument of the book as a whole. As is clear, the task is not to present an exercise of an available method but, as is so common in my intellectual career, to conduct an experiment in the formation of a method. I know the question I wish to answer, which is, what is the Bavli? I have now to develop methods to answer that question. The sequence of chapters that follows forms a single, continuous exercise in developing requisite methods and, by the way, also presenting answers produced by those methods. So the logic of the book begins with a simple question and dictates ways by which that question is to be answered.

In chapter 1 I describe the three sources of truth to which all rabbinic documents after the Mishnah appeal. These are the Mishnah, later called the "oral Torah;" Scripture, afterward called the "written Torah;" and the figure of the sage himself. In this way I place the Bavli into the fundamental context, the one of canonical redaction. Around what prior composition does the Bavli's authorship organize its ideas? The answer, of course, is around the Mishnah. Since the other document to do likewise is the Yerushalmi, chapter 2 turns immediately to the problem of the Yerushalmi and the Bavli as the authors of each book address the Mishnah. We take up a single chapter of the Mishnah and systematically compare the two Talmuds' treatments of that chapter. What I want to know emerges from this comparison. First, do the Talmuds say the same thing or different things? Second, when they say the same thing, do they say it in pretty much the same words or do they say it in different words? Third, when they say much the same thing in different words, does the shared program of exegesis derive from the Mishnah paragraph under discussion or from a common set of exegetical conventions, expressed in diverse ways to be sure, shared by the two Talmuds? So much for the exercise of part 1, establishing that the Bavli exhibits traits of likeness, and traits of difference, when compared to the Yerushalmi.

In part 2 I undertake the differentiation of the two Talmuds against the baseline defined by the common canon—Scripture, Mishnah, sage. Since the two Talmuds refer back to all three sources of torah, I ask how they compare in the relationships between each of them and the three sources, respectively. That accounts for chapters 3, 4, and 5. The three chapters carry out exactly the same exercises of comparison and differentiation, expressed through the charts. I aim at establishing proportions and comparing wholes. The reference system is such that the reader may refer to my translations of the three tractates both in the Yerushalmi and the Bavli and assess whether or not my entries are dictated by the application of a single criterion in a consistent way. I did my best to follow a clear and simple criterion throughout, but error in judgment surely enters such an exercise as this. Still, my conclusions are based on only one-sided and unequivocal data.

In part 3 I turn to the exploitation of the results of part 2. Once we have compared the Bavli to the Yerushalmi and shown how the two documents are alike and not alike when set against the baseline of the three components of the canon, we find important differences. These then yield two further exercises—the comparison of the Bavli to the Yerushalmi in the topical program common to the documents, and then the comparison of the Bavli to the Yerushalmi as well as to many other, prior documents, in the rhetorical preferences revealed by the Bavli's treatment of materials it holds in common with prior compositions. Through topical and rhetorical comparisons the Bavli's literary distinctiveness emerges.

In part 4, finally, I move on to the matter of Judaism, that is to say, definitive aspects of that system of belief and behavior laid forth in the two Talmuds and in related canonical compositions. In chapter 9 I take as my probe the topic of the Messiah, asking how the two Talmuds relate to one another and to the canon when they treat that single topic. That choice is natural because of the centrality of the theme of the Messiah in the Judaism that emerges from late antiquity. Also it is a topic I worked out in *Messiah in Context: Israel's History and Destiny in Formative Judaism* (Philadelphia, 1984: Fortress). I show two facts. First, when we parse the canonical documents by asking how each one treats a common theme, we find that the Yerushalmi and the Bavli form one distinct pole around which a few other documents cluster, while the Mishnah, with the Tosefta, forms another distinct pole around which further compositions cluster. In the middle, divided more or less at random, are some intermediate compositions, tending decisively neither to the one pole nor to the other. At the same time, I point out that the Yerushalmi's account of Judaism emerges, by contrast to the Bavli's, as partial and incomplete.

That fact is underlined in the concluding chapter, in which I turn to the definitive symbol of Judaism, Torah, in its distinctive mythic expression, the myth of the dual Torah. I ask where and how that myth comes to expression and show, this last time, exactly how the Bavli's expression of the myth relates to the Yerushalmi's version of the same myth. The close relationship of the Bavli to the Yerushalmi again emerges to the naked eye. But the distinctive contribution of the authors of the Bavli also comes to the fore. At the end, I state what I think truly differentiates the second Talmud from the first and specify what that distinction is and why the distinction does make a difference.

That, in a few words, constitutes the procedure, methodological experiment, and argument of the book. I move step by step from one exercise to the next, at each point building upon the results of the prior one. The upshot is a thesis on why the Bavli served as it did to define Judaism. Hence I claim to know why the Bavli constitutes the encyclopaedia of the faith, the definitive statement, the conclusion of Judaism, in its formative age.

My former student, Joseph M. Davis, provides a bibliography of books and articles on the same subject as is treated here. I am grateful for his painstaking and gallant search for books and articles in which I might find assistance in my inquiry. The reader will not be surprised to learn that, in the entire antecedent bibliography, I could find not a single piece of writing that addressed the question at hand: How does the Bavli, viewed whole and complete as a redactional structure and construction, relate to the antecedent compositions of the canon that, temporally at least, the Bavli draws to conclusion? Most of what Davis found dealt with episodic items, this text and that. Only one prior scholar, E. Z. Melammed, cited in context, ever even raised the questions that seem to me fundamental to the study of the two Talmuds and of the canon of Judaism. I am used to such a bibliographical impasse.

As often in the past, the shank of this book comprises texts, tables, and charts. Of such as these great literature is not made. But I know no better way to move off the beaten path than by clearing away underbrush and making my own way in uncharted paths. The familiar paths lead nowhere because they no longer direct us to answers to questions worth asking. They carry us only to familiar answers that do not persuade anyone not already persuaded by them or even compel much attention any longer.

The Argument of This Book

The Bavli marks the conclusion of the formation of the rabbinic canon in late antiquity. The contents of the Bavli assuredly place the document at the end of the formative age. How so? Pretty much anything presented in the other documents we find in this one too. But what we find here we do not necessarily locate elsewhere, in compositions assumed to be of earlier date. The Bavli thus serves as an encyclopedia of Torah—that is, of Judaism. It contains almost everything we can demonstrate circulated earlier, while also preserving much else. The Talmud's modes of discourse are four: (1) exegesis of Mishnah and Tosefta, (2) abstract discourse on law in general, (3) exegesis of Scripture, and (4) abstract discourse on mythic or theological themes of Scripture in general. So the Bavli joins together the available types of discourse on the Mishnah and on Scripture, making them into a single composition. In its redactional character it does the same, an achievement entirely unique to the Bavli.

Once the Talmud of Babylonia had reached conclusion, Judaism—Torah as we know it—had taken shape. True, once formed, the Bavli's Judaism of Torah would grow and develop. But its fundamental character, its definitive symbolic structure both of myth and law, and its complete expression in writing, by the time of the closure of the Bavli, had reached full development. Its laws would grow and change. Its theological and mythic components would flourish in new and unprecedented ways. But its fundamental symbolic structure would endure to our own day, ever changing and always vital, never intact but always essentially unimpaired.

The Bavli thus drew together the two principal components of the Torah, the written and the oral parts, not only in detail and episodically but in their main lines of order and structure, wholly and completely. In doing so, the Bavli's authors resolved that canonical dilemma presented by the advent of the

Mishnah, a document clearly written by mortals, by sages, bearing this-worldly authority and making an impact upon everyday and concrete, material reality, yet demanding status as Torah. The first stage of the process, accomplished in Abot, Tosefta, Sifra, and in the Mishnah-centered pericopes of the two Talmuds, was to link the specific statements of the Mishnah to specific statements of Scripture. The second and complementary stage was to make a place for Scripture, in large and substantial sequences, in the arena of discourse defined solely by the Mishnah. The Yerushalmi did not do so. The Bavli did.

In consequence, it is in the Bavli in particular that Scripture and the Mishnah join together, in nearly equal measure, to lay forth the structure and boundaries of discourse. Together they define the lines of order. Together they dictate the foci and determine the range of permissible dispute. In the union (the Torah myth would say, reunion) of Scripture and the Mishnah, the Bavli accomplished that public exposition of "the one whole Torah of Moses our rabbi" that no prior document had accomplished, but at which all prior documents had aimed. It is hardly a surprise, therefore, that the framers of the perfected union should also make explicit what at least some prior documents had implied. One whole Torah of Moses, our rabbi, part in writing, part in memory, here and now in the Bavli emerges wholly and completely one.

Judaism here comes under study as an artifact of the human will and imagination, a way of creating a human society and of living out a human life, a mode of being woman and man in the circumstances of time and change. In forming a society they called sacred, in reaching out to God beyond, in offering up the sacrifice of humility and to the future giving the gift of hope, the Jewish people along the way produced the records at hand. They tell us how a small, despised people found wellsprings of hope in a human situation of despair and why that people found in reason the way to endure and to prevail. That is a story well worth trying to record.

Part One

From the Yerushalmi to the Bavli

The Literary Context

1

Mishnah and Scripture, Yerushalmi and Midrash Collections

Principles of Composition

Introduction

When the final organizers of the Talmud of Babylonia, who, it is commonly alleged, flourished circa A.D. 500–600, considered the redactional choices made by their predecessors, two appeared the most likely. The organizers might take up and arrange such materials as they had in their hands around the categories—books or verses or themes—of Scripture, as had their precursers in bringing into being compositions made up of exegeses of Scripture (midrashim). Or they might follow the order of the Mishnah and compose a systematic commentary and amplification of that document, as had their precursers who created the Talmud of the Land of Israel a century or so before. When they considered their task, however, they had to recognize that they had in hand a tripartite corpus of inherited materials awaiting composition into a final, closed document. First, they took up materials, in various states and stages of completion, pertinent to the Mishnah or to the principles of laws that the Mishnah had originally brought to articulation. Second, they had in hand received materials, again in various conditions, pertinent to the Scripture, both as the Scripture related to the Mishnah and also as the Scripture laid forth its own narratives. Finally, they had in hand materials focused on sages. These were framed around twin biographical principles, either as strings of stories about great sages of the past or as collections of sayings and comments drawn together solely because the same name stands behind the sayings.

The decision the framers of the Bavli reached was to adopt the two redactional principles inherited from the antecedent century or so and to reject the one already rejected by their predecessors, even while honoring it. That is to say, first, they organized the Bavli around the Mishnah. But, second, they adapted and included vast tracts of antecedent materials organized as scriptural commentary. These they inserted whole and complete, not at all in response to the Mishnah's program. And, finally, while making provision for compositions built upon biographical principles, preserving both strings of sayings from a given master (and often a given tradent of a given master) as well as tales about authorities of the preceding half millennium, they did nothing new. That is to say, they never created redactional compositions, of a sizable order, that focused upon given authorities, even though sufficient materials lay at hand to allow doing so. In the three decisions, two of what to do and one of what not to do, the final compositors of the Bavli indicated what they proposed to accomplish: to give final form and fixed expression, through their categories of the organization of all knowledge, to the Torah as it had been known, sifted, searched, approved, and handed down, even from the remote past to their own day. So in our literary categories the compositors of the Bavli were encyclopaedists. Their creation turned out to be the encyclopaedia of Judaism, its summa, its point of final reference, its court of last appeal, its definition, it conclusion, its closure—so they thought, and so said those that followed, to this very day.

Shall we then draw so grand a conclusion from so modest a fact as how people sorted out available redactional categories? Indeed so, if we realize that the modes by which thinkers organize knowledge leads us deep into the theses by which useful knowledge rises to the surface while what is irrelevant or unimportant or trivial sinks to the bottom. If we want to know what people thought and how they thought it, we can do worse than begin by asking about how they organized what they knew, on the one side, and about the choices they made in laying out the main lines of the structure of knowledge, on the other. When we approach a document so vast and complex as the Bavli, resting as it does on a still larger and more complex antecedent corpus of writings, we do best to begin at the very beginning, at the surface of things.

The document as a whole lays itself out as a commentary to the Mishnah. So the framers wished us to think that whatever they wanted to tell us would take the form of Mishnah commentary. But as we shall see in part 2, a second glance indicates that the document is made up of enormous composites, themselves closed prior to inclusion in the Bavli. Some of these composites— around 35% to 40% of Bavli's, if our sample is indicative—were selected and arranged along lines dictated by a logic other than that deriving from the requirements of Mishnah commentary. In these the logic of redaction—what (self-evidently) comes first, what (obviously) goes below—emerges from a different sort of exegetical task from Mishnah commentary. As I said, people focused upon passages of Scripture in making up their compositions of exegesis. And again, as already suggested, sorting out the large-scale compositions of which the document at hand is made up produces yet a third type of composite, this one drawn together around a given name and made up of sayings, often on diverse subjects, attributed to that name, or of stories told about that name.

It goes without saying that people who copy what others had earlier done on the surface lay no claim upon originality. That would be so for Bavli except for one fact. Before the time of the Bavli's authors, as I just pointed out, three principles of composition and redaction—Mishnah exegesis, Scripture exegesis, and biographical collection—flourished more or less in isolation from one another. How do we know? The first is fully exposed in the Talmud of the Land of Israel, the second in earlier compilations of scriptural exegeses. The third accounts for the available biographical composites. To be sure these never were gathered into tractates or other large and autonomous units of literary expression before the time of the nineteenth- and early-twentieth-century biographers of talmudic rabbis. What is clear, therefore, is that the antecedent redactors, before the age of the Bavli's own compositors, thought that the three things could be done fairly separately.

The framers of the Bavli drew together the results of these three types of work, which people prior to their own labors already had created in abundance. Using the two I specified as definitive redactional structures, the framers made of them all one document, the Bavli, or, in the later tradition of Judaism, *the* Talmud. Whatever the place and role of the diverse types of compositions circulating before and in the time of the Bavli—compilations of scriptural exegeses, the Yerushalmi, not to mention the exegeses of Pentateuchal laws in Sifra and the Sifres, the Tosefta, Pirqe Abot and Abot de R. Natan, and on and on—the Bavli superseded them all. It took pride of place. It laid the final seal upon the past and defined not only what would succeed for an unknown tomorrow but the very form, topical order, and program of all that would pass into the hands of the future. Thus, once more, the thesis is validated that when we take up the problem of principles of composition, we take our first step into the path that, at the other side, leads us to a clear picture of how Judaism, as it flourished from the time of the Bavli to our own day (and, I hope, for ages to come as well), reached completion. We confront the Bavli's evidence about Judaism in conclusion. And the Bavli's testimony, to begin with, concerns matters of ultimate redaction, namely, how it was put together out of its largest available building blocks. So that is where we must start. To begin with, let me briefly describe the earlier modes of selection, arrangement, and large-scale composition. Then, in part 2, I turn to those that dictated the logical order and sense of the Bavli.

The Talmud of the Land of Israel and the Mishnah

To describe the Yerushalmi we first take up the whole and proceed to ask about its principal parts. Looking at the Yerushalmi whole, we notice two totally distinct sorts of materials: statements of law, then discussions of, and excurses on, those statements. We bring no substantial presuppositions to the text if we declare these two sorts of materials to be, respectively, primary and constitutive, secondary and derivative. Calling the former the declaration of law, the Mishnah passage, and the latter the exegesis of these laws, the Yerushalmi proper, imposes no a priori judgment formed independent of the literary evidence in hand. We might as well call the two the "code" and the "commentary." The result would be no different.

In fact, the Yerushalmi is made up of two elements, each with its own liter-

ary traits and program of discussion. Since the Mishnah passage at the head
of each set of Yerushalmi's units of discourse defines the limits and determines
the theme and, generally, the problematic of the whole, our attention is drawn
to the traits of the Mishnah passages as a group. Here, of course, a certain
measure of descriptive work has been done. But even if we for the first time
saw these types of pericopes of the Mishnah (embedded as they are in the
Yerushalmi and separated from one another), we should discern that they adhere to a separate and quite distinctive set of literary and conceptual canons
from what follows and surrounds them. Hence at the outset, with no appreci-
able attention to anything beyond the text, we should distinguish two "layers"
of the Yerushalmi and recognize that one "layer" is formed in one way, the
other in another way. (I use *layer* for convenience only; it is not an apt
metaphor.)

If then we were to join together all the Mishnah pericopes, we should notice
that they are stylistically and formally coherent and also different from everything else in the Yerushalmi. Accordingly, for stylistic reasons alone we are on
firm ground in designating the layer of the Mishnah as the base point for all
further inquiry. For the Mishnah layer has been shown to be uniform while the
Yerushalmi layer is not demonstrably so. Hence, itself undifferentiated,
the former—the Mishnah layer—provides the point of differentiation. The
latter—the Yerushalmi layer—presents the diverse materials subject to differentiation. In the first stage in the work of making sense of the Yerushalmi and
describing it whole, what is the initial criterion through which the Yerushalmi's
diverse types of units of discourse are differentiated? It is the varied relationships, to the Mishnah's rule, exhibited by the Yerushalmi's several, diverse
units of discourse. When we compare the Mishnah to the Yerushalmi we find
two intertwined documents, quite different from one another both in style and
in values. Yet they are so tightly joined that the Yerushalmi appears in the main
to provide mere commentary and amplification for the Mishnah.

If, then, we wish to differentiate among the Yerushalmi's units of discourse,
we do so by specifying how a unit of discourse may relate to the Mishnah
paragraph with which it is associated. Let me then spell out the relationships
that characterize one or another type of unit of discourse.

The Yerushalmi invariably does to the Mishnah one of these four things:
(1) text criticism; (2) exegesis of the meaning of the Mishnah, including glosses
and amplifications; (3) addition of scriptural proof texts of the Mishnah's central propositions; and (4) harmonization of one Mishnah passage with another
such passage or with a statement of Tosefta. These four taxa encompass all the
Yerushalmi's units of discourse that relate to the Mishnah at all, 90% of the
whole of the Yerushalmi tractates surveyed in volume 35, *Introduction: Taxonomy*. The first two of these four procedures remain wholly within the narrow frame of the Mishnah passage subject to discussion. The second pair take
an essentially independent stance vis-à-vis the Mishnah pericope at hand.

The Mishnah is read by the Yerushalmi as a composite of discrete and essentially autonomous rules, a set of atoms, not an integrated molecule, so to speak. In so doing, the most striking formal traits of the Mishnah are obliterated. More important, the Mishnah as a whole and complete statement of a viewpoint no longer exists. Its propositions are reduced to details. On occasion, the details may be restated in generalizations encompassing a wide variety of other details across the gaps between one tractate and another. This immensely creative and imaginative approach to the Mishnah vastly expands the range of discourse. But the first, and deepest, consequence is to deny to the Mishnah both its own mode of speech and its distinctive and coherent message.

We turn to amplify the matter of how the Yerushalmi proposes to provide a systematic exegesis of selected passages of the Mishnah. I review a taxonomy of these exegeses. What are the sorts of approaches we are apt to find? These are four, of which two are nearly indistinguishable, the third highly distinctive, and the fourth barely consequential.

1. *Citation and gloss of the language of the Mishnah (meaning of a phrase or concrete illustration of a rule).* A unit of discourse of this type will contain a direct citation of a sentence of the Mishnah. The word choices or phrasing of the Mishnah will be paraphrased or otherwise explained through what is essentially a gloss. Or the rule of the Mishnah will be explained through an example or a restatement of some kind.

2. *Specification of the meaning of the law of the Mishnah or the reason for it.* Items of this type stand very close to those of the former. What differentiates the one from the other is the absence, in the present set of units of discourse, of direct citation of the Mishnah or close and explicit reading of its language. The discussion then tends to allude to the Mishnah or to generalize, while remaining wholly within its framework. In some units of discourse scriptural proof texts are adduced in evidence of a Mishnah passage. These frequently spill over into discussion of the reason for a rule.

3. *Secondary implication or application of the law of the Mishnah.* Units of discourse of this catalog generalize beyond the specific rule of the Mishnah. The discussion will commonly restate the principle of the rule at hand or raise a question invited by it. Hence if the Mishnah's law settles one question, participants in this type of discourse will use that as the foundation for raising a second and consequent question. Two or more rules of the Mishnah (or of the Mishnah and Tosefta) will be contrasted with one another and then harmonized, or two or more rulings of a specific authority will be alleged to conflict and then shown not to stand at variance with one another.

4. *The matter of authorities and their views: case law.* In a handful of items, concrete decisions are attached to specific laws of the Mishnah, or the harmonization or identification of the opinions of Mishnah's authorities forms the center of interest.

From this taxonomy it follows that there was a severely circumscribed repertoire of intellectual initiatives available to the authorities of the Yerushalmi.

Approaching a given rule of the Mishnah, a sage would do one of two things: (1) explain the meaning of the passage, or (2) extend and expand the meaning of the passage. In the former category fall all the items in the first and second approaches, as well as those units of discourse in which either a scriptural proof text is adduced in support of a law or an alleged variant reading of a text is supplied. In the latter category fit all items in the third and fourth approaches, as well as those in which the work is to harmonize laws or principles, on the one side, or to cite and amplify Tosefta's complement to the Mishnah passage, on the other. Within these two categories, which produce, in all, four subdivisions, we may find a place for all units of discourse in which the focus of discussion is a passage of the Mishnah. Of the two sorts, the work of straightforward explanation of the plain meaning of a law of the Mishnah by far predominates. If we may state the outcome very simply: what the framers of the Yerushalmi want to say—whatever else their purpose or aspiration—is what they think the Mishnah means in any given passage.

What about types of units of discourse that stand separate and independent of the Mishnah? We want to know when the Yerushalmi speaks for itself, not for the Mishnah. If we collect all units of discourse, or larger parts of such units, in which exegesis of the Mishnah or expansion upon the law of the Mishnah is absent—about 10% of all the Yerushalmi's units of discourse in my probe—we find at most four types, which in fact are only two.

1. *Theoretical questions of law not associated with a particular passage of the Mishnah.* Some tendency exists to move beyond the legal boundaries set by the Mishnah's rules themselves. More general inquiries are taken up. These of course remain within the framework of the topic of one tractate or another, although some larger modes of thought are characteristic of more than a single tractate. To explain, I point to the mode of thought in which the scriptural basis of the law of the Mishnah will be investigated, without regard to a given tractate. Along these same lines, I may point to a general inquiry into the count under which one may be liable for a given act, comments on the law governing teaching and judging cases, and the like. But these items tend not to leave the Mishnah far behind.

2. *Exegesis of Scripture separate from the Mishnah.* It is under this rubric that we find the most important instances in which the Yerushalmi presents materials essentially independent of the Mishnah. They pursue problems or themes through what is said about a biblical figure, expressing ideas and values simply unknown to the Mishnah. We return to this matter in chapter 4.

3. *Historical statements.* The Yerushalmi contains a fair number of statements that something happened or narratives about how something happened. While many of these are replete with biblical quotations, in general they do not provide exegesis of Scripture, which serves merely as illustration or reference point. We revert to this topic in chapter 5.

4. *Stories about, and rules for, sages and disciples, separate from discussion of a passage of the Mishnah.* The Mishnah contains a tiny number of

tales about rabbis. These serve principally as precedents for, or illustrations of, rules. The Yerushalmi, by contrast, contains a sizable number of stories about sages and their relationships to other people. Like the items in the second and third lists, these too may be adduced as evidence of the values of the people who stand behind the Yerushalmi, the things they thought important. These tales rarely serve to illustrate a rule or concept of the Mishnah. The main, though not the only, characteristic theme is the power of the rabbi, the honor due to the rabbi, and the tension between the rabbi and others, whether the patriarch, on the one side, the heretic on the second, or the gentile on the third. We take up this type of unit of discourse in chapter 6.

Units of discourse (or large segments of such units) independent of the interests of the Mishnah are not numerous. Varying in bulk from one tractate to the next, as I said, in my probe of five tractates of the Yerushalmi they added up to not much more than 10% of the whole. Furthermore, among the four types of units of discourse before us, the items on the first do not move far from the principles and concerns of the Mishnah.

So where we do find extensive passages in which the Mishnah is left far behind, they normally are of two kinds: (1) exegesis of narrative or theological passages of Scripture, and (2) fables about heroes. These latter are divided, artificially to be sure, into tales about rabbis and historical accounts. But no important distinction exists between the two, except that the former speaks of what rabbis said and did while the latter tells about events on a more generous scale. Accordingly, when the Yerushalmi presents us with ideas or expressions of a world related to, but fundamentally separate from, that of the Mishnah, that is, when the Yerushalmi wishes to say something other than what the Mishnah says and means, it will take up one of two modes of discourse. Either we find exegesis of biblical passages, with the value system of the rabbis read into the scriptural tales, or we are told stories about holy men and paradigmatic events, once again through tales told in such a way that a didactic purpose is served.

It remains to stress that the Yerushalmi's exegetes of the Mishnah brought to the document no distinctive program of their own. I perceive no hidden agenda. To state matters negatively, the exegetes did not know in advance of their approach to a law of the Mishnah facts about the passage not contained (at least implicitly) within the boundaries of the language of the Mishnah passage itself (except only for facts contained within other units of the same document). Rejecting propositions that were essentially a priori, they proposed to explain and expand precisely the wording and the conceptions supplied by the document under study. I cannot point to a single instance in which the Yerushalmi's exegetes in retrospect appear to twist and turn the language and message of a passage, attempting to make the words mean something other than what they appear to say. Whether the exegetical results remain close to the wording of a passage of the Mishnah, or whether they leap beyond the bounds of the passage, the upshot is the same. There is no exegetical pro-

gram revealed in the Yerushalmi's reading of the Mishnah other than that defined, to begin with, by the language and conceptions of one Mishnah passage
or another.

The Compilations of Scriptural Exegeses (Midrashim) and the Scriptures

The second principle by which compositors of documents selected and organized materials, in addition to that dictated by Mishnah exegesis, was Scripture exegesis. What did this mean? Quite simply, redactors would gather
materials of Scripture exegesis and organize them in the order of appearance
of verses of Scripture or of the unfolding of a story in Scripture. At the outset,
in the earliest scriptural-exegetical documents (generally assumed to be Sifra,
the two Sifres, followed by Genesis Rabbah and Leviticus Rabbah), people
adhered to the exegetical and redactional pattern already established for the
Mishnah. That is to say, they followed the order of verses of a biblical book,
just as the framers of the Yerushalmi followed the order of Mishnah sentences
of a given tractate. They undertook to explain' words or phrases, imposing
upon Scripture that set of values they regarded as self-evident and factual, the
values of sages' worldview and way of life. Since, it is usually alleged, the
Yerushalmi took shape circa A.D. 400 and the earlier compilations of scriptural exegeses occurred in that same time (Genesis Rabbah, then Leviticus
Rabbah in the period of, and shortly after, the Yerushalmi, with less certain
dates for Sifra and the two Sifres, probably prior to the Yerushalmi), we need
hardly be surprised at a simple fact. The same modes of exegesis and organization—that is, the same logoi and topoi—that determined the content of
self-evident comment in self-evident order on the Mishnah also dictated what
would be done on Scripture. So the original work of collecting and arranging
the compilations of exegeses of Scripture followed the patterns set in collecting and arranging exegeses of the Mishnah. Just as the Talmud, which is
Mishnah exegesis, treats the Mishnah, so the earliest collections of scriptural
exegesis treat Scripture.

My thesis, as is clear, may be expressed as a simple formula:

$$\frac{\text{Talmud}}{\text{Mishnah}} = \frac{\text{Exegetical Collection}}{\text{Scripture}}$$

To put the matter in words, Genesis Rabbah on Genesis is to be compared to a
Talmud tractate devoted to a particular tractate of the Mishnah on that tractate. Let me spell this out. Since the compilation of scriptural exegeses closest in time to the Yerushalmi is Genesis Rabbah, we focus attention on that
document. When we do, we see that Genesis Rabbah is composed of units of
discourse as cogent, in their way, as the ones in the Talmud of the Land of
Israel. These units of discourse fall into precisely the same taxonomical cate-

gories as those of the Talmud of the Land of Israel. Accordingly, the way in which the rabbinical exegetes who selected passages of the Mishnah and so constructed the Talmud of the Land of Israel did their work turns out to be the same as the way in which rabbinical exegetes who selected passages of Scripture and so constructed Genesis Rabbah did *their* work.

Self-evidently, what the one group had to say about the Mishnah bears no material relationship to what the other group had to say about Genesis. But the modes of thought, the ways of framing inquiries and constructing the results into formations of protracted and cogent discourse, so accomplishing quite specific, limited hermeneutical purposes—these are taxonomically uniform. Furthermore, even when we employ a taxonomical system defined not by the Mishnah's continuum but solely by formal traits of Genesis Rabbah's units of discourse, specifically the placement of a verse of Scripture and the mode of analysis of that verse within an exegetical construction, the result is the same. What the masters of biblical exegesis did in Genesis was what the masters of Mishnaic exegesis did in whatever Mishnah tractate they chose for study. It follows that the compiling of the first collection of biblical exegesis falls into the same intellectual framework as the Talmud of the Land of Israel, whether this was before, at the same time as, or in the aftermath of the composition of the Yerushalmi.

Like the Yerushalmi, Genesis Rabbah emerges in two distinct literary stages: first, people worked out its components; second, people arranged them. These may well have been the same people at much the same time, but the literary work divides into separate and distinct stages. First came writing compositions expressive of complex ideas, framed in sophisticated ways. Second came selecting and arranging these units of discourse into the composition now before us. As I said, the taxonomical framework suitable for all units of discourse of the Yerushalmi moves, without significant variation or revision, to encompass and categorize the materials of the earliest composition of scriptural exegesis, Genesis Rabbah. This fact I demonstrated in *Midrash in Context* (Philadelphia, 1984). Let me summarize it. We recall that the framer of an exegetical unit of discourse in the Yerushalmi ordinarily would do one of two things: first, a phrase-by-phrase exegesis of the Mishnah; second, amplification of the meaning of a passage of the Mishnah. So a Talmudic sage confronting the Mishnah had the choice of explaining the meaning of a particular passage or expanding upon the meaning, or the overall theme, of a particular passage. The same was so for scriptural verses. True, in dealing with Scripture a sage might systematically interpret one thing in terms of something else, a verse of Scripture in light of an autonomous set of considerations not explicit in Scripture but (in his mind) absolutely critical to its full meaning. But that is still not much more than the exegesis of the passage at hand for a given purpose, established a priori. That is an exercise fully familiar to the framers of the units of discourse of the Talmud in their confrontation with the Mishnah.

To move on to the taxonomical categories for a scriptural book, these are four, of which the first two are closely related and the fourth of slight consequence. The first category encompasses close exegesis of Scripture, by which I mean a word-for-word or phrase-by-phrase interpretation of a passage. In such an activity, the framer of a discrete composition will wish to read and explain a verse or a few words of a verse of the Scripture at hand, pure and simple. The second category, no less exegetical than the first, is made up of units of discourse in which the components of the verse are treated as part of a larger statement of meaning rather than as a set of individual phrases, stichs requiring attention one by one. Accordingly, in this taxon we deal with wide-ranging discourse about the meaning of a particular passage, hence an effort to amplify what is said in a verse. Here the amplification may take a number of different forms and directions. But the discipline imposed by the originally cited verse of Scripture will always impose boundaries on discourse. The useful third taxon encompasses units of discourse in which the theme of a particular passage defines a very wide-ranging exercise. In this discussion the cited passage itself is unimportant. It is the theme that is definitive. Accordingly, in this third type we take up a unit of discourse in which the composer of the passage wishes to expand on a particular problem, (merely) illustrated in the cited passage. The problem, rather than the cited passage, defines the limits and direction of discourse. The passage at hand falls away, having provided a mere pretext for the real point of concern. The fourth and final taxon, also deriving from the Yerushalmi, takes in units of discourse shaped around a given topic but not intended to constitute cogent and tightly framed discourse on said topic. These units of discourse then constitute topical anthologies rather than carefully composed essays.

But we note that the taxonomic structure just now described derives from the categories inductively discovered for the Yerushalmi. That is suspect. So I have now to specify a different criterion for differentiation among units of discourse and indicate that it yields the same results. Specifically, we take as our point of departure a trait distinctive to the compilation of exegeses at hand rather than one important to the Yerushalmi's treatment of the Mishnah. What do we see? The trait will be the simple facts of the location and role of the proof text in the unit of discourse—(1) beginning, middle, end, on the one side, and (2) probative or merely decorative, on the other. When we ask whether or not a verse or key word is cited, and, if so, where and for what purpose, we locate two main types of units of discourse: (1) a great number in which the key word or verse is cited, and (2) a few in which the key verse is not cited. Among the former we find close counterparts to familiar taxa. The taxon that encompasses units of discourse in which a key verse is cited and then give word-for-word exegesis takes in precisely the same sort of units of discourse as fall into the category of exegesis of Scripture or the Mishnah. The formal taxon composed of units of discourse in which there is a citation of the key verse followed by amplification or expansion on the theme of the verse, without word-for-word exegesis, is familiar. It corresponds to the substantive taxon of units of discourse presenting amplification on the meaning of a given verse of Scripture or the Mishnah. The third formal taxon normally constitutes a mere variation on the second. That is, the location of the key verse—fore or aft—makes no difference in the principle of cogency established within the unit of discourse. There entries normally serve a purpose no different from the one met by the foregoing. If, therefore, we differentiate units of discourse through the use and placement of key verses or words, we discover that that principle of taxonomy produces fairly similar results as those attained when we ask about the purpose or function of a unit of discourse. That is to say, the real point of differentiation is not the position of the key verse, or even whether it is cited, but whether or not it is amplified in a direct way.

In *Midrash in Context* I showed that the two taxonomic schemes just now outlined encompass vast stretches of materials of Genesis Rabbah. Since Sifra and the two Sifres consist of phrase-by-phrase exegeses of verses of Leviticus, Numbers, and Deuteronomy, respectively, the same taxonomy self-evidently serves. But I have to introduce an important qualification. In exegetical compilations produced later, after the time of the Yerushalmi, on the one side, and in earliest compilations of exegeses of Scripture, on the other, matters went their own way. For our purposes, however, that fact bears no material consequences.

The main point is simple. Types of units of discourse that we find in the Yerushalmi and the ones that comprise Genesis Rabbah fall into precisely the same categories and only into those categories. Second, this simple fact of taxonomy then is joined to a further datum. It is generally supposed that the work of composing the first rabbinic collection of exegeses of Scripture to take up nonlegal portions of the Pentateuch (or any other part of the Hebrew Bible), Genesis Rabbah, came at about the same time as the labor of composing the Yerushalmi. Whatever the origin of the materials brought together and formed into a composition, the final composition turns out to be made of materials framed in accord with the same principles of cogent discourse and, hence for the purpose of the same sort of exegesis, as the ones in the Yerushalmi. Taxonomically, all that changes is the document subjected to exegesis (as well, of course, as what is said about it). Because the modes of thought and discourse turn out to exhibit precisely the same definitive traits and only those traits, they sustain a remarkably monothetic taxonomy. Third, that is why I propose the simple equation: The Yerushalmi is to the Mishnah as compilations of exegesis are to Scripture.

The Compositions No One Made: Collections of Wise Sayings and Biographies

The Yerushalmi and the collections of scriptural exegeses comprise compositions made up of already-worked-out units of discourse focused upon the Mishnah and Scripture, respectively. Other such completed compositions deal with individual sages. The two cited components of the canon of Judaism as well as the Bavli contain a sizable quantity of sage units of discourse. These could have coalesced in yet a third type of book. Specifically, sayings and stories about sages could have been organized into collections of wise sayings attributed to various authorities (like Abot), on the one side, or brief snippets of biographies or lives of the saints, on the other. Since the pertinent materials for biographical compositions occur in profusion in the Bavli, we jump ahead and turn to the Bavli's materials of this sort, with the clear stipulation that the same type of materials occur also both in the Yerushalmi and in collections of scriptural exegeses.

Let me define more fully the present unit of discourse. The third type of unit of discourse focuses upon the sage. In this type things that a given authority said are strung together or tales about a given authority are told at some length. Whoever composed and preserved units of discourse on the Mishnah and on Scripture did the same for the sage. What that fact means is simple. In the circles responsible for making up and writing down completed units of discourse, three distinct categories of interest defined the task: (1) exegesis of the Mishnah, (2) exegesis of Scripture, and (3) preservation and exegesis, in exactly the same reverential spirit, of the words and deeds of sages.

We are able, moreover, to show that precisely the same modes of explanation and interpretation found suitable for the Mishnah and the Scripture served equally well for the sayings and doings of sages. That fact may be shown in three ways. First, just as Scripture supplied proof texts, so deeds or statements of sages provided proof texts. Second, just as a verse of Scripture or an explicit statement of the Mishnah resolved a disputed point, so what a sage said or did might be introduced into discourse as ample proof for settling a dispute. And third, it follows that just as Scripture or the Mishnah laid down Torah, so what a sage did or said laid down Torah. In the dimensions of the applied and practical reason by which the law unfolded, the sage found a comfortable place in precisely the taxonomic categories defined, to begin with, by both the Mishnah and Scripture.

Before proceeding to the implications, for our inquiry, of discourse about the sage, let us examine a few substantial examples of the sorts of sustained discourse in biographical materials turned out by circles of sages. What we shall see is an important fact. Just as these circles composed units of discourse about the meaning of a Mishnah passage, a larger theoretical problem of law, the sense of scriptural verse, and the sayings and doings of scriptural heroes seen as sages, so they did the same for living sages themselves. In the simplest example we see that two discrete sayings of a sage are joined together. The principle of conglomeration, therefore, is solely the name of the sage at hand. One saying has to do with overcoming the impulse to do evil, and the other has to do with the classifications of sages' program of learning. What the two subjects have in common is slight. But to the framer of the passage, that fact meant nothing. For he thought that compositions joined by the same tradent and authority—Levi and Simeon—should be made up.

B. Berakhot 4b.XXIII.

A. Said R. Levi bar Hama said R. Simeon b. Laqish, "A person should always provoke his impulse to do good against his impulse to do evil,

B. "as it is said, 'Provoke and do not sin' (Ps. 4:5).

C. "If [the good impulse] wins, well and good. If not, let him take up Torah study,

D. "as it is said, 'Commune with your own heart' (Ps. 4:5).

E. "If [the good impulse] wins, well and good. If not, let him recite the Shema,

F. "as it is said, 'upon your bed' (Ps. 4:5).

G. "If [the good impulse] wins, well and good. If not, let him remember the day of death,

H. "as it is said, 'And keep silent. Sela' (Ps. 4:5)."

I. And R. Levi bar Hama said R. Simeon b. Laqish said, "What is the meaning of the verse of Scripture, 'And I will give you the tables of stone, the law and the commandment, which I have written, that you may teach them' (Exod. 24:12).

J. " 'The tables' refers to the Ten Commandments.

K. " 'Torah' refers to Scripture.

L. " 'Commandment' refers to Mishnah.

M. " 'Which I have written' refers to the Prophets and the Writings.

N. " 'That you may teach them' refers to the Gemara.

O. "This teaches that all of them were given to Moses from Sinai."

The frame of the story at hand links A–H and I–O in a way unfamiliar to those accustomed to the principles of conglomeration in legal and biblical-exegetical compositions. In the former, a given problem or principle of law will tell us why one item is joined to some other. In the latter, a single verse of Scripture will account for the joining of two or more otherwise discrete units of thought. Here one passage, A–H, takes up Ps. 4:5; the other, I–O, Exod. 24:12. The point of the one statement hardly goes over the ground of the other. So the sole principle by which one item has joined the other is biographical: a record of what a sage said about topics that are, at best, contiguous, if related at all.

A second way of stringing together materials illustrative of the lives and teachings of sages is to join incidents involving a given authority or (as in the following case) two authorities believed to have stood in close relationship with one another, disciple and master, for instance. Often these stories go over the same ground in the same way. In the following, the two farewell stories make essentially the same point but in quite different language. What joins the stories is not only the shared theme but the fact that Eliezer is supposed to have studied with Yohanan b. Zakkai.

B. Sanhedrin 68A.II.

   A.   Our rabbis have taught on Tannaite authority:

   B.   When R. Eliezer fell ill, his disciples came in to pay a call on him. They said to him, "Our master, teach us the ways of life, so that through them we may merit the world to come."

   C.   He said to them, "Be attentive to the honor owing to your fellows, keep your children from excessive reflection, and set them among the knees of disciples of sages, and when you pray, know before whom you stand, and on that account you will merit the life of the world to come."

   D.   And when R. Yohanan b. Zakkai fell ill, his disciples came in to pay a call on him. When he saw them, he began to cry. His disciples said to him, "Light of Israel! Pillar at the right hand! Mighty hammer! On what account are you crying?"

   E.   He said to them, "If I were going to be brought before a mortal king, who is here today and tomorrow gone to the grave, who, should he be angry with me, will not be angry forever, and, if he should imprison me, will not imprison me forever, and if he should put me to death, whose sentence of death is not for eternity, and whom I can appease with the right words or bribe with money, even so, I should weep.

   F.   "But now that I am being brought before the King of kings of kings, the Holy One, blessed be he, who endures forever and ever, who, should he be angry with me, will be angry forever, and if he should imprison me, will imprison me forever, and if he should put me to death, whose sentence of death is for eternity, and whom I cannot appease with the right words or bribe with money,

   G.   "and not only so, but before me are two paths, one to the Garden of Eden and the other to Gehenna, and I do not know by which path I shall be brought,

   H.   "and should I not weep?"

   I.   They said to him, "Our master, bless us."

   J.   He said to them, "May it be God's will that the fear of Heaven be upon you as much as the fear of mortal man."

   K.   His disciples said, "Just so much?"

   L.   He said to them, "Would that it were that much. You should know that, when a person commits a transgression, he says, 'I hope no man sees me.'"

   M.   When he was dying, he said to them, "Clear out utensils from the house, because of the uncleanness [of the corpse, which I am about to impart when I die], and prepare a throne for Hezekiah king of Judah, who is coming."

The links between B – C and D – M are clear. First, we have stories about sages' farewells. Second, people took for granted, because of the lists of M. Abot 2:2ff., that Eliezer was disciple of Yohanan b. Zakkai. Otherwise, it is difficult to explain the joining of the stories, since they scarcely make the same point, go over the same matters, or even share a common literary or rhetorical form or preference. But a framer of a composition of lives of saints, who is writing a tractate on how saints die, will have found this passage a powerful one indeed.

Yet another approach to the utilization of tales about sages was to join together stories on a given theme but told about different sages. A tractate or a chapter of a tractate on a given theme, for example, suffering and its reward, can have emerged from the sort of collection that follows. The importance of the next item is that the same kinds of stories about different sages are strung together to make a single point.

B. Berakhot 5B.XXXI.

A.   R. Hiyya bar Abba got sick. R. Yohanan came to him. He said to him, "Are these sufferings precious to you?"

B.   He said to him, "I don't want them, I don't want their reward."

C.   He said to him, "Give me your hand."

D.   He gave him his hand, and [Yohanan] raised him up [out of his sickness].

E.   R. Yohanan got sick. R. Hanina came to him. He said to him, "Are these sufferings precious to you?"

F.   He said to him, "I don't want them. I don't want their reward."

G.   He said to him, "Give me your hand."

H.   He gave him his hand and [Hanina] raised him up [out of his sickness].

I.   Why so? R. Yohanan should have raised himself up?

J.   They say, "A prisoner cannot get himself out of jail."

B. Berakhot 5B.XXXII.

A.   R. Eliezer got sick. R. Yohanan came to see him and found him lying in a dark room. [The dying man] uncovered his arm, and light fell [through the room]. [Yohanan] saw that R. Eliezer was weeping. He said to him, "Why are you crying? Is it because of the Torah that you did not learn sufficiently? We have learned: 'All the same are the ones who do much and do little, so long as each person will do it for the sake of heaven.'

B.   "Is it because of insufficient income? Not everyone has the merit of seeing two tables [Torah and riches, as you have. You have been a master of Torah and also have enjoyed wealth].

C.   "Is it because of children? Here is the bone of my tenth son [whom I buried, so it was no great loss not to have children, since you might have had to bury them]."

D.   He said to him, "I am crying because of this beauty of mine which will be rotting in the ground."

E.   He said to him, "For that it certainly is worth crying," and the two of them wept together.

F.   He said to him, "Are these sufferings precious to you?"

G.   He said to him, "I don't want them, I don't want their reward."

H.   He said to him, "Give me your hand."

I.   He gave him his hand, and [Yohanan] raised him up [out of his sickness].

B. Berakhot 5B.XXXIII.

A.   Four hundred barrels of wine turned sour on R. Huna. R. Judah, brother of R. Sala the Pious, and rabbis came to see him (and some say it was R. Ada bar Ahba and rabbis). They said to him, "The master should take a good look at his deeds."

B.   He said to them, "And am I suspect in your eyes?"

C.   They said to him, "And is the Holy One, blessed be he, suspect of inflicting a penalty without justice?"

D.   He said to them, "Has anybody heard anything bad about me? Let him say it."

E.   They said to him, "This is what we have heard: the master does not give to his hired hand [the latter's share of] vine twigs [which are his right]."

F.   He said to them, "Does he leave me any! He steals all of them to begin with."

G.   They said to him, "This is in line with what people say: 'Go steal from a thief but taste theft too!' [Simon: If you steal from a thief, you also have a taste of it.]"

H.   He said to them, "I pledge that I'll give them to him."

I.   Some say that the vinegar turned back into wine, and some say that the price of vinegar went up so he sold it off at the price of wine.

The foregoing composite makes the same point several times: "Not them, not their reward." Sufferings are precious, but sages are prepared to forego the benefits. The formally climactic entry at XXXIII makes the point that, if bad things happen, the victim has deserved punishment. In joining these several stories about sages—two involving Yohanan, the third entirely separate—the compositor of the passage made his point by juxtaposing two like biographical snippets to a distinct one. Collections of stories about saints can have served quite naturally when formed into tractates on pious virtues, expressing these virtues through strong and pictorial language such as is before us.

The foregoing sources have shown two important facts. First, a principle of composition in the sages' circles was derived from interest in the teachings associated with a given sage, as well as in tales and stories told about a sage or groups of sages. The first of the passages shows us the simplest composition of sayings, the latter, an equivalent conglomeration of related stories. Up to this point, therefore, the reader will readily concede that biographical materials on sages, as much as Mishnah exegesis and Scripture exegesis, came forth out of circles of sages. But I have yet to show that such materials attained sufficient volume and cogency from large-scale compilations—conglomerates so substantial as to sustain entire books.

At the risk of taxing the reader's patience, I shall now demonstrate that, had the framers of large-scale rabbinic compositions wished, they could readily have made up tractates devoted to diverse sayings of a given authority (or, tradent-and-authority). What follows to demonstrate the possibility are two enormous compositions, which together can have made up as much as half of a Talmud chapter in volume. If anyone had wanted to compose a chapter around rabbinical authorities' names, he is thus shown to have had the opportunity.

The first shows us a string of sayings not only in a single set of names but also on discrete subjects. We also see how such a string of sayings could form the focus of exactly the kind of critical analysis and secondary amplification to which any other Talmudic passage would be subjected. So there can have been not only a Talmud based on the Mishnah and a midrash composition based on the Scripture but also a life of a saint (a gospel?) based on a set of rabbis' sayings. Here is the Talmud that can have served a collection of sayings of Yohanan-in-the-name-of-Simeon b. Yohai.

B. Berakhot 7B–8A.LIX.

    A.   [7B] Said R. Yohanan in the name of R. Simeon b. Yohai, "From the day on which the Holy One, blessed be he, created the world, there was no man who called the Holy One, blessed be he, 'Lord,' until Abraham came along and called him Lord.

    B.   "For it is said, 'And he said, O Lord, God, whereby shall I know that I shall inherit it' (Gen. 15:8)."

    C.   Said Rab, "Daniel too was answered only on account of Abraham.

    D.   "For it is said, 'Now therefore, O our God, hearken to the prayer of your servant and to his supplications and cause your face to shine upon your sanctuary that is desolate, for the *Lord's* sake' (Dan. 9:17).

    E.   "'For your sake' is what he should have said, but the sense is, 'For the sake of Abraham, who called you Lord.'"

B. Berakhot 7B–8A.LX.

    A.   And R. Yohanan said in the name of R. Simeon b. Yohai, "How do we know that people should not seek to appease someone when he is mad?

    B.   "As it is said, 'My face will go and then I will give you rest' (Exod. 33:14)."

B. Berakhot 7B–8A.LXI.

    A.   And R. Yohanan said in the name of R. Simeon b. Yohai, "From the day on which the Holy One, blessed be he, created his world, there was no one who praised the Holy One, blessed be he, until Leah came along and praised him.

    B.   "For it is said, 'This time I will praise the Lord' (Gen. 29:35)."

    C.   As to Reuben, said R. Eleazar, "Leah said, 'See what is the difference [the name of Reuben yielding *reu* (see) and *ben* (between)] between my son and the son of my father-in-law.

    D.   "The son of my father-in-law, even knowingly, sold off his birthright, for it is written, 'And he sold his birthright to Jacob' (Gen. 25:33).

    E.   "See what is written concerning him: 'And Esau hated Jacob' (Gen. 27:41), and it is written, 'And he said, is he not rightly named Jacob? for he has supplanted me these two times' (Gen. 27:36).

    F.   "My son, by contrast, even though Joseph forcibly took away his birthright, as it is written, 'But for as much as he defiled his father's couch, his birthright was given to the sons of Joseph' (1 Chron. 5:1), did not become jealous of him, for it is written, 'And Reuben heard it and delivered him out of their hand' (Gen. 37:21)."

    G.   As to the meaning of the name of Ruth, said R. Yohanan, "It was because she had the merit that David would come forth from her, who saturated (RWH) the Holy One, blessed be he, with songs and praises."

    H.   How do we know that a person's name affects [his life]?

    I.   Said R. Eleazar, "It is in line with the verse of Scripture: 'Come, behold the works of the Lord, who has made desolations in the earth' (Ps. 46:9).

    J.   "Do not read 'desolations' but 'names' [which the same root yields]."

B. Berakhot 7B–8A.LXII.

    A.   And R. Yohanan said in the name of R. Simeon b. Yohai, "Bringing a child up badly is worse in a person's house than the war of Gog and Magog.

B. "For it is said, 'A Psalm of David, when he fled from Absalom, his son' (Ps. 3:1), after which it is written, 'Lord how many are my adversaries become, many are they that rise up against me' (Ps. 3:2).

C. "By contrast, in regard to the war of Gog and Magog it is written, 'Why are the nations in an uproar? And why do the peoples mutter in vain?' (Ps. 2:1).

D. "But it is not written in that connection, 'How many are my adversaries become.'"

E. "A Psalm of David, when he fled from Absalom, his son (Ps. 3:1):

F. "'A Psalm of David'? It should be, 'A *lamentation* of David'!

G. Said R. Simeon b. Abishalom, "The matter may be compared to the case of a man against whom an outstanding bond was issued. Before he had paid it, he was sad. After he had paid it, he was glad.

H. "So too with David, when he the Holy One had said to him, 'Behold, I will raise up evil against you out of your own house,' (2 Sam. 2:11), he was sad.

I. "He thought to himself, 'Perhaps it will be a slave or a bastard child, who will not have pity on me.'

J. "When he saw that it was Absalom, he was happy. On that account, he said a psalm."

B. Berakhot 7B–8A.LXIII.

A. And R. Yohanan said in the name of R. Simeon b. Yohai, "It is permitted to contend with the wicked in this world,

B. "for it is said, 'Those who forsake the Torah praise the wicked, but those who keep the Torah contend with them' (Prov. 28:4)."

C. It has been taught on Tannaite authority along these same lines:

D. R. Dosetai bar Matun says, "It is permitted to contend with the wicked in this world, for it is said, 'Those who forsake the Torah praise the wicked, but those who keep the Torah contend with them' (Prov. 28:4)."

E. And if someone should whisper to you, "But is it not written, 'Do not contend with evildoers, nor be envious against those who work unrighteousness' (Ps. 37:1)," say to him, "Someone whose conscience bothers him thinks so.

F. "In fact, 'Do not contend with evildoers' means, do not be like them, 'nor be envious against those who work unrighteousness,' means, do not be like them.

G. "And so it is said, 'Let your heart not envy sinners, but fear the Lord all day' (Prov. 23:17)."

H. Is this the case? And lo, R. Isaac has said, "If you see a wicked person for whom the hour seems to shine, do not contend with him, for it is said, 'His ways prosper at all times' (Ps. 10:5).

I.   "Not only so, but he wins in court, as it is said, 'Your judgments are far above, out of his sight' (Ps. 10:5).

J.   "Not only so, but he overcomes his enemies, for it is said, 'As for all his enemies, he farts at them' (Ps. 10:5)."

K.   There is no contradiction. The one [Isaac] addresses one's own private matters [in which case one should not contend with the wicked], but the other speaks of matters having to do with Heaven [in which case one should contend with them].

L.   And if you wish, I shall propose that both parties speak of matters having to do with Heaven. There is, nonetheless, no contradiction. The one [Isaac] speaks of a wicked person on whom the hour shines, the other of a wicked person on whom the hour does not shine.

M.   And if you wish, I shall propose that both parties speak of a wicked person on whom the hour shines, and there still is no contradiction.

N.   The one [Yohanan, who says the righteous may contend with the wicked] speaks of a completely righteous person, the other [Isaac] speaks of someone who is not completely righteous.

O.   For R. Huna said, "What is the meaning of this verse of Scripture: 'Why do you look, when they deal treacherously, and hold your peace, when the wicked swallows up the man that is more righteous than he' (Hab. 1:13)?

P.   "Now can a wicked person swallow up a righteous one?

Q.   "And lo, it is written, 'The Lord will not leave him in his hand' (Ps. 37:33). And it is further written, 'No mischief shall befall the righteous' (Prov. 12:21).

R.   "The fact therefore is that he may swallow up someone who is more righteous than he, but he cannot swallow up a completely righteous man."

S.   And if you wish, I shall propose that, when the hour shines for him, the situation is different.

B. Berakhot 7B–8A.LXIV.

A.   And R. Yohanan said in the name of R. Simeon b. Yohai, "Beneath anyone who establishes a regular place for praying do that person's enemies fall.

B.   "For it is said, 'And I will appoint a place for my people Israel, and I will plant them, that they may dwell in their own place and be disquieted no more, neither shall the children of wickedness afflict them any more as at the first' (2 Sam. 7:10)."

C.   R. Huna pointed to a contradiction between two verses of Scripture: "It is written, 'To afflict them,' and elsewhere, 'To exterminate them' (1 Chron. 17:9).

D. "To begin with, merely to afflict them, but, at the end, to exterminate them."

B. Berakhot 7B–8A.LXV.

A. And R. Yohanan said in the name of R. Simeon b. Yohai, "Greater is personal service to Torah than learning in Torah [so doing favors for a sage is of greater value than studying with him].

B. "For it is said, 'Here is Elisha, the son of Shaphat, who poured water on the hands of Elijah' (2 Kings 3:11).

C. "It is not said, 'who learned' but 'who poured water.'

D. "This teaches that greater is service to Torah than learning in Torah."

It is not difficult to pick up the main beams of the foregoing construction, since they are signified by Yohanan-Simeon sayings, LIX.A, LX.A, LXI.A, LXII.A, LXIII.A, LXIV.A, LXV.A—seven entries in line. The common theme is not prayer; no other topic is treated in a cogent way either. The sort of inner coherence to which any student of the Bavli is accustomed is not before us. Rather we have a collection of wise thoughts on diverse topics, more in the manner of Proverbs than in the style of the great intellects behind the sustained reasoning in passages of the Bavli and much of the Yerushalmi as well. What is interesting is that, at a later stage, other pertinent materials have been inserted, for example, Rab's at LIX.C–E, and so on down. There is no reason to imagine that these sayings were made up in response to Yohanan-Simeon's statement. Quite to the contrary, framed in their own terms, the sayings were presumably tacked on at a point at which the large-scale construction of Yohanan-Simeon was worked over for a purpose beyond the one intended by the original compositor. For what he wanted to do he did, which is, compose a collection of Yohanan-Simeon sayings. If he hoped that his original collection would form part of a larger composition on Yohanan, he surely was disappointed. But even if he imagined that he would make up material for compositions of lives and sayings of saints, he cannot have expected his little collection to end up where and how it did, as part of a quite different corpus of writing from one in which a given authority had his say or in which stories were told in some sort of sensible sequence about a particular sage. The type of large-scale composition, for which our imagined compositor did his work, in the end never came into being in the rabbinic canon.

In the following, still longer example I begin with the passage to which the entire composition, organized in the name of a tradent and a sage, is attached. At B. Berakhot 6B/1:1 XLI, we have a statement that a synagogue should have a regular quorum. Then the next passage, 1:1 XLII, makes the secondary point that a person should pray in a regular place—a reasonable amplification of the foregoing. That is, just as there should be a quorum routinely organized in a given location, so should an individual routinely attach himself to a given quorum. This statement is given by Helbo in Huna's name. What follows is a sizable set of sayings by Helbo in Huna's name, all of them on the general theme of prayer but none of them on the specific point at hand. Still more interesting, just as in the foregoing, the passage as a whole was composed so that the Helbo-Huna materials themselves are expanded and enriched with secondary accretions. For instance, at XLIII the base materials are given glosses of a variety of types. All in all, we see what we may call a little tractate in the making. But, as we shall hardly have to repeat, no one in the end created a genre of rabbinic literature to accommodate the vast collections of available compositions on sages' sayings and doings.

B. Berakhot 6B.XLI.

A. Said R. Yohanan, "When the Holy One, blessed be he, comes to a synagogue and does not find ten present, he forthwith becomes angry.

B. "For it is said, 'Why when I came was there no one there? When I called, there was no answer' (Isa. 50:2)."

B. Berakhot 6B.XLII.

A. Said R. Helbo said R. Huna, "For whoever arranges a regular place for praying, the God of Abraham is a help, and when he dies, they say for him, 'Woe for the humble man, woe for the pious man, one of the disciples of Abraham, our father.'

B. "And how do we know in the case of Abraham, our father, that he arranged a regular place for praying?

C. "For it is written, 'And Abraham got up early in the morning on the place where he had stood' (Gen. 19:27).

D. "'Standing' refers only to praying, for it is said, 'Then Phinehas stood up and prayed' (Ps. 106:30)."

E. Said R. Helbo to R. Huna, "He who leaves the synagogue should not take large steps."

F. Said Abayye, "That statement applies only when one leaves, but when he enters, it is a religious duty to run [to the synagogue].

G. "For it is said, 'Let us run to know the Lord' (Hos. 6:3)."

H. Said R. Zira, "When in the beginning I saw rabbis running to the lesson on the Sabbath, I thought that the rabbis were profaning the Sabbath. But now that I have heard what R. Tanhum said R. Joshua b. Levi said,

I. "namely, 'A person should always run to take up a matter of law, and even on the Sabbath, as it is said, "They shall walk after the

Lord who shall roar like a lion [for he shall roar, and the children shall come hurrying]" (Hos. 11:10),'

J.   "I too run."

B. Berakhot 6B.XLIII.

A.   Said R. Zira, "The reward for attending the lesson is on account of running [to hear the lesson, not necessarily on account of what one has learned.]"

B.   Said Abayye, "The reward for attending the periodic public assembly [of rabbis] is on account of the crowding together."

C.   Said Raba [to the contrary], "The reward for repeating what one has heard is in reasoning about it."

D.   Said R. Papa, "The reward for attending a house of mourning is on account of one's preserving silence there."

E.   Said Mar Zutra, "The reward for observing a fast day lies in the acts of charity one performs on that day."

F.   Said R. Sheshet, "The reward for delivering a eulogy lies in raising the voice."

G.   Said R. Ashi, "The reward for attending a wedding lies in the words [of compliment paid to the bride and groom]."

B. Berakhot 6B.XLIV.

A.   Said R. Huna, "Whoever prays behind the synagogue is called wicked,

B.   "as it is said, 'The wicked walk round about' (Ps. 12:9)."

C.   Said Abayye, "That statement applies only in the case of one who does not turn his face toward the synagogue, but if he turns his face toward the synagogue, we have no objection."

D.   There was a certain man who would say his prayers behind the synagogue and did not turn his face toward the synagogue. Elijah came by and saw him. He appeared to him in the guise of a Tai Arab.

E.   He said to him, "Are you now standing with your back toward your master?" He drew his sword and killed him.

F.   One of the rabbis asked R. Bibi bar Abayye, and some say, R. Bibi asked R. Nahman bar Isaac, "What is the meaning of the verse, 'When vileness is exalted among the sons of men' (Ps. 12:9)?"

G.   He said to him, "This refers to matters that are exalted, which people treat with contempt."

H.   R. Yohanan and R. Eleazar both say, "When a person falls into need of the help of other people, his face changes color like the *kerum,* for it is said, 'As the *kerum* is to be reviled among the sons of men' (Ps. 12:9)."

I.   What is the meaning of *kerum?*

J.   When R. Dimi came, he said, "There is a certain bird among the coast towns, called the *kerum.* When the sun shines, it turns many colors."

K.   R. Ammi and R. Assi both say, "[When a person turns to others for support], it is as if he is judged to suffer the penalties of both fire and water.

L.   "For it is said, 'When you caused men to ride over our heads, we went through fire and through water' (Ps. 66:12)."

B. Berakhot 6B.XLV.

A.   And R. Helbo said R. Huna said, "A person should always be attentive at the afternoon prayer.

B.   "For lo, Elijah was answered only at the afternoon prayer.

C.   "For it is said, 'And it came to pass at the time of the offering of the late afternoon offering, that Elijah the prophet came near and said, "Hear me, O Lord, hear me" ' (1 Kings 18:36–37)."

D.   "Hear me" so fire will come down from heaven.

E.   "Hear me" that people not say it is merely witchcraft.

F.   R. Yohanan said, "[A person should also be attentive about] the evening prayer.

G.   "For it is said, 'Let my prayer be set forth as incense before you, the lifting up of my hands as the evening sacrifice' (Ps. 141:2)."

H.   R. Nahman bar Isaac said, "[A person should also be attentive about] the morning prayer.

I.   "For it is said, 'O Lord, in the morning you shall hear my voice, in the morning I shall order my prayer to you, and will look forward' (Ps. 5:4)."

B. Berakhot 6B.XLVI.

A.   And R. Helbo said R. Huna said, "Whoever enjoys a marriage banquet and does not felicitate the bridal couple violates five 'voices.'

B.   "For it is said, 'The voice of joy and the voice of gladness, the voice of the bridegroom and the voice of the bride, the voice of those who say, "Give thanks to the Lord of hosts"' (Jer. 33:11)."

C.   And if he does felicitate the couple, what reward does he get?

D.   Said R. Joshua b. Levi, "He acquires the merit of the Torah, which was handed down with five voices.

E.   "For it is said, 'And it came to pass on the third day, when it was morning, that there were voices [thus two], and lightnings, and a thick cloud upon the mount, and the voice of a horn, and when the voice of the horn waxed louder, . . . Moses spoke and God answered him by a voice . . .' (Exod. 19:16, 19) [thus five voices in all]."

F. Is it so [that there were only five voices]?

G. And lo, it is written, "And all the people saw the voices" (Exod. 20:15). [So this would make seven voices.]

H. These voices came before the giving of the Torah [and do not count].

I. R. Abbahu said, "It is as if the one [who felicitated the bridal couple] offered a thanksgiving offering.

J. "For it is said, 'Even of them that bring thanksgiving offerings into the house of the Lord' (Jer. 33:11)."

K. R. Nahman bar Isaac said, "It is as if he rebuilt one of the ruins of Jerusalem.

L. "For it is said, 'For I will cause the captivity of the land to return as at the first, says the Lord' (Jer. 33:11)."

B. Berakhot 6B.XLVII.

A. And R. Helbo said R. Huna said, "The words of any person in whom is fear of Heaven are heard.

B. "For it is said, 'The end of the matter, all having been heard: fear God and keep his commandments, for this is the whole man' (Qoh. 12:13)."

C. What is the meaning of the phrase, "For this is the whole man" (Qoh. 12:13)?

D. Said R. Eleazar, "Said the Holy One, blessed be he, 'The entire world has been created only on account of this one.'"

E. R. Abba bar Kahana said, "This one is worth the whole world."

F. Simeon b. Zoma says, "The entire world was created only to accompany this one."

B. Berakhot 6B.XLVIII.

A. And R. Helbo said R. Huna said, "Whoever knows that his fellow regularly greets him should greet the other first.

B. "For it is said, 'Seek peace and pursue it' (Ps. 34:15).

C. "If he greeted him and the other did not reply, the latter is called a thief.

D. "For it is said, 'It is you who have eaten up the vineyard, the spoil of the poor is in your houses' (Isa. 3:14)."

What we noted in connection with the Yohanan-Simeon collection needs no restatement here. The scope and dimensions of the passage prove impressive. Again we must wonder for what sort of composition the framer of the Helbo-

Huna collection planned his writing. Whatever it was, it hardly fit the ultimate destination of his work.

Let us now return to the point with which we began, the position and authority of the sage. As I said at the outset, the sage stood at that same level of authority as did the Torah, on the one side, and the Mishnah, on the other. Let me now show exactly how we know that fact.

What we observe, through a single interesting instance, is that the same modes of exegetical inquiry pertaining to the Mishnah and Scripture apply without variation to statements made by rabbis of the contemporary period themselves. Indeed, precisely the same theological and exegetical considerations come to bear both upon the Mishnah's statements and opinions expressed by talmudic rabbis. Since these were not to be distinguished from one another in the requirement that opinion be suitably grounded in Scripture, they also should be understood to have formed part of precisely the same corpus of Torah truths. What the Mishnah and the later rabbi said expressed precisely the same kind of truth: revelation—whether through the medium of Scripture, or that contained in the Mishnah, or that given in the opinion of the sage himself. The way in which this search for proof texts applies equally to the Mishnah and to the rabbi's opinion is illustrated in the following passage.

Yerushalmi Sanhedrin 10:4.I.

A.   *The party of Korah has no portion in the world to come, and will not live in the world to come [Mishnah Sanhedrin 10:4].*

B.   What is the scriptural basis for this view?

C.   "So they and all that belonged to them went down alive into Sheol; and the earth closed over them; and they perished from the midst of the assembly" (Num. 16:33).

D.   *"The earth closed over them"—in this world.*

E.   *"And they perished from the midst of the assembly"—in the world to come [Mishnah Sanhedrin 10:4D–F].*

F.   It was taught: **R. Judah b. Batera says, "The contrary view is to be derived from the implication of the following verse:**

G.   **" 'I have gone astray like a lost sheep; seek thy servant and do not forget they commandments' (Ps. 119:176).**

H.   **"Just as the lost object which is mentioned later on in the end is going to be searched for, so the lost object which is stated herein is destined to be searched for" [Tosefta Sanhedrin 13:9].**

I.   Who will pray for them?

J.   R. Samuel bar Nahman said, "Moses will pray for them.

K.   [This is proved from the following verse:] " 'Let Reuben live, and not die, [nor let his men be few]' (Deut. 33:6)."

L.   R. Joshua b. Levi said, "Hannah will pray for them."

M.   This is the view of R. Joshua b. Levi, for R. Joshua b. Levi said,

"Thus did the party of Korah sink ever downward, until Hannah went and prayed for them and said, 'The Lord kills and brings to life; he brings down to Sheol and raises up' (1 Sam. 2:6)."

We have a striking sequence of proof texts, serving (1) the cited statement of the Mishnah, A–C, then (2) an opinion of a rabbi in the Tosefta, F–H, then (3) the position of a rabbi, J–K and L–M. The process of providing proof texts therefore is central; the nature of the passages requiring the proof texts, a matter of indifference. We see that the search for appropriate verses of Scripture vastly transcends the purpose of studying the Mishnah and Scripture, the exegesis of their rules, or the provision of adequate authority for the Mishnah and its laws. In fact, any proposition that is to be taken seriously, whether in the Mishnah, in the Tosefta, or in the mouth of a talmudic sage himself, will elicit interest in scriptural support.

Why does the quest in Scripture for proof texts matter here? It is because we see that the real issue turns out to have been not the Mishnah at all, nor even the vindication of its diverse sayings, one by one. Why not? Once the words of a sage, not merely a rule of the Mishnah, are made to refer to Scripture for proof, it must follow that, in the natural course of things, a rule of the Mishnah or of the Tosefta will likewise be asked to refer to Scripture. That the living sage validated his own words through Scripture explains why the sage in the fourth century validated also the words of the (then) ancient sages of the Mishnah and Tosefta through verses of Scripture. It is one, undivided phenomenon. Distinctions are not made among media—(1) oral, (2) written, or (3) living—of the Torah. The Torah—in our language, the canon of revealed truth—is in three media, not two.

We turn to the way in which the rabbis of the Yerushalmi proposed to resolve differences of opinion. This is important because the Mishnah presents a mass of disputes. Turning speculation about principles into practical law required resolving them. Precisely in the same way in which talmudic rabbis settled disputes in the Mishnah and so attained a consensus about the law of the Mishnah, they handled disputes among themselves. The importance of that fact for our argument again is simple. The rabbis, represented in the Yerushalmi, treated their own contemporaries exactly as they treated the then-ancient authorities of the Mishnah. In their minds the status accorded to the Mishnah, as a derivative of the Torah, applied equally to sages' teachings. In the following instance we see how the same discourse attached to (1) a Mishnah rule is assigned as well to one in (2) the Tosefta and, at the end, to differences among (3) the Yerushalmi's authorities.

Yerushalmi Ketubot 5:1.VI.

    A.   R. Jacob bar Aha, R. Alexa in the name of Hezekiah: "The law accords with the view of R. Eleazar b. Azariah, who stated, *If she was widowed or divorced at the stage of betrothal, the virgin col-*

> *lects only two hundred zuz and the widow, a maneh. If she was widowed or divorced at the stage of a consummated marriage, she collects the full amount [M. Ket. 5:1E,D]."*

B. R. Hananiah said, "The law accords with the view of R. Eleazar b. Azariah."

C. Said Abayye, "They said to R. Hananiah, 'Go and shout [outside whatever opinion you like.' But] R. Jonah, R. Zeira in the name of R. Jonathan said, 'The law accords with the view of R. Eleazar b. Azariah.' [Yet] R. Yosa bar Zeira in the name of R. Jonathan said, 'The law does not accord with the view of R. Eleazar b. Azariah.' [So we do not in fact know the decision.]"

D. Said R. Yose, "We had a mnemonic: Hezekiah and R. Jonathan both say one thing."

E. For it has been taught:

F. **He whose son went abroad, and whom they told, "Your son has died,"**

G. **and who went and wrote over all his property to someone else as a gift,**

H. **and whom they afterward informed that his son was yet alive—**

I. **his deed of gift remains valid.**

J. **R. Simeon b. Menassia says, "His deed of gift is not valid, for if he had known that his son was alive, he would never have made such a gift" [T. Ket. 4:14E–H].**

K. Now R. Jacob bar Aha [=A] said, "The law is in accord with the view of R. Eleazar b. Azariah, and the opinion of R. Eleazar b. Azariah is the same in essence as that of R. Simeon b. Menassia."

L. Now R. Yannai said to R. Hananiah, "Go and shout [outside whatever you want].

M. "But, said R. Yose bar Zeira in the name of R. Jonathan, 'The law is not in accord with R. Eleazar b. Azariah.'"

N. But in fact the case was to be decided in accord with the view of R. Eleazar b. Azariah.

What is important here is that the Talmud makes no distinction whatever when deciding the law of disputes (1) in the Mishnah, (2) in the Tosefta, and (3) among talmudic rabbis. The same already-formed colloquy applied at the outset to the Mishnah's dispute is then held equally applicable to the Tosefta's. The process of thought is the main thing, without regard to the document to which the process applies.

Still more important than the persistence of a given mode of thought applicable to Scripture, to the Mishnah, and to the sayings of Yerushalmi's rabbis themselves is the presentation of the rabbi as a lawgiver in the model of Moses. The capacity of the sage himself to participate in the process of revelation is illustrated in two types of materials. First, tales told about rabbis' behavior on specific occasions immediately were translated into rules for the entire community to keep. Accordingly—and for us this is crucial—he was a source not merely of good example but of prescriptive law.

Y. Abodah Zarah 5 :4.III.

X.   R. Aha went to Emmaus, and he ate dumpling [prepared by Samaritans].
Y.   R. Jeremiah ate leavened bread prepared by them.
Z.   R. Hezekiah ate locusts prepared by them.
AA.   R. Abbahu prohibited Israelite use of wine prepared by them.

These reports of what rabbis had done enjoyed the same authority as statements of the law on eating what Samaritans cooked, as did citations of traditions in the names of the great authorities of old. What someone did served as a norm, if he was a sage of sufficient standing.

Far more common are instances in which the deed of a rabbi is adduced as an authoritative precedent for the law under discussion. It was everywhere taken for granted that what a rabbi did he did because of his mastery of the law. Even though a formulation of the law was not in hand, a tale about what a rabbi actually did constituted adequate evidence on how to formulate the law itself. So on the basis of the action or practice of an authority, a law might be framed that was quite independent of the person of the sage. The sage then functioned as a lawgiver, like Moses. Among many instances of that mode of generating law are the following:

Y. Abodah Zarah 3 :11.II.

A.   Gamaliel Zuga was walking along, leaning on the shoulder of R. Simeon b. Laqish. They came across an image.
B.   He said to him, "What is the law as to passing before it?"
C.   He said to him, "Pass before it, but close [your] eyes."
D.   R. Isaac was walking along, leaning on the shoulder of R. Yohanan. They came across an idol before the council building.
E.   He said to him, "What is the law as to passing before it?"
F.   He said to him, "Pass before it, but close [your] eyes."
G.   R. Jacob bar Idi was walking along, leaning upon R. Joshua b. Levi. They came across a procession in which an idol was carried. He said to him, "Nahum, the most holy man, passed before this idol, and will you not pass by it? Pass before it but close your eyes."

Y. Abodah Zarah 2 :2.III.

FF.   R. Aha had chills and fever. [They brought him] a medicinal drink prepared from the phallus of Dionysian revelers [thus Jastrow I.400.B]. But he would not drink it. They brought it to R. Jonah,

and he did drink it. Said R. Mana, "Now if R. Jonah, the patriarch, had known what it was, he would never have drunk it."

GG.   Said R. Huna, "That is to say, 'They do not accept healing from
something that derives from an act of fornication.'"

The point of these stories requires no repetition. What is important is GG, the
rewording of the point of the story as decided law. The sages of the Yerushalmi
recognized no distinction in authority or standing—hence, in status as revelation—between what the Mishnah said and what the written Torah said. They
also used the same process of validation to demonstrate that what they themselves declared enjoyed the same standing and authority as what they found in
the written Torah. So their intent always was to show that in fact there were no
gradations in revelation. God spoke in various ways and through diverse media: to prophets and to sages, in writing and in memorized sayings, to olden
times and to the present day. We can discern no systematic effort to distinguish
one kind of revelation from another—revelation transmitted in writing, that
transmitted orally, revelation from ancient prophet, an exegesis or a Torah
teaching of a contemporary sage. Sages rejected the concept of layers and lev-
els of revelations, of making distinctions between one medium and another,
and hence between one book and another.

The Three Sources of Judaism in Its Canon: Scripture, Mishnah, Sage

Why did the rabbinic canon take shape around only two of its three foci of
revelation, Scripture and the Mishnah, omitting all systematic reference to the
sage, who was, in fact, the heart and center of the system of Judaism? To state
matters otherwise, the problem at hand is literary and formal, not one of the
system and substance of Judaism. That system rested on a tripartite structure
of revelation: Scripture, Mishnah, sage. God's will reached Israel through
each of these three media equally. That is the premise of the Judaism of the
entire rabbinic canon, of each of the stories that appeal to a verse of Scripture,
a phrase or sentence of the Mishnah, or a teaching or action of a sage.

If we now ask ourselves why sages produced no tractates of biography, an
adequate answer is not readily at hand. One might wish to propose that there
was no biographical document, for example, a collection of sage remarks,
awaiting exegesis and amplification, parallel to the Mishnah, on the one side,
and Scripture, on the other. Such an available book of proverbs would have
supplied the backbone and structure for an equivalent to the two Talmuds and
the several compilations of scriptural exegeses. The authors of the Mishnah-
tractate Abot managed to do quite well in composing a collection of wise sayings attributed to sages, and the framer of the Fathers according to R. Nathan,
commonly described as a kind of "Talmud" to Mishnah-tractate Abot, did
equally well in collecting and arranging biographical stories and additional

sayings. So it is not self-evident that the reason we have no lives of saints is the absence of a canonical text to which to attach the lives. It was done—once. By contrast, we have scores of tractates for the Mishnah and a dozen midrash-collections for Scripture.

To state matters simply: either a teaching was true and authoritative, wherever it was found and however it had reached the living sage, or a teaching was untrue and not authoritative. Scripture, the Mishnah, the sage—the three spoke with equal authority. True, one had to come into alignment with the other, the Mishnah with Scripture, the sage with the Mishnah. But it was not the case that one component of the *Torah*, of God's word to Israel, stood within the sacred circle, another beyond. Interpretation and what was interpreted, exegesis and text, belonged together.

So to conclude: what makes me so certain that the sage, or rabbi, constitutes the third component in a tripartite canon of the Torah? Because while Scripture and the Mishnah govern what the sage knows, in the Yerushalmi (as in the Bavli) it is the sage who authoritatively speaks about them. What sages were willing to do to the Mishnah in the Yerushalmi and Bavli is precisely what they were prepared to do to Scripture—impose upon it their own judgment of its meaning. It is the source of the authority of the sage himself that turns out to pose the fundamental question. With the answer to that question, we also know, first, the status, as to revelation, of the things the sage says, whether he speaks of the Mishnah or of Scripture; second, we know the standing of the books he writes, whether these are tractates of the Yerushalmi or the Bavli or the compositions of exegeses of Scripture.

The sage speaks with authority about the Mishnah and the Scripture. As much as they, he therefore has authority deriving from revelation. He himself may participate in the process of revelation. There is no material difference. Since that is so, the sage's book, whether the Yerushalmi or the Bavli to the Mishnah or Midrash to Scripture, is Torah, that is, revealed by God. It also forms part of the Torah, a fully canonical document. The reason, then, is that the sage is like Moses, "our rabbi," who received torah and wrote the Torah. So while the canon was in three parts—Scripture, Mishnah, sage—the sage, in saying what the other parts meant and in embodying that meaning in his life and thought, took primacy of place. If no document organized itself around sayings and stories of sages, it was because that was superfluous. Why so? Because all documents, equally, whether Scripture, whether Mishnah, whether Yerushalmi, gave full and complete expression of deeds and deliberations of sages, beginning, after all, with Moses, our rabbi.

Let us recover the question with which we began. What we want to know is how framers of the Bavli might have done their work. So we have turned to how their predecessors, authors of units of discourse, did their work. That permits us to compare what the Bavli's authors did with what they had received. In particular, as we shall see in part 3, it allows us to relate the Bavli to the Yerushalmi. How so? We shall see that the two Talmuds took up the three sources of the canon and made decisions about how to organize the materials deriving, to begin with, from those discrete sources—Scripture, the Mishnah, sages. As our exercises unfold, moreover, we shall be struck by the points in which the Bavli's framers followed their predecessors and also those in which they made their own choices. At the end we shall find it possible to differentiate the Bavli from the Yerushalmi only upon the criterion of redactional preferences, modes of choosing and organizing large-scale discourse. Recognizing the three components of the single canon, the written Torah, the oral Torah, and the sage as the living Torah, leads us deep into the investigation at hand.

2

Yerushalmi and Bavli

Alike and Not Alike

Autonomy, Connection, Continuity

Since the Talmud of Babylonia constitutes the second of the two Talmuds, separated from the first by a century or more, the Bavli by definition stands connected to two prior documents, the Mishnah and the Yerushalmi. Also by definition, it stands autonomous of the entirety of the rabbinic canon. Why so? Because it can be, and usually is, studied entirely on its own, delivering its own message in its own terms. But again by definition, the Bavli forms part of, and stands continuous with, "the one whole Torah of Moses, our rabbi." Accordingly, proponents of the document claim in its behalf a critical place within the canon of Judaism. So the Bavli forms part of a larger continuity of texts, all of them making their contribution to Judaism. Among the three perspectives by which we describe and analyze the Bavli—autonomy, connection, continuity—however, it is the issue of connection that seizes and retains our attention.

Until we can identify what makes the Bavli distinctive, thus related to, but essentially autonomous of, its predecessor, we can make no statements about the Bavli in particular. We then are left to speak of Talmudic Judaism or the Talmuds. We lose all possibility of showing that one document, viewed as a whole and analyzed through its recurrent traits of rhetoric and salient, characteristic topical interests, speaks to its world and its age. But, as I said, the Bavli is autonomous. So it delivers its message in a way that is its own. It therefore is in substantial measure distinct from the other Talmud. If therefore we cannot show that the Bavli is more than a secondary development of the Yerushalmi, we cannot hope to explain what the Bavli contributed and why it did so at the particular time and place in which it did. So when we speak of autonomy and connection, the stakes are not small.

To conclude this part of the argument rapidly, the issue of continuity need not detain us here and now. It is part of the larger question of how all the documents of the rabbinic canon express a single Judaism, a harmony, a unity, "one whole Torah." That issue, confronted by the great intellects of Judaism through the ages, once more will have to gain attention in its own terms, when the present tasks have reached fruition. We return to it in chapter 10.

We need hardly dwell on the simple fact that both the Yerushalmi and the Bavli organize their materials as comments on Mishnah sentences or paragraphs. A further important but equally obvious fact is that the two compositions differ from all other documents of the rabbinic canon both in their focus—the Mishnah—and in their mode of discourse. That is to say, Mishnah exegesis and expansion find their place, in the entire corpus of rabbinic writings of late antiquity, solely in the two Talmuds. What is shared between the two Talmuds and the remainder of the canon deals with Scripture exegesis, on the one side, and deeds and sayings of sages, on the other. To give one simple example, while Leviticus Rabbah contains exegeses of Scripture found also in one or another of the two Talmuds, there is not a single passage of the Mishnah subjected, in Leviticus Rabbah, to modes of analysis commonplace in the two Talmuds, even though on rare occasion a Mishnah sentence or paragraph may find its way into Leviticus Rabbah. So the two Talmuds stand together as well as take up a position apart from the remainder of the canon. These two facts make the definitive points in common sufficiently clear so we may address the more difficult issue of whether and how the two Talmuds differ from one another.

To unpack and explore that issue, we shall entertain a series of propositions and examine evidence marshalled to test those propositions. We begin from the simplest point and move to the more complex and subtle ones. I can imagine no more obvious and self-evident point of entry than this: the two Talmuds not only treat the Mishnah paragraphs in the same order, they also say much the same thing about them. That is the first proposition demanding analysis.

The First Chapter of Mishnah-Tractate Sukkah in Yerushalmi and Bavli

We take up the simplest proposition.

> A.   The two Talmuds say pretty much the same thing in the same words. The Bavli, coming later, depends upon and merely amplifies or augments the Yerushalmi.

or:

> B.   The two Talmuds treat the Mishnah paragraph in distinct and distinctive ways. They use different language to make their own points. Where they raise the same issue, it derives from the shared text, the Mishnah, and its logic. Both Talmuds respond to the Mishnah; the Bavli does not depend overall on a conventional program supplied by the Yerushalmi.

The sample at hand will decisively settle matters in favor of B. How so? In what follows, I compare and contrast the exegetical program of the Yerushalmi, given in the left-hand column, against that of the Bavli, given in the right. My précis of each unit of discourse deals only with the issue at hand: what did the exegetes of the Mishnah paragraph wish to ask? Unless there is a clear reproduction of the same discussion in both Talmuds, I do not present the actual texts. The system of division and signification worked out in my translation of Yerushalmi as well as Bavli Sukkah is followed throughout. It has the merit of consistent principles of division, so we are comparing passages that, in a single, consistent way, are identified as whole and complete. Where passages are congruent I indicate in the Bavli column by cf. and the Yerushalmi unit. Where they intersect, I indicate with an equal sign (=).

1:1A–F

A. *A sukkah that is taller than twenty cubits is invalid.*
B. *R. Judah declares it valid.*
C. *And one which is not ten handbreadths high,*
D. *one which does not have three walls,*
E. *or one, the light of which is greater than the shade of which,*
F. *is invalid.*

Yerushalmi	Bavli
I. Basis for Judah's dispute with rabbis: analogy to the Temple's dimensions. M. Er. 1:1.	I. Relationship of M. Suk. 1:1 to M. Er. 1:1: what differentiates sukkah from erub law. = Y. I.
II. Why sages regard a sukkah that is too tall as invalid.	II. Scriptural basis for position of sages at M. 1:1A. [cf. Y. I.]
III. Rab: A larger sukkah is valid even if it is very tall.	III. If sukkah roofing touches walls of sukkah, the sukkah may be higher than twenty cubits.
IV. Hoshaiah: If one builds an intervening floor, so diminishing the distance from roof to floor in part of a sukkah, what is the status of the space unaffected by the intervening floor?	IV. Dispute of Judah/sages + precedent supplied by T. Suk. 1:1A–E = Y. III.
V. If one lowered the sukkah roof by hanging garlands, does that lower the roof to less than the acceptable height?	V. Sukkah must hold person's head and greater part of his body. Discourse: M. Suk. 2:7.
VI. How do we know that air space ten handbreadths above the ground constitutes a domain distinct from the ground? M. Shab. 1:1.	VI. Who stands behind view that house not 4 x 4 cubits is not regarded as a house. = Y. II.
VII. Rabbi, Simeon, Judah: Sukkah must be given dimension in length, breadth, and must have four walls. Dispute.	VII. Diminishing the height of a sukkah by raising the floor. [cf. Y. IV.]
VIII. Hiyya-Yohanan: Sukkah is valid if it has two walls of normal size and a third of negligible dimensions.	VIII. Diminishing the height of a sukkah by lowering the roof with hangings. = Y. V.
	IX. Putting sukkah roofing on posts.
	X. M. 1:1C: Scriptural basis for rule that sukkah less than ten handbreadths in height is invalid.
	XI. Continues X.
	XII. Continues X.
	XIII. Sukkah has to have three walls,

IX. A braided wall as a partition.
X. M. Kil. 4:4.
XI. Tips of lathes that protrude from sukkah roofing are treated as part of the sukkah.
XII. Citation and discourse on M. 1:1E–F: If light is half and half, it is valid/invalid.

with the third of negligible [cf. Y. VIII] dimensions. = Y. VII–VIII.
XIV. Where does builder set the little wall?
XV. Continues foregoing.
XVI. M. 1:1E-F: definition of valid roofing = Y. XII.
XVII. Sukkah must be permanent, not temporary, in character. Various authorities who take that view.
XVIII. Continues XVII.
XIX. Two sukkah, one inside the other.
XX. Sukkah built for gentiles, women, cattle, Samaritans is valid, if the roofing is valid.

Before proceeding to the comparison of the two Talmud's treatment of the same passage, let us briefly review how, overall, each one has composed its materials.

Yerushalmi to M. Suk. 1 : 1A – E. The Yerushalmi provides a substantial discussion for each of the Mishnah's topical clauses in sequence, furthermore bringing together parallel rulings in other tractates to enrich the context for discussion. It would be difficult to point to a more satisfactory inquiry, on the part of either Talmud, into the Mishnah's principles and problems. Unit I takes up the noteworthy parallel between M. 1:1A and M. Er. 1:1A. The main point in both cases is the scriptural basis for the dimensions specified by the law. The effort to differentiate is equally necessary. Hence the difference between one sort of symbolic gateway and another, or between one wall built for a given purpose and another wall built for some other purpose, has to be specified. Unit II undertakes a complementary discourse of differentiation. It is now between a sukkah and a house. The two are comparable, since a person is supposed to dwell in a sukkah during the festival. Unit III, continuous with the foregoing, further takes up the specified measurement and explains it. Unit IV raises a difficult question, dealing with the theory, already adumbrated, that we extend the line of a wall or a roof or a cornice in such a way as to imagine that the line comes down to the ground or protrudes upward. At unit IV we seem to have a sukkah roofing at an angle, extending from the middle of a sukkah outwards, above the limit of twenty cubits. Unit V asks about lowering the sukkah roofing by suspending decorations from it or raising the sukkah floor by putting straw or pebbles on it. Both produce the effect of bringing the sukkah within the required dimensions of its height. Unit VI does not belong at all; it is primary at Y. Shab. 1:1. I assume it was deemed to supplement M. 1:1C. Unit VII takes up the matter of the required walls for the sukkah, M. 1:1D. Once again the scriptural basis for the rule is indicated.

Unit VIII carries forward this same topic, now clarifying the theoretical problems in the same matter. At unit IX we deal with an odd kind of partition, a braid partition. This discussion is primary to Y. Er. 1:9 and is inserted here because of IX and X. The inclusion of unit X is inexplicable, except as it may form a continuous discourse with unit IX. It is primary at Y. Er. 1:8. Units XI and XII are placed where they are as discussions of M. 1:1E. But only unit XII takes up the exegesis of the Mishnah's language.

Bavli to M. Suk. 1:1A–F. The protracted Bavli passage serving M. 1:1A–F not only works its way through the Mishnah paragraph but systematically expands the law applicable to that paragraph by seeking out pertinent principles in parallel or contrasting cases of law. When a unit of discourse abandons the theme or principle connected to the Mishnah paragraph, it is to take up a secondary matter introduced by a unit of discourse that has focused on that theme or principle. Unit I begins with an analysis of the word choice at hand. At the same time it introduces an important point, M. Er. 1:1, namely, the comparison between the sukkah and a contraption erected also on a temporary basis and for symbolic purposes. Such a contraption is a symbolic gateway that transforms an alley entry into a gateway for a courtyard and so alters the status of the alley and the courtyards that open on to it, turning them into a single domain. As one domain, they are open for carrying on the Sabbath, at which time people may not carry objects from one domain (e.g., private) to another (e.g., public). That comparison is repeatedly invoked. Units II and III then move from language to scriptural sources for the law. Unit IV then stands in the same relationship to unit III, and so too unit V. Unit VI reverts to an issue of unit V. Thus the entire discussion, II–VI, flows out of the exegetical requirements of the opening lines of the Mishnah paragraph. But the designated unit-divisions seem to mark discussions that could have stood originally by themselves. Unit VII then reverts to the original topic, the requisite height of the sukkah (= Y. IV–V). It deals with a fresh problem, namely, artificially diminishing or increasing the height of the sukkah by alterations to the inside of the hut. One may raise the floor to diminish the height or lower the floor to increase it. Unit VIII pursues the same interest. It further introduces principles distinct from the Mishnah's rules but imposed upon the interpretation of those rules or the amplification of pertinent cases. This important exercise in secondary expansion of a rather simple rule through the introduction of fresh and rather engaging principles—"curved wall," fictional extension of walls upward or downward and the like—then proceeds in its own terms. Unit IX is continuous in its thematic interest with unit VIII. Unit X reverts to the Mishnah paragraph, now M. 1:1C, and asks the question usually raised at the outset about the scriptural authority behind the Mishnah's rule. This leads us into a sizable digression on scriptural exegesis, with special interest in establishing the analogy between utensils in the temple and dimensions pertinent to the sukkah. The underlying conception, that what the Israelite does on cultic occasions in the home responds to what is done in the cult in the temple, is familiar. Units XI and XII pursue the same line of thought. Then unit XIII reverts once more to the Mishnah's rule, M. 1:1D. Now we take up the issue of the walls of the sukkah. These must be three, in the rabbis' view, and four in Simeon's. Each party concedes that one of the requisite walls may be merely symbolic. The biblical source for the required number of walls forms the first object of inquiry. Unit XIV then takes up the symbolic wall. Unit XV reverts to a statement on Tannaite authority given in unit XIII. Subject to close study is a somewhat complicated notion. There are diverse kinds of sukkah buildings. One, we know, is a sukkah erected to carry out the religious duty of the festival. But a person may build a sukkah to extend the enclosed and private area of his home. If he places such a sukkah by the door, the area in which it is permitted to carry objects—private domain—covers not only the space of the house but also the space of the sukkah. That sukkah, erected in connection with Sabbath observance, is compared to the sukkah erected for purposes of keeping the festival. The issue is appropriate here, since the matter concerns the character of the walls of the sukkah built for Sabbath observance. Unit XVI then returns to the Mishnah paragraph. Unit XVIII moves back from the Mishnah's statements and deals with the general principle, taken by some parties, that the sukkah must bear the qualities of a permanent dwelling. That issue intersects with our Mishnah paragraph in connection with Judah's and Simeon's views on the requirement that there be a roof of a certain height and four walls. But the construction as a whole stands independent of the Mishnah paragraph and clearly was put together in its own terms. XVIII takes up XVII.M. Units XIX and XX evidently are miscellaneous—the only such units of discourse in the entire massive construction. I cannot point to a more thorough or satisfying sequence of Babylonian Talmudic units of discourse in which the Mishnah's statements are amplified than the amplifications themselves worked out on their own. The whole is thorough, beautifully articulated, and cogent until the very end.

Since, intersecting in topic and problematic, the Bavli goes over the ground of the Yerushalmi at several points, pursuing essentially the same problem, we have to ask about possible borrowing by the Bavli from the Yerushalmi, not of theses or conventions of interpretation but of whole constructions. To show the points of word-for-word correspondence such as they are, let us now consider side by side one suggestive item, Y. III = B. IV.

Y. 1:1	B. 1:1
III.	IV.
A. [As to the invalidity of a sukkah more than twenty cubits high,] R. Ba in the name of Rab: "That applies to a sukkah that will hold only the head and the greater part of the body of a person and also his table.	A. [The specification of the cited authorities, II.A, C, E, on the minimum requirements of the sukkah, now comes under discussion in its own terms.] The following objection was raised:
B. "But if it held more than that, it is valid [even at such a height]."	B. A sukkah which is taller than twenty cubits is invalid.

C. [Giving a different reason and qualification,] R. Jacob bar Aha in the name of R. Josiah: "That applies [further] when the walls do not go all the way up with it [to the top, the roofing] but if the walls go all the way up with it to the roofing, it is valid."

D. [Proving that C's reason, not A–B's, is valid, we cite the following:]

E. Lo, the following Tannaite teaching differs [in T.'s version]: Said R. Judah, "M'SH B: The sukkah of Helene was twenty cubits tall, and sages went in and out, when visiting her, and not one of them said a thing."

F. They said to him, "It was because she is a woman, and a woman is not liable to keep the commandment of sitting in a sukkah."

G. He said to them, "Now did she not have seven sons who are disciples of sages, and all of them were dwelling in that same sukkah!" [T. Suk. 1:1].

H. Do you then have the possibility of claiming that the sukkah of Helene could not hold more than the head and the greater part of the body and the table of a person? [Surely, someone of her wealth would not build so niggardly a sukkah.]

I. Consequently, the operative reason is that the sides of the sukkah do not go all the way up [to the sukkah roofing at the top, leaving a space].

J. It stands to reason, then, that what R. Josiah has said is so.

K. [And the Tannaite teaching] does not differ [from sages' view], for it is the way of the rich to leave a small bit of the wall out beneath the sukkah roofing itself, so that cooling air may pass through.

C. R. Judah declares it valid [M. 1:1A–B], even up to forty or fifty cubits.

D. Said R. Judah, "M'SH B: The sukkah of Helene in Lud was twenty cubits tall, and sages went in and out, when visiting her, and not one of them said a thing."

E. They said to him, "It was because she is a woman, and a woman is not liable to keep the commandment of sitting in a sukkah."

F. He said to them, "Now did she not have seven sons [who are disciples of sages, and all of them were dwelling in that same sukkah]" [T. Suk. 1:1A–E].

G. "And furthermore, everything she ever did was done in accord with the instruction of sages."

H. Now what need do I have for this additional reason: "Furthermore, everything she ever did was done in accord with the instructions of sages"?

I. This is the sense of what he said to them: "Now, if you say that the sons were minors, and minors are exempt from the religious duty of dwelling in the sukkah, since she had seven sons, it is not possible that among them was not a single one who no longer needed his mother's tending [and so would be required to dwell on his own in the sukkah]."

J. "And if, further, you should maintain that a minor who no longer needs his mother's tending is subject to the law only on the authority of rabbis, and that woman paid no attention to rules that rested only on the authority of the rabbis, come and note the following: 'And furthermore, everything she ever did was done in accord with the instructions of sages.'"

K. [We now revert to the issue with which we began, namely, the comparison of the story at hand to the reasons adduced by the authorities at unit III:] Now with reverence to the one who said, the dispute applies to a case in which the walls of the sukkah do not touch the sukkah roofing, would a queen dwell in a sukkah, the walls of which do not touch the sukkah roofing?

L. [3A] [Indeed so! The reason is that] the space makes possible good ventilation.

M. But in the view of the one who has said that the dispute pertains to a small sukkah, would a queen ever dwell in a small sukkah?

N. Said Rabbah bar R. Ada, "At issue in the dispute is solely a case of a sukkah which is made with many small cubbies."

O. But would a queen take up residence in a sukkah that was subdivided into many small cubbies?

P. Said R. Ashi, "At issue is only [a large sukkah which had] such recesses.

Q. "Rabbis take the view that the queen's sons were dwelling in a sukkah of absolutely valid traits, while she dwelled in the recesses on account of modesty [i.e., not showing her face among the men], and it was on that account that rabbis said nothing to her [about her dwelling in what was, in fact, an invalid part of the sukkah].

R. "And R. Judah maintains the position that her sons were dwelling along with her [in the cubbyholes of the sukkah], and even so, the rabbis did not criticize what she was doing [which proves that the small cubbies of the sukkah were valid]."

The issue of Y. III.A and B. IV.A is the same. Tosefta's precedent, marked in bold face, is used differently in each Talmud. In the Bavli it makes a point relevant to B. IV.A, the height of the sukkah. It is entirely relevant to the purpose for which it is adduced. The sukkah of the queen was high, so sustaining Judah's view. The secondary issue, IV.K, links the precedent to unit III. The whole is integrated and well composed. By contrast, the Yerushalmi's use of the precedent is odd. The passage is explicit as to the large size of the hut, so Y.III.H is somewhat jarring. It really contradicts Y. III.G. Y. III.I then revises matters to force the precedent to serve Y. III.C. We cannot imagine that Bavli's author has depended on Yerushalmi's composition. He has used the precedent for his own inquiry and in his own way. Where, therefore, Yerushalmi and Bavli share materials, the Bavli's use of those materials—if this case is suggestive—will not depend upon the Yerushalmi's. Both refer back to the Mishnah and to the Tosefta, responding to the former in terms (here) of the exegetical program precipitated by the contents available in the latter.

The first exercise of comparison now requires extension. We shall therefore review the programs of each of the two Talmuds for Mishnah-tractate Sukkah chapter 1.

1:1G–N

G.　*[9A] A superannuated sukkah—*

H.　*The House of Shammai declare it invalid.*

I.　*And the House of Hillel declare it valid.*

J.　*And what exactly is a supernatural sukkah?*

K.　*And which one made thirty days [or more] before the festival [of Sukkot].*

L.　*But if one made it for the sake of the festival,*

M.　*even at the beginning of the year,*

N.　*it is valid.*

I. A qualification of the position of the Hillelites.	I. Scripture's support for the view of the House of Shammai.
II. The dispute of the houses pertains also to Passover.	II. How can the Hillelites accept as valid a sukkah not constructed for the purpose of observing the festival?
III. T. 1:4A–B.	
IV. What blessing is recited over a sukkah when it is made?	

Yerushalmi to M. Suk. 1:2. Unit I glosses M. 1:2A–C. Unit II presents a dispute in a different matter but about the same principle. Unit III supplements M. with T. Unit IV indicates the blessing to be said in connection with making and using the sukkah.

Bavli to M. Suk. 1:1G–N [=Y.M.1:2]. Unit I clarifies the source of the law, and unit II introduces a separate, but related, consideration. The exegesis of the Mishnah's rule in relationship to scriptural proof text is thorough.

1:2

A.　*[9B] He who makes his sukkah under a tree is as if he made it in [his] house.*

B.　*A sukkah on top of a sukkah—*

C.　*the one on top is valid.*

D.　*And the one on the bottom is invalid.*

E.　*R. Judah says, "If there are no residents in the top one, the bottom one is valid."*

I.
Clarification of M. 1:2B–D:
How much space defines the separation of the two roofs, so that
the upper one is deemed distinct
and valid?

II.
Clarification of M. 1:2E.

I. Clarification of M. 1:2A re char-
acter of the tree's foliage.
II. Scriptural basis of M. 1:2B.
III. Augmentation of M. 1:2B–D.
IV. Clarification of M. 1:2B–D:
how much space [= Y. I].

Yerushalmi to M. Suk. 1:2. The point is that the roof of the sukkah must be
exposed to the firmament and not made up, A, in large part by the boughs of
the tree. D follows the same principle, now with reference to a sukkah covered by another. Judah's view is that, without residents, the upper sukkah does
not constitute a dwelling, thus excluding A's consideration. Unit I clarifies M.
1:2B's notion of two sukkah roofs near one another by raising a problem independent of M. Unit II amplifies Judah's meaning, M. 1:3E.

Bavli to M. Suk. 1:2. The point is that the roof of the sukkah must be exposed to the firmament and not covered, I.A, in large part by the boughs of
the tree. D follows the same principle, now with reference to a sukkah covered by another. Judah's view is that, without residents, the upper sukkah does
not constitute a dwelling, thus excluding A's consideration. Unit I then clarifies M. 1:2A. But the real interest is the notion that if invalid and valid forms
of sukkah roofing are intertwined, with a greater portion of valid, the whole is
valid. That principle, not demanded by the Mishnah's rule, clarifies that rule.
Unit II proceeds to the scriptural basis for M. 1:2B. Unit III focuses upon that
same rule, making a point that the Talmud's anonymous voice itself calls self-
evident. Unit IV clarifies a secondary question—the relationship of the
two sukkah constructions, upper and lower—but in so doing also invokes
M. 1:2E. Since Y. I and B. IV go over exactly the same question, we shall
once more compare the two units of discourse side by side to see how, if at all,
they relate:

I.
A. In the case of two *sukkah* roofs, one
on top of the other, in which the upper roofing was such that the light
was greater than the shade [and hence
invalid], while the lower one was
such that the light was not greater
than the shade on its own, but, together with the other roof, the shade
was greater than the light—
B. What is the maximum of space that
may be between the two roofs so that
they should be deemed joined together [into a single sukkah roofing,

IV.
A. And how much space would there be
between one sukkah and the other so
that the lower sukkah would be invalid [as a sukkah beneath a sukkah]?
B. Said R. Huna, "A handbreadth. [If
the space between the upper-sukkah
roofing and the lower-sukkah roofing
is less than a handbreadth, the two
sets of roofing are regarded as one.
[Then we do not have a case of one
sukkah beneath another sukkah at
all.]"
C. [Huna continues,] "For so we find

hence a valid one for the sukkah beneath]?

C. There were two Amoras. One said, "Ten cubits," and the other said, "Four."

D. The one who maintained that ten cubits distance are permissible objected to the one who said that only four are permissible, "If it is because of the principle of forming a tent [that you want the two so close together], we find that a tent may be no more than a handbreadth [in its principal dimensions, hence also height]. [So you permit too broad a space between the two roofs.]"

that the handbreadth is the standard measure in connection with cases of overshadowing of corpse uncleanness, for we have learned in the Mishnah: *A handbreadth of space by a handbreadth at the height of a handbreadth brings uncleanness [should it be left open in a partition between corpse matter in one otherwise closed room and another such room] or interposes against the passage of the same uncleanness [if such a space is closed off], but a space less than a handbreadth in height neither brings uncleanness [if open] nor interposes [if closed] [M. Oh. 3:7].* [The operative measure is a handbreadth. If the roof is higher than that distance, it is deemed a separate roof, and if it is lower, it is deemed part of the contained space]."

D. R. Hisda and Rabbah bar R. Huna say, "Four [handbreadths], for we do not find a contained space taken into account if it is less than four handbreadths."

E. And Samuel said, "Ten."

F. What is the reason for the view of Samuel? The requisite measure for rendering the sukkah valid [ten handbreadths above the ground] also operates to render it invalid.

G. Just as the requisite measure of height is ten handbreadths, so the distance that will invalidate likewise is ten handbreadths.

H. [Arguing to the contrary conclusion on the basis of the same principle as F:] We have learned in the Mishnah: *R. Judah says, "If there are no residents in the top one, the bottom one is valid"* [M. 1:2E].

I. What is the sense of "If there are no residents . . . valid"?

J. If it is in concrete terms, that is, if the issue is that there really are no occupants, is this the governing criterion? [It is a random fact.]

K. But rather is not the sense of there being no residents to mean, any [upper] sukkah which is not suitable for a dwelling [would leave the lower sukkah *valid*]?

L. What would be an example of such a case? One which was not ten handbreadths in height.

M. Would this then bear the implication that, in the view of the first [anonymous] authority [vis-à-vis Judah], even one which is not suitable for dwelling [would leave the lower sukkah] invalid? [This would then refute Samuel's position, above].

N. When R. Dimi came, he said, "In the West they say, If the lower [sukkah's roof] cannot hold the weight of the pillows and blankets of the upper one, the lower one is valid. [The upper sukkah then is not sufficiently strong. Its floor, the roof of the lower sukkah, cannot carry the weight.]"

O. Does this then bear the implication that the first of the two authorities takes the view that even if the [lower sukkah] is not suitable to bear [the weight of the upper, the lower one] is invalid?

P. At issue between [Judah and the first authority] is the case of a [lower] sukkah, the floor-roof of which can bear the weight of the upper sukkah only with difficulty.

There is no reason to belabor the obvious. Once more, when the two Talmuds wish to deal with the same issue, the overlap is in conception; but there is no point of verbal contact, let alone of intersection. Each Talmud undertakes its own analysis in its own way. Each Talmud bases its discussion on the common source (the Mishnah, sometimes also the Tosefta), but each one builds its discussion on the basis of points made by its selection of authorities and pursues matters in terms of its own established conventions of rhetoric.

1:3

A.   *[If] one spread a sheet on top of [a sukkah] on account of the hot sun,*

B.   *or underneath [the cover of boughs] on account of droppings [of the branches or leaves of the bough cover],*

C.   *or [if] one spread [a sheet] over a four-poster bed [in a sukkah],*

D.   *it is invalid [for dwelling or sleeping and so for fulfilling one's obligation to dwell in the sukkah].*

E.   *But one spreads it over the frame of a two-poster bed.*

I. One may not spread rugs over a
sukkah roof, but may spread
them on the sides.
II. M. 1:3B clarified.
III. M. 1:3E clarified.

I. Clarification of M. 1:3B.
II. Continuation of foregoing: what
is put up to decorate a sukkah
does not diminish the height of
the sukkah.
III. Decorations for a sukkah that extend above the roof.
IV. Clarification of M. 1:3C re canopied bed.
V. Sleeping in a canopied bed.
VI. Sleeping in a canopied bed in a
sukkah, framed in accord with
M. 2:1B.

The Yerushalmi's perfunctory discussion clarifies sentences in the Mishnah
paragraph. The Bavli begins with analysis of the implications of the Mishnah's
language, unit I attending to M. 1:3B. Unit II is inserted because it deals with
decorations in a sukkah, important in the discussion of unit I. Unit III carries
forward the same point of interest. Unit IV then reverts to the Mishnah, now
to M. 1:3C, E, the contrast between two types of beds, explained just now.
This leads to the secondary discussion at units V and VI. So the Bavli forms
around the principal clauses of the Mishnah and then extends its discussion to
secondary matters generated by its original inquiry. Obviously, the Bavli's
framers have given a far more elaborate treatment to the Mishnah.

1:4

A. *[If] one trained a vine, gourd, or ivy over it and then spread sukkah roofing on [one of these], it is invalid.*

B. *But if the sukkah roofing exceeded them,*

C. *or if one cut them [the vines] down,*

D. *it is valid.*

E. *This is the general rule:*

F. *Whatever is susceptible to uncleanness and does not grow from
the ground—they do not make sukkah roofing with it.*

G. *And whatever is not susceptible to uncleanness, but does grow
from the ground [and has been cut off]—they do make sukkah
roofing with it.*

I. Clarification of M. 1:4C.
II. Illustration of M. 1:4F–G.
III. Exegetical foundations for M.
1:4E–G about the status, as to
cleanness, of what may be used
for sukkah roofing.

I. Clarification of M. 1:4C–D.
II. Expansion on foregoing, with at-
tention to M. 1:4A.
III. Exegetical foundations for M.
1:4F–G.
IV. Continuation of foregoing.
V. Continuation of foregoing.

Yerushalmi to M. 1:4. Unit I complements the rule of M. 1:4A–D. Units II and III take up M. 1:4F–G, what may be used in sukkah roofing. Unit II provides some facts, and unit III, exegetical foundations for M.'s principle.

Bavli to M. 1:4. The Bavli's elaborate discussion, units I–II, accomplishes two things. First, it raises the question of the procedure to be followed in connection with M. 1:4C. Second, it introduces the underlying principle at issue whether the mere act of cutting down the vines also serves to render them suitable for the specific purpose of use as sukkah roofing, or whether some distinct act of designation, thus preparation, is required. The former view is worked out in unit I. Unit II then produces a striking analogy in which a quite different case—making strings into show fringes—is shown to invoke upon the same principle, namely, whether a mere act of destruction—cutting the vines, severing the string—suffices, or whether a clear-cut deed of deliberate and positive validation also is required. It is clear that the issue of show fringes need not involve the matter of the vines for sukkah roofing, but unit II makes a strong argument that the two cases must be worked out in tandem. Units III–V then present the familiar exercise of locating scriptural proof for a Mishnaic proposition.

Because Y. III and B. IV–VI not only go over the same problem, namely, discovering exegetical foundations for the Mishnah's rule, but also resort to the same antecedent materials in constructing their discussions, we have yet again to compare the two compositions side by side.

III.

A. Said R. Yohanan, "It is written, 'You shall keep the feast of booths seven days, when you make your ingathering from your threshing floor and your wine press' (Deut. 16:13).

B. "From the refuse of your threshing floor and your wine press you may make sukkah roofing for yourself."

C. R. Simeon b. Laqish said, "'But a mist went up from the earth and watered the whole face of the ground' (Gen. 2:6). [The analogy of the covering of the sukkah is to mist, which arises from the ground and is not susceptible to receive uncleanness.]"

D. Said R. Tanhuma, "This one is consistent with opinions held elsewhere, and that one is consistent with opinions held elsewhere.

E. "R. Yohanan has said, 'The clouds came from above,' and so he derives

III.

A. *This is the general rule: Whatever is susceptible to uncleanness, etc. [M. 1:4F–G]:*

B. What is the scriptural basis for this rule?

C. Said R. Simeon b. Laqish, "Scripture has stated, 'And a mist went up from the earth' (Gen. 2:6).

D. "Just as mist is something which is not susceptible to uncleanness and grows from the ground, so a sukkah must be made of some thing which does not receive uncleanness and grows from the ground."

E. That explanation is suitable to the person who holds that the sukkah in which Israel dwelled in the wilderness was clouds of glory.

F. But in the view of him who holds that the sukkah was the genuine article which the Israelites actually made for themselves [and not an the rule from the reference to 'your ingathering.'

F. "R. Simeon b. Laqish said, 'Clouds come from below,' so he derives the rule from clouds [of mist]."

G. Said R. Abin, "This party is consistent with opinions held elsewhere, and that one is consistent with opinions held elsewhere.

H. "R. Yohanan compares the matter to one who sends his fellow a jug of wine, giving him the jug as well as the wine. [Along these same lines God gives the clouds along with the rain from heaven.]

I. "R. Simeon b. Laqish compares the matter to a priest, who said to his fellow, 'Send over your basket and take some grain for yourself.' [Clouds come from below, and God puts rain in them in heaven.]"

analogy to clouds of glory], what sort of proof may one bring?

G. The problem at hand accords with that which has been taught on Tannaite authority:

H. "'For I made the children of Israel dwell in sukkot' (Lev. 23:43), meaning in clouds of glory," the words of R. Eliezer.

I. R. Aqiba says, "They were actually sukkot that people made for themselves."

J. Now [as just noted] the stated proof poses no problems to the view of R. Eliezer, but as to the position of R. Aqiba, what is there to say?

IV.

A. When R. Dimi came, [he said that] R. Yohanan said, "Scripture has stated, 'The festal offering of Sukkot you shall prepare' (Deut. 16:13).

B. "The sukkah thus is compared to the festal offering [brought as an animal sacrifice on the festival day].

C. "Just as the festal offering is something that does not receive uncleanness [animals fed from what grows from the ground are, in Yohanan's view, as if they too grow from the ground] and also grows from the ground [as just now explained], so the sukkah must be made of something that does not receive uncleanness and grows from the ground."

D. [12A] But what if you wish to propose a further analogy, just as the festal offering is of an animate being, so the sukkah must be made of an animate being?

V.

A. When Rabin came, he said that R. Yohanan said, "Scripture has stated, 'After you have gathered in from your threshing floor and from your winepress. . .' (Deut. 16:13). Scripture speaks of what is left on the threshing floor and the dregs of the winepress. [These grow from the ground and are not susceptible to uncleanness, so too the sukkah roofing, of which the verse at hand speaks, must conform to the same traits.]''

B. And may I say that Scripture speaks of the threshing floor itself and the winepress itself? [Perhaps somehow the sukkah must be composed of these objects?]

C. Said R. Zira, "Here it is written, 'Winepress,' and it is hardly possible to make use of a winepress for sukkah roofing!''

D. To this explanation R. Jeremiah objected, "And might I speculate that what is required is use of congealed wine which comes from Senir, like fig cakes? [Perhaps the sense of Scripture is that that is what must be used for sukkah roofing!]''

E. Said R. Zira, "We had a valid proposition in hand, but R. Jeremiah came along and threw an ax at it [and smashed it]!''

F. R. Ashi said, " 'From your threshing floor' and not the threshing floor itself, 'from your winepress' and not the winepress itself [is to be the source of materials used for sukkah roofing].''

G. R. Hisda said, "Proof for the desired proposition derives from here: 'Go forth to the mountain and collect olive branches, branches of wild olive, myrtle branches, palm branches, and branches of thick trees' (Neh. 8:15). [All of these are not susceptible to uncleanness and grow from the ground, and, in context, are specified for use as sukkah roofing].''

H. Myrtle branches fall into the category of branches of thick trees [of Lev. 23:40]. [Why specify the same species twice?]

I. Said R. Hisda, "The wild myrtle is for the sukkah roofing, and the branches of thick trees for the lulab.''

The composition of the Yerushalmi is in two simple parts: first, the citation of Yohanan and Simeon b. Laqish; second, Tanhuma's and Abin's point that the two parties' explanations are coherent with things each says in another context. The contrast presented by the Bavli is stunning. Now we have an extended composition on Simeon b. Laqish's statement, given verbatim as it appears in the Yerushalmi. The Bavli's discussion, fully worked out in unit III, is totally its own. The interest of the framer is not in setting Yohanan up in a dispute with Simeon b. Laqish. Rather, he has chosen fully to analyze Simeon's proof and then to introduce an available composition on Tannaite authority, III.G–J. Yohanan is introduced on his own at unit IV. The proof is the same; but while the Yerushalmi suffices with a virtually unarticulated citation of proof texts, the Bavli beautifully articulates what is at issue and then tests matters. In the presentation of Yohanan's proof, the Bavli's framer gives us two complete versions—one at unit IV, the other at unit V.

For our purposes one question now must be settled. Does the Bavli's compositor draw upon the Yerushalmi's version? The answer is decisively negative. The Bavli's author draws upon a shared tradition, known also to the Yerushalmi's writer, that associates Simeon b. Laqish with Gen. 2:6, Yohanan with Deut. 16:13, and both with the present Mishnah paragraph. If the author of the Bavli version had had access to the Yerushalmi's treatment of the matter, he would not have been much impressed, for the point of interest of the Yerushalmi's expansion—the consistency of the two authorities with positions held elsewhere—simply bears no relevance to Bavli's point of entry.

It remains to observe that the two Talmuds come into contact not only through shared access to the Mishnah and to the Tosefta as well as some materials of earlier Amoraic authorities. The two Talmuds meet also in what appears to be a common exegetical program on questions or principles that bear upon a given Mishnah paragraph. But that common program derives over and over again from the contents of the Mishnah paragraph at hand, that is, the principles of law implied by a given rule. It may emerge from the overall task that, linking the Mishnah to Scripture, formed the center of the hermeneutic labor of everyone who received the Mishnah and proposed to deal with it.

1:5

A. *Bundles of straw, wood, or brush—*
B. *they do not make a sukkah roofing with them.*
C. *But any of them that one untied is valid.*
D. *And all of them are valid [as is] for use for the sides [of the sukkah].*

I. Yohanan's explanation of M. 1:5A–B.
II. What is attached to sheaves for sukkah roofing is not part of the sheaves.
III. Scriptural basis for M. 1:5D.

I. Yohanan's explanation, as in Y.
II. Judah-Rab: Sukkah roofing made with arrow shafts.
III. Sukkah roofing with flax.
IV. Sukkah roofing with licorice wood and wormwood.
V. Sukkah roofing with palm tree, with reeds, etc.

VI. Sukkah roofing with bundles.
VII. A case.
VIII. Interposition.
IX. Grain cut for sukkah roofing.
X. Continuation of foregoing.
XI. Continuation of foregoing.

Yerushalmi to M. Suk. 1 :5. Used when bound up, the bundles look not like roofing but like a storage area. The bundles in any case may serve as sides or side posts. Unit I supplies a rule for M. Unit II points out that used for one purpose, a sheaf will not be susceptible to uncleanness; used for another, it will be. Accordingly, we invoke the principle that protrusions of pieces of food affect the food to which they are attached when the sheaf is planned for use as food, but not when the sheaf is used for another purpose. This is relevant, in a general way, to M. 1:5A. Unit III provides a scriptural basis for M. 1:5D.

Bavli to M. Suk. 1 :5. Unit I provides a discussion for M. 1:5A–B, a rather complex composition. Unit II proceeds to make its own point about other sorts of materials used, or not used, for sukkah roofing. Unit III pursues the same interest, which works its way through units IV and V. Unit VI takes up the secondary theme of what does, and does not, constitute a bundle, clarifying M. 1:5A only in a very general way. Unit VII makes the same sort of contribution. Unit VIII is included because of the appearance, in its catalog, of use for materials for sukkah roofing. Unit IX, with its appended supplements at X and XI, raises an interesting question about the status of the stalks of pieces of fruit as regards uncleanness. The basic principle is that if we regard them as useful, they also are susceptible; but if they are held to be useless, they are insusceptible. This is worked out with exceptional sophistication throughout, and I see no problems in following either the arguments or the relevance of the cases adduced in evidence. Units IX–XI ignore the Mishnah paragraph.

A verbatim comparison now is called for since it will reinforce an important, indeed critical, point. Where the Bavli's authors had access to materials used in the Yerushalmi, they followed their own exegetical program. They in no way limited themselves to whatever program the Yerushalmi may have defined. Quite to the contrary, where the Bavli's framers take over not only the same Mishnah paragraph but also the same antecedent unarticulated lemma (in what follows, Yohanan's explanation), the Bavli's authors do precisely what they want, adhering to a set of conventions distinctive to their own document. That fact cannot be more stunningly illustrated than it is in what follows.

I.	I.
A. [As to M. 1:5A–B,] R. Hiyya in the name of R. Yohanan: "It is because	A. Said R. Jacob, "I heard from R. Yohanan two [explanations], one for

[the sukkah] will look like a storage house."

B. R. Jacob bar Abayye, R. Sheshet in the name of R. Hiyya the Elder: "A bundle is made up of no fewer than twenty-five sticks [of wood].

the rule at hand and the other for the rule that follows:

B. *"He who hollowed out a space in a haystack to make a sukkah therein— it is no sukkah [M. 1:8D–E].*

C. "[The reason for] one [of the rulings] is on account of a [precautionary] decree [on account of the possibility of a person's using a sukkah as a] storehouse.

D. "[The reason for] the other [of the rulings] is on account of the exegesis, '"You shall make" (Deut. 16:13)—and not make use of what is ready-made.'

E. "Now I do not know which of the two rulings [of the Mishnah at hand] is on account of the consideration of not using the sukkah as a storehouse, and which one of them is on account of the exegesis, ' "You shall make"— and not from what is ready-made.' "

F. Said R. Jeremiah, "Let us see [how we may work matters out on the basis of a further ruling in Yohanan's name].

G. "For R. Hiyya bar Abba said R. Yohanan said, 'On what account did they rule: *Bundles of straw, wood, or brush—they do not make a sukkah roofing with them [M. 1:5A–B]?*

H. " '[It is because] there are times that a person will come in from the field in the evening, with his bundle [of produce] on his back, and he might just push it up and leave it on top of his sukkah, so as to allow the produce to dry. Then he will reconsider the matter and determine to make use of [the bundles] for sukkah roofing. Yet the Torah has said, "You will make" (Deut. 16:13)—and not from what is ready-made.'

I. "Now since the rule at hand is on account of a precautionary decree [lest the farmer use the sukkah] as a storehouse [in the scenario just now described, it must follow that] the other ruling [about hollowing out a haystake and turning it into a sukkah] is on account of the exegesis of 'You shall make'—and not what is ready-made."

J. And R. Jacob? [What left him in doubt as to Yohanan's explanations for the two rulings, since, after all, the teaching cited by Hiyya bar Abba was available?]

K. In point of fact, he had not heard the tradition [in Yohanan's name] made available by R. Hiyya bar Abba.

L. Said R. Ashi, "[Can we really say that the operative consideration in the ruling about] *bundles of straw, wood, or brush* is only on account of the precautionary decree [against using the sukkah as a] storehouse, but there is no consideration at all of the exegesis, ' "You shall make for yourself"—and not from what is ready-made'?

M. "And, [as to the ruling concerning] *hollowing out a space in a haystack,* [may we say that the operative consideration is only] on account of the exegesis, ' "You shall make for yourself"—and not from what is ready-made,' while the criterion based on the precautionary decree [against using the sukkah as a] storehouse is not operative? [Surely each of the two rulings is susceptible to both of the available explanations!]"

N. [Then how can we explain the position of] R. Yohanan, [who invokes only a single consideration for each case]?

O. [Yohanan] may say to you, "In the present case, in which it is taught in the Mishnah, *They do not make a sukkah roofing with them [M. 1:5B],* [that prohibition applies] to begin with, [12B], in which case they do not make the sukkah roofing on account of a precautionary decree against [using the sukkah for a] storehouse.

P. "But as to the rule as the Torah would have it, it would be a valid procedure. [Rabbi's decree against it, making the law more strict than the Torah requires, is in fact applicable only to begin with. But if one has actually done so, then after the fact the procedure is acceptable.]

Q. "And in that other case [hollowing out a hole in a haystack for use as a sukkah], in which case the Mishnah is phrased, *It is no sukkah* [at all] then, even after the fact, on the authority of the law of the Torah, it also does not constitute a valid sukkah."

1:6

A. *"They make sukkah roofing with boards,"* the words of R. Judah.

B. *And R. Meir prohibits doing so.*

C. *[If] one put on top of it a board which is four handbreadths broad, it is valid,*

D. *so long as one not sleep underneath [that particular board].*

I. Clarification of the subject of dispute at M. 1:6A, the character of the boards.	I. Clarification of character of the boards under dispute at M. 1:6A–B, in light of M. 1:6C–D.
II. Same for M. 1:6C–D.	II. If one turned the boards on their sides.

The Yerushalmi's contribution is to supply comments on the several clauses of the Mishnah paragraph. Bavli's unit I presents a beautifully articulated dispute between Rab and Samuel, making points along the lines of those of the Yerushalmi but in a vastly expanded range of inquiry. Unit II goes on to a secondary issue. Comparing the Yerushalmi's to the Bavli's treatment of the passage at hand produces results entirely the same as the foregoing comparisons.

1:7

A. *[15A] A timber roofing which had no plastering—*

B. *R. Judah says, "The House of Shammai say, 'One loosens it and removes one [board] between each two.'*

C. *"And the House of Hillel say, 'One either loosens it or removes one [board] from between each two.'"*

D. *R. Meir says, "One removes one from between each two, and does not loosen [the others at all]."*

I. Brief clarification of M. 1:7D.	I. Exegetical basis for the position of the two houses. Analysis of the positions of Judah and Meir.

1:8

A. *One who makes a roof for his sukkah out of spits or with the side pieces of a bed—*

B. *if there is a space between them equivalent to their own breadth,*

C.   *[the sukkah] is valid.*

D.   *One who hollowed out a space in a haystack to make a sukkah therein—*

E.   *it is no sukkah.*

I. Clarification of M. 1:8B.

II. Reason for the rule of 1:9D–E.

I. Does M. 1:8A–C refute the view of Huna, b. R. Joshua, re valid partition?

II. Does M. 1:8A support the view of Ammi bar Tibiomi.

III. Continues II.

IV. Clarification of M. 1:8D.

The Yerushalmi's treatment is brief and routine. As to the Bavli, unit I brings the present passage into confrontation with its exact opposite, concerning the fence erected for creating a distinct domain. The same principle applies in both cases, namely, the fictive filling in of small gaps in a fence, roofing, or partition. If we do not fill in such a gap in one case, we ought not to think the principle applies in the other. On that basis the issue is worked out, and, as usual, the correct solution is to propose a distinction between the one case and the other. Unit II carries on the same exercise of bringing law in one topic to bear upon law in some other, and this is done by invoking the shared principle applicable to both. Unit III then reverts to the explication of the law as it applies to the sukkah in particular. Unit IV then completes the analysis of the Mishnah passage specifying limitations to the invalidity of the arrangement specified in the Mishnah; this further explains the underlying principle.

1:9A–G

A.   *One who suspends the sides from above to below—*

B.   *if the [the partitions] are three [or more] handbreadths above the ground,*

C.   *[the sukkah] is invalid.*

D.   *[If one builds the sides] from the ground upward,*

E.   *if [they are] ten handbreadths above the ground,*

F.   *[the sukkah] is valid.*

G.   *R. Yose says, "Just as [the required height] from below to above [when the wall is built up from the ground] is ten handbreadths, "so [the required height] from above to below [when the wall is suspended from above toward the ground] is ten handbreadths [even though the bottom is not within three handbreadths of the ground]. [The operative criterion is the height of the partitions.]"*

I. Clarification of Yose's view, M. 1:9G.

I. The relationship of this Mishnah paragraph to M. Er. 8:6.

II. Illustration and application of the law at hand.

III. Same as above.

Y. shows that three cited authorities concur that we draw an imaginary wall downward from above, which closes off the area beneath. B. goes over that same principle but in much different context and richer elaboration, and B. then proceeds to spell out the application of the law at hand. A comparison of the whole of Y. to the whole of B. would show that, while the principle at hand is the same—as it should be, since it is dictated by the Mishnah paragraph—the composition that follows in each Talmud is wholly distinct from the one in the other.

1:9H—1:10

H. *[17A] [If] one sets the sukkah roofing three handbreadths from the walls [of the sukkah], [the sukkah] is invalid.*

M. 1:9

A. *A house, [the roof of] which was damaged, and on [the gaps in the roof of which] one put sukkah roofing—*

B. *if the distance from the wall to the sukkah roofing is four cubits, it is invalid [as a sukkah].*

C. *And so too, [is the rule for] a courtyard which is surrounded by a peristyle.*

D. *A large sukkah, [the roofing of which] they surrounded with some sort of material with which they do not make sukkah roofing—*

E. *if there was a space of four cubits below it,*

F. *it is invalid [as a sukkah].*

M. 1:10

I. Clarification of M. 1:10B.

II. If one slept under inadequately roofed-over space, does one carry out his obligation to dwell in the sukkah?

III. Reversion to unit I, now with reference to M. 1:10D–F.

I. Why was it necessary to give all three rulings, M. 1:9H, M. 1:10A–C, M. 1:10D–F? Each ruling had to be made explicit.

II. Amplification of M. 1:9H, M. 1:10A–B.

III. Different version of foregoing.

IV. If one diminished open space in sukkah roofing, the sukkah is validated. Reference to M. Oh. 10:1, 2.

V. M. 1:10A clarified.

VI. If one put sukkah roofing over a peristyle.

VII. Different version of foregoing.

VIII. Same issue as foregoing.

IX. A lath that protrudes from a sukkah.

Yerushalmi to M. 1:9H–1:10. Unit I draws upon the Mishnah paragraph
to support a statement by Hiyya. Unit II clarifies the status of an invalid part
of the roofing of an otherwise valid sukkah. Unit III reverts to the proposition
of unit I.

Bavli to M. 1:9H–1:10. The sizable passage of Bavli at hand pursues its
own interests and intersects with the Mishnah paragraph mainly to invoke that
paragraph for illustrative purposes. Unit I starts with a familiar exercise of
proving that the Mishnah does not repeat itself, the only word-for-word exegesis. Unit II asks an independent question, namely, the comparison between
two sorts of invalid space in sukkah roofing—one, a gap, the other, a filling of
invalid materials. Each is supposedly subject to a distinct minimum measure
for invalidating the sukkah roofing. Unit III provides a second version of the
same dispute, and this, as we see, provides a mirror image of the discussion at
M. 1:6. It seems to me the person who has made up these protracted discussions had a rather sophisticated and comprehensive notion of how he wished
to pursue the issue at hand. To the Mishnah paragraph, the entire discussion is
tangential. Its principle is important in its own right. Unit IV is continuous
with the foregoing. At unit V we revert to the Mishnah paragraph, now to M.
1:10A. This passage has been constructed around its own framework—Ishmael's sayings in his father's name—and not around our Mishnah passage.
Unit VI raises a theoretical question but is inserted because it relates to M.
1:10C. But the issue is the theory of the law, not the amplification of the case
of the peristyle. Unit VII is continuous with the foregoing. Unit VIII provides
an illustration of the same matter. Unit IX does not seem to contribute in any
way to the amplification of the rule of the Mishnah paragraph. As a composition it hangs together on its own.

1:11 A–D

A.   *One who makes his sukkah in the shape of a cone or who leaned it
     up against a wall—*
B.   *R. Eliezer declares it invalid,*
C.   *because it has no roof.*
D.   *And sages declare it valid,*

I. Citation and amplification of T.   I. Same as in Yerushalmi.
   Suk. 1:10B–D.   II. Continuation of foregoing.

At the risk of taxing the reader's patience, I present a comparison of Y. unit
I and B. units I–II. Here, once more, we see that, even when both Talmuds
wish to make use of the same materials and say much the same thing, Bavli
has no inclination to follow matters in the way that the Yerushalmi has done.

I.

A. **R. Eliezer concedes [in regard to M. 1:12A–C] that if its roof is a handbreadth in size,**

B. **or if it was a handbreadth above the ground,**

C. **it is valid [T. Suk. 1:10B–D].**

D. It has been taught: One who makes his sukkah like a house in the forest of Lebanon [so that the tree trunks serve as the walls, and the sukkah roofing is spread above]—it is valid.

E. For whom is such a ruling required?

F. Is it not required to clarify the position of R. Eliezer? [To him the issue is whether or not there is a clearly discernible roof, M. 1:12C, not whether the walls have been erected for the purpose of the sukkah.]

I.

A. It has been taught on Tannaite authority:

B. **R. Eliezer concedes that if one raised [the sukkah] a handbreadth above the ground or moved it a handbreadth away from the wall [as the case may be], it is a valid sukkah.** [Now we have a roof, constituted either by the raised sukkah or by the space between the sukkah and the wall, with the open air space deemed fictively filled in, as we recall] [T. Suk. 1:10B–D].

C. What is the reason behind rabbis' ruling?

D. The inclining wall of the tent is deemed to fall into the category of a tent.

II.

A. Abayye came upon R. Joseph, who was sleeping in a sukkah in a bridal bed [with curtains that sloped down from a point, not forming a roof]. He said to him, "In accord with whose opinion do you do so? [You clearly regard it as all right to sleep in a sukkah in a covered bed. Presumably this is because you do not regard the canopy as intervening and forming a roof between the bed and the sukkah roofing.] Is this in accord with R. Eliezer [who does not regard a sloping roof as a roof at all]? Have you then abandoned the [majority] view of rabbis and acted in accord with R. Eliezer [a minority]?"

B. He said to him, "There is a baraita [a Tannaite teaching alternative to the version now in the Mishnah] that has matters reversed: 'R. Eliezer declares [the arrangement] valid, and sages declare it invalid.'"

C. He said to him, "Do you then abandon the version of the Mishnah and act in accord with the alternative version of a baraita [of lesser reliability]?

D. He said to him, "The version of the Mishnah in any case stands for the viewpoint only of an individual, for

it has been taught on Tannaite
authority:

E.   *"He who makes his sukkah in the
     shape of a cone or who leaned it up
     against a wall—*

F.   *"R. Nathan says, 'R. Eliezer de-
     clares it invalid, because it has no
     roof, and sages declare it valid.'"*

The Yerushalmi's interest in the passage of the Tosefta is in comparing two
teachings, Tosefta's with the one that clarifies Eliezer's position. The whole
then serves to explain what is at issue at M. 1:12C. The Bavli's interest is
expressed at I.C–D, rabbis' position. Unit II then works out the implications
of the matter. At issue for the Bavli are versions of the positions of Eliezer and
sages, on the one side, and the decided law, on the other. The exegetical
focus, then, is practical rather than theoretical. But for our purposes the main
point is not to characterize the one Talmud as against the other. Rather, we
want to see whether, when the two Talmuds deal with the same Mishnah paragraph, they say pretty much the same thing. They do not.

1:11E–J

E.   *A large, reed mat,*

F.   *[if] one made it for lying, it is susceptible to uncleanness, and
     [so] they do not make sukkah roofing out of it.*

G.   *[If one made it] for sukkah roofing, they make sukkah roofing out
     of it, and it is not susceptible to uncleanness.*

H.   *R. Eliezer says, "All the same are a small one and a large one:*

I.   *"[if] one made it for lying, it is susceptible to uncleanness, and
     they do not make sukkah roofing out of it.*

J.   *"[If one made it for] sukkah roofing, they do make sukkah roofing
     out of it, and it is not susceptible to uncleanness."*

I. Clarification of M. 1:11E–G.   I. Contrast of M. 1:11F and M.
   What sort of mats are under   1:11G.
   discussion.   II. T. 1:10E–L.
                                        III. Types of mats and susceptibility
                                             to uncleanness.

The Yerushalmi's treatment of the matter is informative, not speculative. As
to Bavli, unit I subjects the formulation of the Mishnah to a close reading,
which allows reference to secondary considerations. Unit II is cited not only
to complement the Mishnah but also to set the stage for unit III, which alludes

directly to II.I. Unit III amplifies the matter of mats, such as at M. 1:11E. At the same time the issues of M. 1:11E–J—the consideration for what is susceptible to uncleanness—are worked out. So the entire construction is devoted to the exegesis of the Mishnah-paragraph.

Alike and Not Alike

We revert to the issue of continuity, connection, and autonomy, asking about the Bavli whether it is autonomous from, connected to, or continuous with the Yerushalmi and the canon of which both form a principal part.

The Bavli and the Yerushalmi assuredly stand autonomous from one another. How so? Each in its own way works out its own program of exegesis and amplification of the Mishnah. Word-for-word correspondences are few. Where materials are shared, moreover, they derive from either the Mishnah or the Tosefta or some antecedent convention of exegesis. But in all instances of shared language or conventional hermeneutics the framers of the Bavli worked things out on their own. They in no way accepted the Yerushalmi as a model for how they said things or for the bulk of what they said. What is shared, moreover, derives principally from the Mishnah. It comes, secondarily, from some sort of conventional program (partly encapsulated, also, in the Tosefta). But the Bavli's authors developed inherited intellectual conventions in a strikingly independent way.

On the other hand, the Bavli and the Yerushalmi most certainly do form a cogent part of a larger, continuous statement, that of "the one whole Torah of Moses, our rabbi" or, in modern theological language, Judaism. That premise of all study of the canon of formative Judaism stands firm. Nothing we have reviewed leads us to doubt its validity for those documents. The particular aspect of continuity at hand, however, requires specification. How is the Bavli continuous with the Yerushalmi? The Bavli meets the Yerushalmi in the Mishnah. The two also come together, to a markedly diminished measure, in the Tosefta and, still less, in some shared phrases deriving from post-Mishnaic authorities (e.g., those of the third-century masters Yohanan and Simeon b. Laqish). So in one specific way the two documents prove at one and continuous.

In somewhat more general ways, too, they wish to do much the same thing, which is to subject the Mishnah to a process of explanation and amplification. While the authors of the Bavli developed their own principles of hermeneutics, composition, and redaction, still, the upshot of their work, the Bavli as a whole, did not baffle their predecessors, who created the Yerushalmi. Apart from disagreements on tertiary details, the two sets of authorities found themselves entirely at home in the conceptions, rhetoric, and documents created by their counterparts. That seems self-evident proof of the continuity of the Bavli with the Yerushalmi.

If the two then turn out to be autonomous as well as continuous with one another, the real problem of nuance and differentiation is presented by matters of connection. These have forthwith to be divided into two parts: first, the connection of one document to the other; second, the connection of both documents to other components of the larger rabbinic canon. Here, once more, we find ourselves making self-evident observations.

To deal with the second question in summary fashion, the two documents are not only connected to one another but also stand essentially autonomous of the rest of the rabbinic canon, except (by definition) for the Mishnah and the Tosefta, which they serve. How so? In various passages, as we have noticed, we find shared materials in the two Talmuds and a common program of logic and rhetoric. What is shared between them, however, rarely also finds a place in other components of the canon of ancient Judaism. That is to say, while the two Talmuds constantly quote and explain the Mishnah, no other rabbinic document takes so sustained an interest in the Mishnah, or, indeed, much interest at all. So in the rabbinic canon the Talmuds occupy a place entirely their own, secondary to and continuous with the Mishnah-Tosefta. That place turns out to be set apart from the remainder of the canon. Counterparts to the Talmuds' treatment of the Mishnah rarely appear in any other rabbinic composition. The exception to the rule will be Sifra and, to a lesser degree, the two Sifres. These in places do go over the same matters in much the same way as do the two Talmuds. But the exception proves null when we realize that, where Sifra and the two Sifres share sizable statements with the two Talmuds (severally or together), it is ordinarily a common interest in the scriptural foundations of a Mishnaic law or, to a markedly diminished degree, one of the Tosefta. So that is hardly an exception since both Talmuds and the exegetical compilations on Leviticus, Numbers, and Deuteronomy meet in a common interest in the Mishnah and Tosefta. Why—to conclude with the obvious—do the two Talmuds stand essentially apart from the remainder of the canon? The two Talmuds form around the Mishnah, while most of the rest of the canon takes shape around books of the Hebrew Scriptures.

The other question—the connection of Bavli to Yerushalmi—is more important. Let me unpack the question at hand and review the aspect of the question relevant to the argument of this book. What we want to know concerns the Bavli in particular. The first and most fundamental question is this: Does the Bavli bear a message of its own? Or does the document essentially rest upon, and continue, the work of the Yerushalmi? If the Yerushalmi dictates the program and policy—the hermeneutic and rhetoric—of the Bavli, then we cannot speak of the Bavli as a document on its own. Its logic, its mode of inquiry, its rhetoric, its mode of thought—all these will turn out to belong to its precursors. What would define the Bavli then would be its authors ability to do better or to say at greater length what others had already done and said. In that case the Bavli would have to take its place as a secondary and subordinate component of that sector of the canon of Judaism defined, for all time, by the concerns and the circumstances of the framers of the Yerushalmi.

The contrary proposition is that while the Bavli shares with the Yerushalmi a common program and purpose, its authors carry out that program in their own way. By this thesis they should appear to define that purpose in response to interests shaped in their distinct context and framework. Then we may claim that the Bavli presents its own message. It accomplishes its own goals. True, its logic, its inquiry, its mode of thought may run parallel to those of the Yerushalmi. But that is only because they derive from sources common to both documents. In terms of this second hypothesis, the Bavli flows not from the Yerushalmi but from the Mishnah. That is the source, also, of the Yerushalmi and hence the cause of the parallel course of both documents. According to this second proposition, the Bavli is not secondary. It is not subordinate to the Yerushalmi in that larger sector of the canon of Judaism defined by the Mishnah.

As between these two propositions, the materials we have examined decisively settle the question in favor of the second. At point after point, we found the two documents connected not only to the common source but mainly or solely through that source. Where they go over the same problems, it is because the shared source presented these problems to the authors of both documents. In our comparison of the two documents, we found that the rhetoric and literary program of the Bavli owed remarkably little to those of its predecessor.

The comparisons of actual texts yielded decisive evidence for several propositions. First, there is little verbatim correspondence. The Bavli's authors scarcely ever made use of extensive constructions and only rarely of brief formulations also found in the Yerushalmi. So far as our modest sample suggests, they never did so when it came to detailed expository arguments and analyses. Where there is verbatim sharing, it is a Mishnah paragraph or Tosefta passage that is held in common, on the one side, or a prior, severely abbreviated lemma of an earlier Amoraic authority, on the other. Where the two sets of authors deal with such a shared lemma, however, each group does exactly what it wishes, imputing words to the prior authority (as if the said authority had actually spoken those words) simply not known to the other group. More important, what the framers of the Bavli wished to do with a saying of an earlier Amoraic authority in no way responded to the policy or program of the Yerushalmi's authors. Quite to the contrary, where both sets of authors shared sayings of Yohanan and Simeon b. Laqish, we noted that each set went its own way. In no aspect did the Yerushalmi's interest in these shared sayings affect the Bavli's treatment of them. The point in common was that prior authorities explained the same passage of the Mishnah. From that simple starting point, the Bavli's authors went in a direction not imagined by the Yerushalmi's. The power and intellectual force of the Bavli's authors in that context vastly overshadowed the capacities of the Yerushalmi's.

What the systematic analysis of a single chapter tells us, therefore, may be stated very briefly. The Yerushalmi and the Bavli are alike in their devotion to the exegesis and amplification of the Mishnah. Viewed as literary constructions, they share, in addition, a basic exegetical program, which flows from the Mishnah. The Bavli's framers pursued their own interests in their own way. They reveal independence of mind and originality of taste. It must follow that the Bavli is sufficiently unlike the Yerushalmi to be judged autonomous, disconnected—unlike in all the ways that matter. How so? In general the Bavli falls into the same classification as does the Yerushalmi. But in detail, it presents its own message in its own way. The genus is the same, the species not. Since that is the fact, we may now proceed to ask how, over all, that message takes shape. In respect to its treatment of the three principal components of the canon of revelation—the Mishnah, Scripture, the sage—we want to know how the Bavli actually differs from the Yerushalmi.

Part Two

The Talmuds and the Canonical Truth of Judaism

Alike and Not Alike

3

The Talmuds and the Mishnah

Differentiating Documents

Now that we realize the Bavli is essentially independent of the Yerushalmi, connected to the former composition principally by shared documents, our task becomes clear. We must differentiate the one Talmud from the other so as to discern what, if any, traits in the Bavli speak in particular for the authors of the Bavli. To compare and contrast the Yerushalmi and the Bavli, we seek a criterion for comparison, a point in common allowing controlled differentiation. In this part of the argument of the present book, the canon's three sources of torah—Scripture, Mishnah, sage—serve as the fixed point against which we compare the two documents. How each relates to materials formed around the redactional framework provided by the tripartite canon forms the consistent criterion, for both Talmuds' authors made ample use of and reference to each component of the one whole Torah. We begin with the Mishnah because of its priority in the redactional structure of both Talmuds and because that priority separates the two Talmuds from all other canonical writings.

When I undertook the parallel exercise for the Yerushalmi alone (in *Talmud of the Land of Israel*, volume 35, *Introduction: Taxonomy* [Chicago, 1983], pp. 2–3), I turned to the Talmud's units of discourse, which vary from one another in diverse ways. First I classified those units by type. Then I set them against the unchanging horizon of the Mishnah. Since in the present chapter I carry forward that same exercise but now encompass both the Yerushalmi and the Bavli, I believe a restatement of the reasoning behind the original go-around serves a useful purpose.

Since both the Yerushalmi and the Bavli carry forward and depend upon the Mishnah, to describe the Talmuds we have to begin with their relationships to the Mishnah. That is the Talmuds' own starting point. While the Mishnah admits to no antecedents and rarely alludes to or cites anything prior to its own materials, a passage of the Yerushalmi or the Bavli is often incomprehensible without knowledge of the passage of the Mishnah around which the talmudic discourse centers. Yet in describing and defining the Yerushalmi and the Bavli, we should grossly err if we were to say they are only, or mainly, step-by-step commentaries on the Mishnah or defined solely by the Mishnah's interests. We may not even say—though it is a step closer to the truth—that the Talmuds constitute a commentary on or secondary development of the Mishnah and important passages of the Tosefta. Units of discourse that serve these sorts of materials stand side by side with many that in an immediate sense do not. Accordingly, while a description of the Talmuds requires attention to the interplay between them and the Mishnah and Tosefta, the diverse relationships between the Talmuds and one or the other of those two documents constitute only one point of description and differentiation. For the authors of the Talmuds take full command of their own programs of thought and inquiry. These framers, responsible for the construction and organization of the units of discourse, chose what in the Mishnah they wished to analyze and what ignore. True, there could be no Yerushalmi or Bavli without the Mishnah and Tosefta. But knowing only those two works, we could never have predicted in a systematic way the character of the Talmuds' discourse at any point. The Mishnah, nonetheless, permits us at the outset to gain perspective on the character of both Talmuds because the Mishnah exhibits a remarkable unity of literary and redactional traits. By that standard the Talmuds present none. That is why the Mishnah defines the constant, the fixed stars, by which we differentiate the Talmuds not only from the Mishnah but, more important, from one another.

Mishnah in the Talmuds

Our first point of inquiry is the simplest. Let me express it in a question: Does one Talmud devote proportionately more of its time to the exegesis of the Mishnah that does the other? That is to say, we wish to find out whether the framers of one of the two Talmuds take for themselves a more limited task than the framers of the other. Speaking of the earlier as the more likely, we wonder whether the authors of the Yerushalmi define their work principally in exegesis of the Mishnah while the authors of the Bavli take on not only that task but others as well. How are we to find out?

The answer lies in comparing in detail the character of the units of discourse of which passages of the two Talmuds serving a single Mishnah tractate are made up. Working Mishnah paragraph by Mishnah paragraph, we shall see exactly where and how the framers of the Bavli took up tasks other than those of Mishnah exegesis. For the present purpose, we consider Mishnah tractate Sotah, itself a composite of legal and scriptural-theological interest. Our point of differentiation then is quite simple. I list units of discourse devoted to Mishnah exegesis (including amplification of the Mishnah's laws and their underlying principles) as against units of discourse of all types other than Mishnah exegesis.

Sotah	Mishnah Exegesis		Other Types of Discourse	
	Yerushalmi	Bavli	Yerushalmi	Bavli
1:1	I, II, III, IV, V, VI, VII, VIII, IX, [X]	II, III, IV, V, VI, VIII, IX, XII, XIII, XIV,	—	I, VII, X, XI, XVI, XVII, XVIII, XIX, XX,
1:2	I, II, III, IV, V, VI, [VII, VIII, IX]	XX, XV, XXX, XXXI		XXI, XXII, XXIII, XXIV, XXV, XXVI, XXVII, XXVIII, XXIX
1:3	I, II, III, IV, V	I (1:3A–D), I (1:3E–G), II		
1:4	I, III,	(1:4–6:) I, II,	II	
1:5	I, II, III, IV, V	III, IV, V, VI, VII, VIII, IX,		
1:6	I, II, II	X, XI, XII, XIII		
1:7	I, II, III	I, II, IV, V		III
1:8	I, II, III, IV, V, VI, VII, VIII, IX	(1:8–9:) I, II, III, IV, V, VI, VII, VIII, IX,		XV, XVI, XVIII, XIX, XX, XXI, XXII, XXIII,
1:9	I	X, XI, XII,		XXIV, XXV,
1:10	I, II, III, IV, V, VI, VII, VIII	XIII, XIV, XVII, XVIII, XXVII, XXVIII, XXIX, XXX, XXXI, LXXII, LXXIII, LXXIV, LXXV, LXXVI, LXXVII, LXXVIII, LXXIX, LXXX, LXXXI, LXXXII, LXXXIII, LXXXIV, LXXXV, LXXXVI, LXXXVII		XXVI, XXXII, XXXIII, XXXIV, XXXV, XXXVII, XXXVIII, XXXIX, XL, XLI, XLII, XLIII, XLIV, XLV, XLVI, XLVII, XLVIII, XLIX, L, LI, LII, LIII, LIV, LV, LVI, LVII, LVIII, LIX, LX, LXI, LXII, LXIII, LXIV, LXV, LXVI, LXVII, LXVIII, LXIX, LXX, LXXI

The opening chapter of Mishnah tractate Sotah tells us the principal difference between the Yerushalmi's and the Bavli's treatment of the Mishnah. Both Talmuds pay devout attention to the successive sentences of the Mishnah paragraph. Where the Bavli differs is in what its authors add. We see this most clearly in reference to M. Sot. 1:1–2 and M. Sot. 1:7–10. In both cases, the Yerushalmi provides what is needed for Mishnah exegesis and amplification. The Bavli adds a vast secondary collection of materials joined together without reference to the interests of the Mishnah, then further tacked on to materials that are relevant to those interests. (Later I shall characterize these additional materials.) To make this point clear, let us review the Bavli's composites that serve M. 1:1–2 and M. 1:7–10.

The Bavli to M. 1:1–2 begins the tractate from the most distant perspective, asking about the place of a given tractate in relation to its neighbors, fore
and aft. The exegesis of the Mishnah's language begins at unit II. Unit III goes
on to the substance of M. 1:1A, Eliezer's view of the sort of testimony that is
required. The main point is that in the present case a single witness suffices
for part of the procedure, just as Eliezer says. At unit IV we proceed to
Joshua's statement, M. 1:1B. The proof text for his statement is compared to
that for Eliezer's. Unit V proceeds to Tosefta's version of Eliezer's view and
to the difficulty the Talmud's authorities had in squaring Tosefta's criticism of
Yose's position in Eliezer's name with the Mishnah's version of Eliezer's view
since the same criticism applies to both. Unit VI carries forward unit V and is
continuous with it, since it refers back to Yose b. R. Judah. But the main focus
of unit VI is on whether or not the rite of expressing jealousy goes forward
beyond the destruction of the temple, with the secondary focus on the meaning of the phrase *express jealousy* and whether that meaning is positive or
negative. The construction is neatly balanced and carefully spelled out. Unit
VII begins with a set of exegetical exercises in which verses of the present
passage figure. VII provides two of them. VIII then turns to the exegesis of
the passage as foundation for a detail of the law of evidence. Since Ishmael
figures in unit VIII, unit IX, providing a capacious and systematic account of
exegetical disputes involving Ishmael, is tacked on whole. I am not sure why
unit X was added, although it would accord with the editorial program of unit
XII. Unit XI, of course, is simply part of the set of materials of the same
classification as unit X. But I see nothing to explain why unit XI was joined to
unit X, or why both units were found pertinent, other than the general theme
of unfaithfulness. Perhaps VII, X, and XII formed a larger essay on that
theme. The relevance of the whole to the present setting derived, then, from
VII. VIII–IX formed a whole and, as we see, XII pursues the interest of VIII
in the matter of evidence against the accused wife. Unit XII completes the
discussion of the effect of the testimony of a single witness and why such testimony is acceptable in one circumstance but not the other. The issue is
worked out in terms of its locus classicus at M. 6:1–2. Units XIII, XIV, and
XV proceed to deal with the detail of how much time is involved in "going
aside" and in conducting sexual relations—that is, that to which witnesses
testify. The issue is not the Mishnah's. Tosefta's entry on the subject begins
with XIII. XIV then follows with a further formulation, autonomous of both
Mishnah and Tosefta. This is then compared to Tosefta's. A systematic gloss
of Ashi characterizes the whole. XV then takes up a still more carefully composed set of glosses in Ashi's name. The entire set must be seen as a protracted
composition. XVI–XXIX present a thematic collection, mainly on humility.
Perhaps having sexual relations with married women is the detail that made
the entire composition appear to be relevant here. XXX and XXXI complete
the analysis of the Mishnah paragraph. The person who arranged the Talmud

at hand clearly was guided by the sequence of statements of the Mishnah paragraph since he left his comments on the last lines until he had completed his repertoire of materials he deemed pertinent to the theme of the earlier lines of the Mishnah paragraph. So there is no visible intent to deal with legal, then exegetical and theological or moral themes or to arrange the Talmud in such a way that we take up one type of material, then another type. The redactional program was to deal with the language of the Mishnah paragraph, then its broader implications where pertinent; then the corresponding materials of the Tosefta; then the larger themes relevant in a general way to both, with long passages of thematically relevant materials assembled to fill out the picture.

To grasp what the framers of the Bavli to M. 1:7–10 have given us, let me report on the organization of this vast tract: Samson (M. 1:8A): I–XXVI (including Judah and Tamar); Absalom (M. 1:8B–D): XXVII–XXIX; Miriam (M. 1:9B): XXX–LXXI (including exegesis of Exod. 1–2); Joseph (M. 1:9C–D): LXXII–LXXX; Moses (M. 1:9E–F): LXXXI–LXXXVII. In general, the materials follow the thematic order dictated by the Mishnah paragraph. But they are laid out in terms of their own interests. The prevailing impression of extreme prolixity derives from two facts. First, the framer of a given set of units deals not only with his primary texts, for example, about Samson, but also with secondary ones, such as Judah and Tamar. Second, the theme of Miriam draws in its wake a very long and systematical exegetical exercise on the verses of Exod. 1–2 in which Miriam plays some part. The focus, of course, is scarcely on Miriam in particular; it is on the verses in general. Where the sort of massive secondary accretion does not figure, as with Joseph and Moses, we see a clearer picture of the framers of the original thematic units as they did their work. The net effect of the construction as a whole may only be called tedious. There is no large-scale goal or direction. I discern no organizing point beyond that stated by the Mishnah itself. But the materials of which the Talmud is constructed have not been selected because of the Mishnah's proposition but only because of its theme. The treatment of Moses, at the end, produces a sublime conclusion and leaves the false impression that a deft editorial hand has done its work. But that is not true. The contrast between the encyclopaedic collection at hand and the sort of purposive compositions we may see in Leviticus Rabbah, in which materials are chosen and assembled to make a point and illustrate and substantiate a proposition, is clear.

Let us rapidly collect the facts of the remainder of the tractate in both Talmuds.

Sotah	Mishnah Exegesis		Other Types of Discourse	
	Yerushalmi	Bavli	Yerushalmi	Bavli
2:1	I, II, III, IV, V, VI	I, II, III, IV, V, VI, VII, VIII, IX, X, XI, XII, XIII, XIV, XV, XVI, XVII, XVIII, XIX (Much devoted to Tosefta.)		
2:2	I, [II], III, V, VI, VII, VIII	I, II, III, IV, V, VI, VII, VIII	IV	
2:3	I	I		II
2:4	I, II, III, IV, V	I, II, III		
2:5	I, II, III, IV, V, VI, VII, VIII, IX, X	(2:5–6:) I, II, III, IV, V		
2:6	I			
3:1	I, II, III, IV, V, VI,	(3:1–2:) I, II, III, IV, V		
3:2	I			
3:3	I, II, III, IV	(3:3–4:) I, II		
3:4	I, II, III, IV, V, VI, VIII, IX, X, XI, XII	III, IV, V, VI, VII, VIII, IX, XIII, XIV,	VII	X, XI, XII,
3:5	I, II, III	(3:5–8:) I, II,		
3:6	I, II, III, [IV]	III, IV, V, VI, VII, VIII, IX, X, XI, XII, XIII		
3:7	I, II, III, IV			
3:8	I, II, III, IV, V, VI, VII			
4:1	I, II, III, IV, V, VI	(4:1–5:) I, II, III, IV, V, VI,		XIII, XV
4:2	I	(4:1–5:) I, II, III, IV, V, VI, VII, VIII, IX, X,		
4:3	I, II, III	XI, XII, XIV, XVI,		
4:4	I, II, III	XVII, XVIII		
4:5	I		II	
5:1	I, II	(5:1–5:) I, II,		IV
5:2	I, II, III, IV, V, VI, VII, VIII	III, V, VI, VII, VIII, IX, X, XI, XII, XIII, XIV		
5:3	I, II, [IV]		IV	
5:4	I		II	
5:5	I, II, III, IV			
5:6	I		II, III	
6:1	I, II, III	(6:1–4:) I, II		
6:2	I, II, III			

Sotah	Mishnah Exegesis		Other Types of Discourse	
	Yerushalmi	Bavli	Yerushalmi	Bavli
6:3	I			
6:4	I, II, III, IV, V, VI, VII			
7:1	I, II, III, IV, V, VI	(7:1–5:) I, II, IV, V, VI, VII,		III, XIII, XV, XIX, XXI, XXII
7:2	I, II	VIII, IX, X, XI,	III	
7:3	I, II, III, IV	XII, XIV, XVI,		
7:4	I, II, III, IV, V	XVII, XVIII, XX, XXIII, XXIV, XXV,		
7:5	I, II, III, IV, V	XXVI		
7:6	I, II, III, IV	I, II, III, IV, V, VI, VII, VIII, XVIII, XXVI, XXVII		IX, X, XI, XII, XIII, XIV, XV, XVI, XVII, XIX, XX, XXI, XXII, XXIII, XXIV, XXV
7:7	I, II	I, II, III, IV, V, VI		
7:8	I, II	I, II, III, IV, V		VI, VII
8:1	I	I, II, III, IV, V, IX, XII	II, III	VI, VII, VIII, X, XI, XIV
8:2	—	(8:2–4:) I, II III, IV, V, XII, XIII, XIV, XV, XVI, XVII	I	VI, VII, VIII, IX, X, XI
8:3	I, II		III, IV, V, VI, VII, VIII, IX	I
8:4	I, II, III, IV, V			
8:5	I, III, IV	(8:5–7) I, II	II, V	
8:6	I, II, III	III		
8:7	I, II			
8:8	I, II			
8:9	I, II			
8:10	I, II, III		IV	
9:1	I, II, III, IV, V, VI, VII	(9:1–2:) I, II III, IV–VI, VII, VIII, IX, X		
9:2	I, II, III, IV, V, VI, VII,	(9:2–4:) I, II III, IV, V		
9:3	I			
9:4	I			
9:5	I, II, III, IV, V, VI, VII, VIII, IX, X, XI, XII	(9:5–6) I, II III, IV, V, VI, VII, VIII, IX, X		XI, XII, XIII, XIV, XV, XVI, XVII, XVIII, XIX, XX, XXI,
9:6	I, II, III, IV, V, VI	—[a]		XXII, XXIII, XXIV, XXV
9:7	I, II	(9:7–10:) I, II,		
9:8	I	III, IV, V, VI,		

| | Mishnah Exegesis | | Other Types of Discourse | |
Sotah	Yerushalmi	Bavli	Yerushalmi	Bavli
9:9	I	VII, VIII, IX, X		
9:10	I, II			
9:11	I, II, III, IV, V, VI, VII, VIII, IX	(9:11–13:) I, IV, V, VI, VII, VIII, IX, X,		II, III, XII, XIII
9:12	I, II, III	XI, XIV, XV		
9:13	I, II, III, IV, V, VI	—ᵇ		
9:14	I, II, III, IV	(9:14–15:) I, II,		
9:15	I, II, III, IV, V, VI	III, IV, V, VI, VII, VIII		
9:16	I, II			

ᵃUnit I pursues the analysis of the logical and exegetical bases for M. 9:5C's rule. Unit II is continuous with the foregoing. Unit III clarifies the matter of labor and the yoke, N. 9:5B. Unit IV proceeds to the theme of M. 9:5C; unit V to M. 9:5D; unit VI, M. 9:5E; and unit VII to M. 9:5F. Unit VIII runs through the same sort of exercise for M. 9:5F that is accomplished at unit I for M. 9:5C. Unit IX proceeds to M. 9:6A. Once the theme of providing an escort comes to the fore, however, we have a rather substantial exercise of expounding on that theme and on biblical passages that illustrate it, from unit X through unit XXV. As is common, when a passage of Scripture is adduced in evidence, discussion may veer off to treat that passage in its own terms. But so far as the whole reveals a simple plan, it is to spell out what is important about the statements of the Mishnah, then to discourse in a more expansive way about its theme.

ᵇUnit I explains the relevance of a proof text at M. 9:11. This leads to a sizable collection on what is wrong with singing or excessive merriment, units II–III. Unit IV proceeds to M. 9:12A, introducing Tosefta's date. Units V and VI do the same for M. 9:12B, which then is augmented at unit VII. Units VIII and IX provide material pertinent to the word choice of the Mishnah. Unit X glosses M. 9:12C. Inclusion at unit XI of a pertinent saying of Ilai about the power of prayer leads to the addition of a run of materials in the same authority's name, unit XII, and then, unit XIII adds further materials on the theme of unit XII, now in another authority's name. Unit XIV brings us back to M. 9:12E, and unit XV, to M. 9:13.

The foregoing tables leave no doubt as to the facts. Both Talmuds devote the bulk of their attention to Mishnah exegesis (defined broadly). However, the Bavli differs from the Yerushalmi in one important aspect. The Bavli includes sizable collections of units of discourse not devoted to Mishnah exegesis while the Yerushalmi does not. Self-evidently, the Yerushalmi contains some modest volume of this other sort of material. But when it occurs, it is in the form of singletons. In the tractate under study, the Yerushalmi's nonexegetical units rarely present sustained and vigorous discourse. Ordinarily, though not always, the Yerushalmi's nonexegetical units take up a single story or pursue the exegesis of a verse or two of Scripture. The Bavli's sorts of vast thematic conglomerates, for example, on the importance of humility or on various verses of Scripture such as those dealing with the birth of Moses, enjoy no counterpart in the Yerushalmi. So where the Bavli differs is in the addition, in volume and in quality, of materials of a type absent in most compositions of the Yerushalmi and rare and ordinarily brief and perfunctory even in those in which they occur.

The Talmuds on the Mishnah

Having isolated those units of discourse of both Yerushalmi and Bavli Sotah that address the explanation and amplification of the Mishnah, we move to the next stage of differentiation. We have now to ask whether the two Talmuds treat the Mishnah in much the same way or whether the Bavli approaches Mishnah exegesis in a manner different from the Yerushalmi. For the present purpose, we shall resort to the simple taxonomy for types of units of discourse in the broad classification of Mishnah exegesis that I developed for the analysis of the Yerushalmi's relationship to the Mishnah (*Talmud of the Land of Israel* 35:9–12). These taxa permit us to divide the Yerushalmi's and Bavli's units of discourse devoted to the Mishnah along consistent and reasonably objective lines. The main issue before us is whether a single taxonomic system serves both Talmuds' Mishnah exegeses or whether one of the two Talmuds requires an essentially distinct taxonomic system from that of the other. Of special interest in the present context is whether or not the Bavli's framers explore essentially fresh approaches to what is to be said in response to Mishnah paragraphs. We shall now see that they do not.

1. Mishnah exegesis. Here I list each unit in which there is citation of the Mishnah passage or clear-cut reference to it without direct citation followed by an explanation of the plain sense of the cited passage. There is reason, of course, to differentiate among types of treatments of the Mishnah, for example, citation and gloss, rephrasing or restatement of the rule, and so on. For the present purpose, for self-evident reasons, there is no purpose in such differentiation.

Yerushalmi		Bavli	
1:1	III	1:1–2	II, III, IV,
1:2	III		XIII, XXX, XXXI
1:3	III, IV	1:3A–D	I
1:4	III	1:3E–G	I, III
1:5	III	1:4–6	II, III, IV, V, VI, VIII, IX,
1:6	I, II, III		X, XI, XII, XIII
1:8	VII, X	1:7	I, V,
		1:8–9	XXX
2:1	II, IV, V, VII	2:1	I, XVIII, XIX
2:2	I	2:2	II, III
2:4	II, IV, V	2:3	I
2:5	I, IV	2:5–6	II
3:1	II, IV	3:1–2	II
3:3	II, III	3:3–4	II, III, IV, V, VI, VII, VIII,

Yerushalmi		Bavli	
3:4	I, II, VII, IX, X, XI, XII		IX, XIII, XIV
		3:5–8	VII, VIII
3:6	II		
3:8	X		
4:1	II, III, IV, VI	4:1–5	V, VI, VII, VIII, IX, X, XII,
4:2	I		XVI, XVIII
4:3	I, III		
4:4	I		
4:5	II		
5:1	I, II	5:1–5	I, VII, X
5:2	I, II, III		
5:3	II		
5:5	I, III, IV		
6:1	I, II, III	6:1–4	II
6:2	II		
6:4	I, IV, V, VI		
7:1	V	7:1–5	V
7:3	III	7:6	XXXVII
7:5	I, XX	7:7	I, II, III, IV, V, VI, VII
7:6	I, II, III, IV	7:8	I, II, III, IV
7:7	I		
7:8	I		
8:4	II, V	8:1	III, IV, V, IX, XII
8:5	III	8:2	XIV, XV
8:9	II	8:5–7	I, II, III
9:2	II, III, VI	9:1–2	III, IV, X
9:3	I	9:2G–4	III, IV
9:4	I	9:5–6	III
9:5	II, IV, VII, X	9:7–10	II, VII, VIII, X, XII
9:6	V, VI	9:11–13	IV, VIII, IX, X, XIV, XV
9:7	I	9:14–15	II, III, IV, V, VIII
9:8	I		
9:11	I, II, V, VI, VII, VIII, IX, X		
9:12	I		
9:13	I, IV, V, VI		
9:14	III, IV		
9:15	I, III, IV, V, VI		

2. *Mishnah-Scripture relationships.* The basis in Scripture for a rule in the Mishnah forms a common point of inquiry in these units of discourse.

Yerushalmi		Bavli	
1:1	I, VI	1:1–2	XII
1:2	VII	1:4–6	I
1:3	II	1:8–9	XXVII, LXXII, LXXX
1:5	I, IV		
1:7	III, IV		

Yerushalmi		Bavli	
1:8	I, IX		
1:9	I		
2:1	I, VI	2:1	(II–XVII [Scriptural basis
2:2	III, V, VIII		is for Tosefta's rules.])
		2:2	I, IV
3:1	I, V	3:1–2	I, III
3:2	I	3:3–4	I
3:4	III	3:5–8	II, III, IV, V, VI, IX, X,
3:5	II, III		XI, XII, XIII
3:6	IV		
3:7	I, II, III, IV		
3:8	I, III, IV, V, VI, VII		
4:1	I, V	4:1–5	I, XI, XIV, XVIII
4:4	III		
4:5	I		
5:2	VI	5:1–5	II, III, IV, V, VI, XIII, XIV
6:2	I	6:1–4	I
7:1	I, II	7:1–5	I, II, IV, VI, VII, VIII, IX,
7:2	I		X, XI
7:3	I, II	7:6	I, II, III, IV, V, VI, VII
7:4	II, IV, V		
7:5	III		
8:1	I	8:1	I
8:4	I, III, IV	8:2–4	I, II, III, IV, V, XVI, XVII
8:5	I		
8:6	I		
8:9	I		
8:10	I		
9:1	I, II, IV, VII	9:1–2	I, II, VII, VIII, IX
9:2	VII	9:2G–4	I, II, V
9:5	I, III, XII	9:5–6	I–II, V, VI, VII, VIII, IX
9:6	I, II	9:7–10	I, IV, V, IX
9:9	I	9:11–13	I
9:15	I	9:14–15	

3. Tosefta: Citation and exegesis. The two Talmuds frequently cite ver-batim, or nearly verbatim, statements found in the Tosefta. In a fair number of instances where there is no clear-cut discourse on the Mishnah passage itself, the Talmuds will cite the Tosefta and discuss that. The Talmud's contribution to the exegesis of the Mishnah consists in the elucidation of the Tosefta's complement to the Mishnah.

Yerushalmi		Bavli	
1:1	IV, VII	1:1–2	V
1:2	IV, VI	1:3E–G	II
1:3	V	1:4–6	VII
1:4	I	1:7	II, IV

Yerushalmi		Bavli	
1:7	I, II	1:8–9	I, II, LXXV, LXXXIV
1:10	VII		
2:2	VI	2:2	VI, VIII
		2:5–6	III
3:3	I, IV	3:5–8	I
3:4	V, VI, IX		
3:6	I, III		
4:3	II	4:1–5	VI
4:5	III		
5:2	VII	5:1–5	VII, XI, XII
5:3	I		
5:4	I		
6:3	I		
7:1	IV, VI	7:1–5	XII, XIV, XVI, XVII,
7:4	I, III		XVIII, XXIV
7:5	II, IV	7:7	V
8:3	II, III	8:2	XII, XIII
8:5	IV		
8:6	II		
8:7	I, II		
8:8	I, II		
8:10	III		
9:1	V	9:7–10	III, VI, VIII, IX, XI
9:2	I	9:11–13	IV, V, VI
9:5	XI	9:14–15	I, III, VI, VII
9:6	II		
9:10	I		
9:11	I, III, IV		
9:12	II, III		
9:13	II, III		
9:14	II		
9:15	II		
9:16	I		

4. Legal speculation and reflection primary to the Mishnah. A unit of discourse may well carry forward a discussion superficially separate from the Mishnah. Yet upon close inspection we notice that the discussion at hand speculates on principles introduced, to begin with, in the Mishnah's rule or in Tosefta's complement to that rule.

Yerushalmi		Bavli	
1:1	II, V, VIII, IX	1:1–2	VII, VIII, IX, XIV, XV
1:2	I, II, IX		
2:1	III	2:2	V, VII
2:2	VII	2:4	I, II, III
2:3	I	2:5–6	I, IV
2:4	I, II		

Yerushalmi		Bavli	
2:5	II–III, V		
3:1	III	3:1–2	IV
3:5	I		
4:4	II	4:1–5	II, III
5:2	IV, V, VIII	5:1–5	IX
6:2	III		
6:4	II, III, VII		
7:8	II		
8:1	III		
8:5	V		
8:6	III		
8:10	II		
9:1	III, VI	9:1–2	VI
9:2	IV		
9:5	V, VI, VIII		
9:7	II		

5. Harmonization of distinct laws of the Mishnah. One of the more interesting kinds of units of discourse is that in which principles are abstracted from utterly unrelated rules of the Mishnah (less commonly, of the Tosefta). These are then shown to intersect and conflict; or opinions and principles of a given authority on one such matter will be shown to differ from those of that same authority on another, intersecting matter. These units tend in Yerushalmi to occur verbatim at several different tractates, since they serve equally well (or poorly) each Mishnah pericope cited therein. Items on this list stand side by side with those on the foregoing. Both sorts of units of discourse relate to the Mishnah in essentially the same way. They vastly amplify the principles of the Mishnah. But they do not serve for a close exegesis of its wording or specific rule. These entries are few but always substantial and difficult because several different kinds of law have to be mastered, then the underlying principles made explicit and brought into juxtaposition with those of other laws on other topics.

Yerushalmi		Bavli	
1:1	V, VIII		
1:3	III		
1:5	V		
2:2	II	2:1	II–XVII
3:1	VI		
5:3	III, IV		
[9:1	VIII]		
9:2	V		
9:5	IX		

6. Legal speculation and reflection independent of the passage of the Mishnah at hand. There are units of discourse essentially independent of the Mishnah pericope with which they are associated. These pursue questions not even indirectly generated by the law in hand. From time to time we may guess at why the redactor thought the discourse belonged where he placed it. While there are not a great many of these, as in the foregoing instance, they are long and involved, always difficult, and unusually interesting.

Yerushalmi	Bavli	
	1:1–2	I
	2:5–6	V
	4:1–5	XV
	8:2	VI, VII, VIII, IX, X, XI
9:2 VIII	9:1–2	V

7. Anthology of laws relevant to the Mishnah only in theme. Sizable units of discourse are joined together only by a common theme and joined to the Mishnah pericope at which they occur only because, in some general way, someone supposed their themes to intersect with those of the Mishnah passage at hand. This type of unit of discourse predominates in those chapters where the Mishnah's statements, for their part, pertain not to law but to lore. Most such anthologies are rich in citation of, and comment upon, verses of Scripture. But the present category includes by no means the bulk of the Talmud's scriptural exegeses and comments in the tractate at hand.

Yerushalmi	Bavli
2:5 VI, VII, VIII, IX, X	
[7:5 III–V]	

Alike and Not Alike

The current question is whether one Talmud exhibits marked preferences in Mishnah exegesis over those displayed in the other Talmud. The answer is that that is not the case. Both devote substantial efforts to the several basic forms of Mishnah exegesis, specifically, explanations of words and phrases and amplifications thereof (list 1), interpretation of how Scripture supplies a basis for the Mishnah paragraph's ruling (list 2), citation of a passage of Tosefta and amplification of that passage, whether or not in relationship to the Mishnah (list 3), large-scale legal speculation on the Mishnah (list 4), exercises of harmonization of distinct laws of the Mishnah (list 5). List 6 suggests a greater tendency in the Bavli to speculate on law beyond the framework of a Mishnah paragraph. List 7 suggests that the Yerushalmi will construct anthologies of the law while the Bavli will not. But the sample at hand is too small to permit any conclusion on the matter.

Our purpose has now been served. We see very clearly that, where the Yerushalmi and the Bavli take up Mishnah exegesis in its various types, the authors of the two documents tend to do more or less the same thing, though in different proportions. More probative than the contents of the lists is the simple fact that a single taxonomy serves both documents. That proves beyond doubt the essential identity of the Mishnah hermeneutics of the authors of the two Talmuds. The upshot is that if we wish to ask how the Bavli differs from the Yerushalmi, we cannot ask the two Talmuds' approaches to the Mishnah to answer our question. The authors of the Bavli responded to the same document in much the same way as did those of the Yerushalmi, even though, as we saw in the preceding chapter, their rhetoric and logic in many ways were their own. But doing the same thing in a different, perhaps more sophisticated way, the authors of the Bavli simply improved upon their predecessors. From such improvements an autonomous and powerful, independent statement will not come forth. We have then to look elsewhere to find out what is distinctive about the Bavli: what makes the Bavli the Bavli, not just more of the Yerushalmi-Tosefta-Mishnah.

4

The Talmuds and Scripture

Differentiating Documents

Scripture, the next component of the tripartite canon of Judaism represented in the Talmuds, presents more interesting results. We already have recognized that the approach to the problem of Mishnah exegesis in the Bavli differs from that of the Yerushalmi, in its treatment of verses of themes of Scripture. We have now to test and refine that observation. What we want to know is where and how the authors of each Talmud took up units of discourse devoted not to the Mishnaic part of the one whole Torah of Moses, our rabbi, but to the scriptural component. Let me first explain the character of Scripture units of discourse and spell out how they constitute a distinct species of the genus of Torah, along with the other two species, Mishnah units of discourse and sage units of discourse (treated in chapter 5).

Sizable units of discourse in both Talmuds take up the exegesis of verses of passages of Scripture. The purpose in composing such Scripture units proves diverse. As we already know, some such compositions take shape around problems of law, either to link rules of the Mishnah to proof texts of Scripture or to explore in a context autonomous of the Mishnah the legal implications of legal passages of Scripture. These units of discourse in general link up to the Mishnah, one way or the other, and prove common in both Talmuds. We have cataloged them in chapter 3. But other Scripture units exhibit no link to the Mishnah or to problems of legal theory. They prove propositions through statements of Scripture. They elaborate values or ideals by reference to scriptural cases. They focus upon the meaning of a verse or a sequence of verses of Scripture. While the intent of the authors of units of discourse such as these cannot be exhaustively described, we can point to at least one reason they did their work. It is clear that, in some cases, their purpose was to expound systematically, in terms of a quite separate set of issues from those explicit in the passage at hand, the sense of a verse or sequence of verses in Scripture. In other such constructions we find a manifest interest in a virtue or a vice, with verses of Scripture supplying ample proof texts or examples to prove that said virtue brings reward, or vice, punishment. In further instances we have a single verse subjected to close reading and exposition. In others, there are groups of verses.

The main point is simply that Scripture, as much as the Mishnah, served some authors of units of discourse and editors of conglomerates of units of discourse as the frame, the structure, around which to organize ideas. What we now ask is only how much of the work of those authors of Scripture units of discourse found its way into one Talmud as against the other. Then we inquire about what sort of work each set of compositors—those for the Yerushalmi, those for the Bavli—appears to have preferred. The question at hand therefore remains the same: whether or not on the basis of proportions of Scripture units of discourse in each of the two Talmuds, we are able to differentiate one Talmud from the other. As we shall now see, the evidence is decisive.

Scripture in the Talmuds

Our first point of differentiation between Yerushalmi and Bavli asks whether one Talmud devotes a larger proportion of its interest to Scripture units of discourse than does the other. That matter proves fundamental. While we do not know what choices the framers of the Talmuds faced, the sorts of material they rejected not now being available, we do have in our hands precisely what has survived of what they preferred. The Talmuds tell us. So we begin with their policies of selection and composition: where and how units of discourse devoted to systematic exposition of a verse or verse of Scripture for other than legal-exegetical purposes made their appearance. In surveying three tractates—Sotah, Sukkah, and Sanhedrin—we simply review the particular items devoted to Scripture and indicate their proportion of the larger composite in which they appear. Let me state the question simply. How many units of discourse serving a given Mishnah paragraph focus upon not the Mishnah but Scripture, and what proportion of the total units of discourse serving said paragraph is devoted to Scripture?

The catalogs that follow omit reference to the units of discourse in which Scripture serves in the illumination of the Mishnah. Units of discourse of that classification have already been dealt with in the last chapter. What we now review is units of discourse in which Scripture, not the Mishnah, forms the focus, on the one side, or supplies the probative facts, on the other. Where the Mishnah introduces a scriptural theme, for example, Ahab, Jeroboam, or David, I omit those items in which the Mishnah's main point about the scriptural theme dominates discussion. I include the items in which the scriptural theme on its own defines the range of interest. For example, I enter references to units made up of sequences of verses on the scriptural theme subjected to analysis entirely in their own terms, out of all relationship to the purposes or terms of the Mishnah's allusions to that same topic or theme. While the distinction introduces an element of subjectivity, in making the catalogs I tried with reference to both Talmuds to sort matters out in a consistent way. Where, further, units of discourse make reference to verses of Scripture as proof texts, even though said units of discourse make their own points, not those generated by the plain sense of Scripture, I catalogue those items. These will be differentiated in the next section of this chapter, where I review the units of discourse in which Scripture sets the agenda.

Scripture Units of Discourse
(In parentheses: total number of Scripture units and total number of units of discourse serving the Mishnah paragraph signified at the left.)

Sotah	Yerushalmi		Sotah	Bavli	
1:1	—	(0/10)	1:1–2	XI, XVI, XVII, XVIII,	
1:2	—	(0/9)		XIX, XX, XXI, XXII,	
1:3	—	(0/4)		XXIII, XXIV, XXV,	
1:4	III	(1/3)		XXVI, XXVIII, XXIX	(15/31)
1:5	—	(0/5)	1:3A–D	—	(0/1)
1:6	—	(0/3)	1:3E–G	—	(0/3)
1:7	—	(0/4)	1:4–6	—	(0/13)
1:8	II, III, IV, V,		1:7	III	(1/4)
	VI, VIII	(6/9)	1:8–9	III–XXVI, XXVIII–	
	[Omitted: items			XXIX, XXXI–LXXI,	
	explicitly			LXXIII–LXXIV,	
	referring to M.]			LXXXI–LXXXIII,	
1:9	—	(0/10)		LXXXVI–LXXXVII	(74/87)
1:10	III, V, VI, VIII	(4/8)			
2:1	—	(0/7)	2:1	—	(0/19)
2:2	—	(0/8)	2:2	—	(0/8)
2:3	—	(0/1)	2:3	—	(0/2)
2:4	—	(0/5)	2:4	—	(0/3)
2:5	—	(0/10)	2:5–6	—	(0/5)
2:6	—	(0/1)			
3:1	—	(0/6)	3:1–2	—	(0/5)
3:2	—	(0/1)	3:3–4	VI, XI, XII	(3/14)
3:3	—	(0/4)	3:5–8	—	(0/13)
3:4	—	(0/12)			
3:5	—	(0/3)			
3:6	—	(0/4)			
3:7	—	(0/4)			
3:8	—	(0/7)			
4:1	—	(0/6)	4:1–5	—	(0/18)
4:2	—	(0/1)			
4:3	—	(0/3)			
4:4	—	(0/3)			
4:5	—	(0/2)			
5:1	—	(0/2)	5:1–5	—	(0/14)
5:2	—	(0/8)			
5:3	—	(0/4)			

Sotah	Yerushalmi		Sotah	Bavli	
5:4	—	(0/2)			
5:5	III	(1/4)			
5:6	I, II, III	(3/3)			
6:1	—	(0/3)	6:1–4	—	(0/2)
6:2	—	(0/3)			
6:3	—	(0/1)			
6:4	—	(0/6)			
7:1	II	(1/6)	7:1–5	XIII, XV, XX, XXI,	
7:2	—	(0/3)		XXII	(5/26)
7:3	—	(0/4)	7:6	IX–XVI	(8/27)
7:4	—	(0/5)	7:7	—	(0/6)
	[All serve Mishnah exegesis.]		7:8	VI, VII	(2/7)
7:5	—	(0/5)			
7:6	—	(0/4)			
7:7	—	(0/2)			
7:8	—	(0/2)			
8:1	—	(0/3)	8:1	VI, VII, VIII, XIII	(4/13)
8:2	—	(0/1)	8:2–4	—	(0/17)
8:3	I, VI, VII	(3/9)	8:5–7	—	(0/3)
8:4	—	(0/4)			
8:5	—	(0/5)			
8:6	—	(0/3)			
8:7	—	(0/2)			
8:8	—	(0/2			
8:9	—	(0/2)			
8:10	—	(0/4)			
9:1	—	(0/8)	9:1–2	—	(0/10)
9:2	—	(0/8)	9:2G–4	—	(0/5)
9:3	—	(0/1)	9:5–6	X–XXV	(16/25)
9:4	—	(0/1)	9:7–10	—	(0/12)
9:5	—	(0/12)	9:11–13	III, XI–XIII	(4/15)
9:6	—	(0/6)	9:14–15	—	(0/8)
9:7	—	(0/2)			
9:8	—	(0/1)			
9:9	—	(0/1)			
9:10	—	(0/2)			
9:11	—	(0/10)			
9:12	—	(0/3)			
9:13	—	(0/6)			
9:14	—	(0/4)			
9:15	—	(0/6)			
9:16	—	(0/2)			
TOTAL	19/319			132/411	
PERCENTAGE	5.9%			32.1%	

Sukkah	Yerushalmi		Sukkah	Bavli	
1:1	—	(0/12)	1:1	—	(0/20)
1:2	—	(0/3)	1:2	—	(0/2)
1:3	—	(0/2)	1:3	—	(0/3)
1:4	—	(0/1)	1:4	—	(0/6)
1:5	—	(0/3)	1:5	—	(0/11)

Sukkah	Yerushalmi		Sukkah	Bavli	
1:6	—	(0/3)	1:6	—	(0/2)
1:7	—	(0/2)	1:7	—	(0/1)
1:8	—	(0/1)	1:8	—	(0/4)
1:9	—	(0/2)	1:9	—	(0/3)
1:10	—	(0/1)	1:10	—	(0/9)
1:11	—	(0/3)	1:11	—	(0/2)
1:12	—	(0/2)	1:12	—	(0/3)
2:1	—	(0/3)	2:1	—	(0/3)
2:2	—	(0/1)	2:2A–B	—	(0/1)
2:3	—	(0/2)	2:2C–H	—	(0/3)
2:4	—	(0/3)	2:3	—	(0/8)
2:5	—	(0/4)	2:4	—	(0/11)
2:6	—	(0/1)	2:5	—	(0/2)
2:7	—	(0/3)	2:6	—	(0/8)
2:8	—	(0/3)	2:7–8	—	(0/4)
2:9	—	(0/1)	2:9	—	(0/8)
2:10	—	(0/3)			
3:1	—	(0/12)	3:1	—	(0/14)
3:2	—	(0/2)	3:2	—	(0/10)
3:3	—	(0/1)	3:3	—	(0/5)
3:4	—	(0/4)	3:4	—	(0/4)
3:5	—	(0/2)	3:5–7	—	(0/19)
3:6	—	(0/5)	3:8	—	(0/3)
3:7	—	(0/3	3:9A–D	—	(0/2)
3:8	—	(0/3)	3:9E–H	—	(0/1)
3:9	—	(0/1)	3:10–11D	—	(0/6)
3:10	—	(0/8)	3:11E–F	—	(0/4)
3:11	—	(0/3)	3:12	—	(0/2)
3:12	—	(0/1)	3:13–14	—	(0/5)
			3:15	—	(0/2)
4:1	—	(0/3)	4:1–4	—	(0/12)
4:2	—	(0/1)	4:5–7	IV	(1/15)
4:3	V	(1/5)	4:8A–B	—	(0/1)
4:4	—	(0/1)	4:8C–F	—	(0/1)
4:5	—	(0/3)	4:9–10	II, III, VIII, XII,	
4:6	—	(0/3)		XIII, XV	(6/17)
4:7	—	(0/3)			
TOTAL	1/139				7/237
PERCENTAGE	0.7%				2.9%

Sanhedrin	Yerushalmi		Sanhedrin	Bavli	
1:1	—	(0/7)	1:1–6	XVIII, XX, XXI,	
1:2	—	(0/19)		XXIII, XXV, XXVI,	
1:3	—	(0/8)		XXIX, XXX, LXXXV,	
1:4	V, VI	(2/6)		LXXXVI	(10/91)
3:3	—	(0/1)	3:1	XI	(7/11)
3:2	—	(0/2)	3:2	—	(1/11)
3:3	—	(0/2)	3:3	XI	(0/3)
3:4	—	(0/3)	3:4–5	—	(0/16)
3:5	—	(0/3)	3:6–7	—	(0/27)
3:6	—	(0/6)	3:8	—	(0/7)
3:7	—	(0/1)			
3:8	—	(0/4)			

Sanhedrin	Yerushalmi		Sanhedrin	Bavli	
3:9	—	(0/6)			
3:10	—	(0/1)			
3:11	—	(0/1)			
3:12	—	(0/3)			
4:1	—	(0/4)	4:1–2	XXII	(1/27)
4:2	I	(1/1)	4:3–4	III, IV	(2/6)
4:3	—	(0/2)	4:5	IV, VI, VIII, IX,	
4:4	—	(0/1)		X, XI, XII, XIII,	
4:5	—	(0/1)		XV–XXIII, XXX–XXXV	(28/35)
4:6	—	(0/2)			
4:7	—	(0/5)			
4:8	—	(0/2)			
4:9	II	(1/2)			
5:1	—	(0/6)	5:1–5	XVII	(1/22)
5:2	—	(0/2)			
5:3	—	(0/2)			
5:4	—	(0/2)			
5:5	—	(0/3)			
6:1	—	(0/2)	6:1A–G	—	(0/8)
6:2	—	(0/1)	6:1H–J	III	(1/3)
6:3	I	(1/3)	6:2	I–XII	(12/16)
6:4	—	(0/1)	6:3	—	(0/2)
6:5	—	(0/3)	6:4A–G	—	(0/5)
6:6	—	(0/2)	6:4H–M	—	(0/4)
6:7	II	(1/2)	6:4N–6:6	VI, VIII, XVI,	
6:8	—	(0/1)		XVII	(5/17)
6:9	—	(0/1)			
6:10	—	(0/3)			
7:1	—	(0/4)	7:1	—	(0/15)
7:2	—	(0/4)	7:2	—	(0/6)
7:3	—	(0/3)	7:3A–F	—	(0/2)
7:4	—	(0/2)	7:3G–J	—	(0/2)
7:5	—	(0/4)	7:4A–R	—	(0/3)
7:6	—	(0/5)	7:4S–V	—	(0/10)
7:7	—	(0/5)	7:5	XIII, XIV–XVI,	
7:8	—	(0/7)		XIX	(5/26)
7:9	—	(0/5)	7:6	XI, XII, XIII, XIV,	
7:10	—	(0/10)		XV	(5/18)
7:11	—	(0/4)	7:7A–E	—	(0/6)
7:12	—	(0/4)	7:7F–I	—	(0/6)
7:13	—	(0/7)	7:8	—	(0/4)
			7:9	—	(0/3)
			7:10–11	VIII, X	(2/13)
8:1	—	(0/2)	8:1	VI	(1/7)
8:2	—	(0/5)	8:2	IV–VIII	(5/15)
8:3	—	(0/3)	8:3	—	(0/2)
8:4	—	(0/2)	8:4	—	(0/6)
8:5	—	(0/2)	8:5	—	(0/1)
8:6	—	(0/2)	8:6	—	(0/7)
8:7	—	(0/2)	8:7	—	(0/11)
8:8	—	(0/3)			
8:9	—	(0/4)			
9:1	—	(0/8)	9:1A–C	X	(12/11)
9:2	—	(0/3)	9:1–D–M	—	

Sanhedrin	Yerushalmi		Sanhedrin	Bavli	
3)					
9:3	—	(0/5)	9:1N–T	—	(0/2)
9:4	—	(0/2)	9:2	—	(0/4)
9:5	—	(0/1)	9:3	—	(0/4)
9:6	—	(0/3)	9:4	—	(0/4)
9:7	—	(0/4)	9:5	—	(0/5)
			9:6	VII–X	(4/13)
10:1	II, III, V, VI,		10:1	—	(0/18)
	VII	(5/11)	10:2	—	(0/6)
10:2	III	(1/12)	10:3	—	(0/1)
10:3	—	(0/2)	10:4	—	(0/1)
10:4	—	(0/2)	10:5–6	VIII, X	(2/13)
10:5	—	(0/4)			
10:6	—	(0/3)			
10:7	—	(0/2)			
10:8	—	(0/1)			
11:1	—	(0/2)	11:1–2	II–X, XXII–LXXXIII,	
11:2	—	(0/4)		LXXXVII–LXXXIX,	
11:3	—	(0/3)		XCIII–CI, CVI–CVII,	
11:4	I	(1/2)		CIX–CXV, CXVII,	
11:5	I, III, IV	(3/4)		CXIX–CXXIV,	
11:6	—	(0/2)		CXXVIII–CXXIX,	
				CXXXII–CXXXIII, CXLIV,	
				CXLVIII, CLIII–CLX,	
				CLXXVII–CLXXXI,	
				CLXXVI–CLXXVII, CLXXXV,	
				CLXXXIX, CXC–CXCIV,	
				CXCLI–CCIII,	
				CCVII–CCIX,	
				CCXIV–CCXIX, CCXXI,	
				CCXXIII–CCVI,	
				CCLIX–CCLVI	(178/256)
			11:3A–CC	IV–XIX, XXI–XXIV,	
				XXVII–XXVIII, XXX,	
				XXXII, XXXVI–XLVII	(35/48)
			11:3DD–FF	II, III, IV, V,	
				VI–VIII	(7/8)
			11:4–6	XX, XXI–XXII	(3/24)
TOTAL	21/322			321/909	
PERCENTAGE	6.5%			35.3%	

The result is consistent and one sided. While the Yerushalmi contains a negligible proportion of Scripture units of discourse—5.9% in Sotah, 0.7% in Sukkah, and 6.5% in Sanhedrin—the Yerushalmi's successors in the Bavli made use of sizable numbers and vastly larger proportions of the same sort of units. In proportion to the whole, these are 32.1% in Sotah, 2.9% in Sukkah, and 35.3% in Sanhedrin—five times the percentage for Sotah, four times for Sukkah, and five times for Sanhedrin. We need not suppose that the work of composing Scripture units of discourse took place mainly in Babylonia. Nor can we imagine that the work got underway after the Yerushalmi had come to closure. These hypotheses are not relevant here. The sole evidence at hand hardly permits us to entertain such propositions. All we know, after all, is what the framers on the two Talmuds have given us, not what they decided not to include. Thus far, therefore, all we have done is differentiate the two documents by showing that the compositors of the Bavli have made far more extensive use of Scripture units of discourse than did those of the Yerushalmi. To point toward the meaning of the facts at hand, we have now to undertake a further exercise of differentiation.

The Talmuds and Scripture

At issue is whether or not a single taxonomy serves both Talmuds. If it does, the difference in proportion proved just now bears one set of meanings. If it does not, that same difference requires a different set of interpretations. So the heart of matters lies in the sort of taxonomic structure I am able to propose for sorting out the types of Scripture units of discourse.

In fact I take up two distinct exercises of taxonomy. In one I distinguish one type of Scripture unit of discourse from another. Second, I differentiate one reason for the utilization of a Scripture unit of discourse from another. In this exercise I want to know whether one Talmud exhibits marked preference for one sort of Scripture unit of discourse as against some other sort. In the other exercise I want to know whether one group of compositors or redactors had in mind, when including Scripture units of discourse, the same purposes or intentions distinct from those that impelled the other group to make use of the same sort of materials. Proceeding to the former of the two exercises, I begin each catalog with a clear example of the type of unit of discourse listed and an explanation of what makes such a type of unit of discourse readily identified. In the latter of the two exercises it would not be equivalently convenient to provide a simple illustration. But the categories themselves are so gross and objective that a quick look at the sources will persuade the reader of the aptness of the differentiation and the correctness of the division among the differentiated categories.

Let me elaborate on these brief remarks. The trait in common among the units of discourse at hand—their focus upon Scripture—has now to yield to consideration of the traits that differentiate one type of such unit of discourse from the next. One fundamental and ubiquitous question is simple: on what basis did the author or composer of a given sustained unit of discourse gather and join the materials that he used? That is to say, we ask what struck the framer as a point in common among the diverse materials he assembled. Once we define as our point of differentiation the principle of aggregation of materials, we see two completely distinct theories. In one, a sequence of verses of Scripture, for example, a chapter of Scripture, clearly formed the center of interest for the compositors. What the authors of the passage proposed, therefore, is to collect sayings relevant to the sequence of verses and to arrange them into a composite. In a second, a fundamental ideal or value formed the focus of discourse. Verses of Scripture, drawn from diverse passages, find their way into such a unit of discourse because they serve in some way to exemplify or clarify the virtue of value at hand. The differentiation for taxonomic purposes then is both formal and functional. In a formal sense, a unit of discourse finds structure in the framework of a chapter or of a large sequence of verses, of Scripture. Or second, a unit of discourse takes shape around the inner logic or sense of a given ideal or virtue. It is that ideal, for example, study of Torah, that will guide the author to verses of Scripture suitable for his larger Scripture unit of discourse. In that case, in a formal sense, a unit of discourse will skip about biblical books, picking and choosing verses out of their own context and moving those verses into the context of the ideal or value under discussion. So the questions are why and how the framer of a given unit of discourse focused upon Scripture chose and joined the items at hand. In that case, we seek to differentiate among Scripture units of discourse not in terms of the function these units serve in their larger, talmudic context.

We begin at the surface, then work our way to the substrate. We look at the larger setting, not upon the inner architectonic. Thus we ask the reason for including a Scripture unit. The reason the framers inverted the construction will occupy our attention. At issue is the evident basis or reason for the utilization of a Scripture unit of discourse: in context or not in context.

1. Scripture unit of discourse illustrates a point of law or theology in the antecedent analytical composition, even though the unit stands independent of the composition that it serves. The Scripture unit of discourse therefore fits into context and serves an exemplary purpose. The Scripture unit of discourse relates to the larger argument constructed by the compositors or to the substance of the point they wish to make, not merely to the topic viewed in general terms. Here, therefore, Scripture units of discourse serve a larger redactional purpose and do not establish their own redactional structure.

Sotah	Yerushalmi	Sotah	Bavli
1:4	III	1:8–9	III–XVII, XXVIII–XXIX,
1:8	II, III, IV, V, VI, VIII		XXXI–LXXI, LXXIII–LXXIV, LXXXI–LXXXIII, LXXXVI–LXXXVII
1:10	V, VI, VIII	3:3–4	VI, XI–XII
5:6	I, II, III	7:1–5	XIII, XV, XX–XXII
8:3	I, VI	7:6	IX, XVI
		7:8	VI–VII
		8:1	VI–VIII, XIII
		9:5–6	X–XXV
		9:11–13	III, XI–XIII
15/319	4.7%	87/411	21.1%

Sukkah	Yerushalmi	Sukkah	Bavli
4:3	V	4:5–7	IV
		4:9–10	II, III, VIII
1/139	0.7%	74/237	1.6%

Sanhedrin	Yerushalmi	Sanhedrin	Bavli
1:4	V–VI	1:1–6	XXIX
2:3	V	2:1–2	XIII
2:4	III	4:3–4	III–IV
2:5	III–IV	4:5	IV, VI, IX–XIII
2:6	II	6:1H–J	III
4:2	I	6:2	I–XII
4:9	II	8:1	VI
6:3	I	9:6	VII–X
6:7	II	10:5–6	VIII
10:1	II, III, V, VI, VII	11:1–2	II–X, XXII–LIII, CLIII–CLX,
10:2	III		CLXVII–CLXXVII, CLXXX,
11:4	I		CLXXXIX, CCXIV–CCXIX, CCXXI,
11:5	I, III, IV		CCXXIII–CCVI
		11:3A–CC	IV–XIX, XXI–XXIV, XXVII–XXVIII
			XXX, XXXVI–XLVII
		11:4–6	XX–XXII
21/322	6.5%	137/909	15%

2. *Scripture unit of discourse is autonomous of the point of law or theology in the antecedent analytical context (all the more so, in the Mishnah). The unit is introduced "for its own sake," that is to say, without clear relationship to the established context of discourse. The Scripture unit of discourse therefore serves no exemplary purpose established by the compositors' larger plan for the arrangement of a sequence of units of discourse. The visible connection is topical, that is, the intent to provide more materials relevant in theme but not in substance or argument.*

Sotah	Yerushalmi	Sotah	Bavli
7:1	*II*	*1:1–2*	*XI, XVI–XXIX*
		1:7	*III*
		1:8–9	*XVIII–XXVI*
1/319	*.03%*	*25/411*	*6%*

Sukkah	Yerushalmi	Sukkah	Bavli
		4:9–10	*XII–XIII, XV*
0/139	*0%*	*3/237*	*1.2%*

Sanhedrin	Yerushalmi	Sanhedrin	Bavli
		1:1–6	*XVIII, XX, XXI, XXIII, XXV,*
			XXVI, XXX, LXXXV–LXXXVI
		2:3	*III*
		2:4A–D	*IV*
		2:4E–I	*III*
		2:5	*I–VI, VIII*
		3:1	*XI*
		3:3	*XI*
		4:1–2	*XXII*
		4:5	*VIII, XV–XXIII, XXX–XXXV*
		5:1–5	*XVII*

Sanhedrin	Yerushalmi	Sanhedrin	Bavli
		6:4N–6	*VI–VIII, XVI–XVII*
		7:5	*XIII–XVI, XIX*
		7:6	*XI–XV*
		7:10–11	*VIII, X*
		8:2	*IV–VIII*
		10:5–6	*X*
		11:1–2	*LXXXVIII–CXXXIX, XLIII–CI,*
			CVI–CVII, CIX–CXV, CXVII,
			CXIX–CXXIV, CXXVIII–CXXIX,
			CXXXII–CXXXIII, CXLIV, CXLVIII,
			CXC–CXCIV, CXCVI–CCIII,
			CCVII–CCIX
		11:3A–CC	*XXXII*
		11:3DD–FF	*II–VIII*
0/322	*0%*	*160/909*	*17.6%*

The important result derives from the contrast between the two catalogs. For purposes that fit into a larger context of continuing discourse, the Yerushalmi and the Bavli make roughly comparable use of Scripture units. This means that, so far as the Yerushalmi is concerned, Scripture units of discourse, available and quite useful, always serve a redactional purpose beyond themselves. The second possible utilization of the same classification of unit of discourse—out of rhetorical context, thus, for instance, out of phase with Mishnah exegesis—presents a stunning contrast. Here the Yerushalmi presents no counterpart at all to the Bavli. A single taxonomy does not serve both Talmuds.

Unlike the Yerushalmi, the Bavli makes proportionate use of Scripture units of discourse for a purpose other than Mishnah exegesis, on the one side, or the amplification of points established in the context of legal or theological exposition, on the other. Scripture units of this course occur out of context, one might say "for their own sake." The Bavli's framers therefore were prepared to organize their larger composition around more than the single focus of a context of discourse dictated by the Mishnah or by points of law or theology deemed pertinent to the Mishnah. For Sotah and Sukkah the latter sort of redactional utilization presents lower proportions—21% versus 6%, 1.6% versus 1.25%. For Sanhedrin the comparison yields nearly equal proportions—15% versus 17.6%. The main point, however, is not what the Bavli's compositors found more useful than the Yerushalmi's. Let me state the contrast with emphasis: *It is that they were prepared to build large-scale discourse around a framework deriving from other than that context that commenced with sustained Mishnah exegesis.*

One might wish to call the contrast at hand "contextual" as against "noncontextual" redaction of units of discourse. But I think the point is other. It is that, for the Bavli's authors, two distinct principles guided selection and large-scale redactional arrangement of Scripture units of discourse. One, available from the Yerushalmi, instructed them to use Scripture units of discourse because these served the larger and established purposes of Mishnah exegesis and amplification. The other, not generated by the needs of Mishnah exegesis and amplification, told them to allow Scripture units of discourse, especially substantial ones, to find a place within their composition out of all relationship with the frame of reference and context of discourse defined by the available program of inquiry.

In this simple, redactional framework, therefore, we may say that, while the Yerushalmi builds its lines of structure around paragraphs of the Mishnah alone, the Bavli utilizes a second redactional focus. It is redactional construction upon passages of Scripture, which, linked one way or another, serve as suitably as do passages of the Mishnah. So the Yerushalmi rests upon a simple, and the Bavli upon a complex, principle of what defines redactional logic as well as dictates inner cogency between units of discourse. The one speaks to the Mishnah, the other to the Mishnah and also Scripture.

Having carried out one taxonomic exercise and shown that a single taxonomy based on redactional utilization of Scripture units of discourse does not serve, we proceed to the next question. If we now ignore the compositors' purposes in inserting Scripture units of discourse and deal only with the diverse principles of conglomeration, may we resort to a single taxonomy for both Talmuds? That is to say, do all, or nearly all, units of discourse concerning Scripture in both Talmuds fall into the same framework? Or do we find that one Talmud contains greater diversity of types of Scripture units of discourse than the other? These questions define the next exercise.

Let me spell out what I mean by principles of conglomeration, for this second taxonomic exercise focuses on a fresh criterion of differentiation. What I now ask is how, viewed on its own—out of redactional context—as a cogent unit of discourse, a Scripture unit of discourse hangs together. What makes the parts of such a single composite form a whole?

The simplest answer to this question, based both on formal and rhetorical traits, derives from the point of origin of the verses cited in a given construction, on the one hand. Then we distinguish Scripture units of discourse that are organized around a sequence of verses, for instance, half a chapter of Scripture. Some of these sequences of verses will follow the exact order of verses, much as the Talmuds will take up a paragraph of the Mishnah and explain each of its sentences, one by one. Other sequences of verses will take shape around a single biblical figure, for example, Samson or Ahab or Korah (as in Sanhedrin).

A second principle of conglomeration derives from a theological or moral value or principle, for example, the importance of study of Torah, the danger of strong drink, and the like. Then many verses, from diverse passages of Scripture, will come forth to give testimony. The principle of organization derives from the ideal or value under discussion (normally for purposes of exposition and advocacy). The logic of that principle or value will dictate which verses will make an appearance.

The framer of the former type of Scripture unit of discourse will have resorted to Scripture, as much as his colleague at the next table will have resorted to the Mishnah, when he wanted to string together various singleton sayings into a cogent unit of discourse. The author of the latter type of Scripture unit of discourse, by contrast, will have followed a different theory of utilization of Scripture in the composition of a cogent and sizable statement.

A third taxon exists in which a single verse all by itself forms the focus of discourse and holds together a unit of discourse on its own. That third type constitutes little more than a variation of the first, and cataloging entries of that type serves as a test to verify or falsify the results of the comparisons made possible by catalogs of the first two types. If the thesis at hand proves valid, then the third catalog should replicate the results of the first. In each catalog that follows I begin with an example of what I regard as the differentiating and distinctive principles of inner cogency characteristic of all the items on the catalog that follows.

Before proceeding, I have to address the question now troubling readers knowledgeable in the texts at hand. What of the many units of discourse in which verses of Scripture occur miscellaneously? In such units of discourse, verses of Scripture provide proof texts. But they do not supply the framework of composition or conglomeration, let alone the principle of redaction in the larger context, for the passage in which they occur. The unit of discourse using Scripture only for scriptural proof texts holds together for reasons unrelated to the proof texts. These have little to do with either the sequence of biblical verses, on the one side, or the inner cogency of a value or principle to the exegesis and amplification of which chains of biblical verse prove vital, on the other. Let me spell this out by an example of what might have characterized a fourth catalog, one that I did not find worth drawing up.

B. Sotah 22A, 3:3–4.XI.

    A.   Our rabbis have taught on Tannaite authority:

    B.   What is the definition of an am haares?

    C.   "It is anyone who does not recite the recitation of the Shema morning and night, along with its associated blessings," the words of R. Meir.

    D.   And sages say, "It is anyone who does not put on phylacteries."

    E.   Ben Azzai says, "It is anyone who does not have show fringes on his garment."

    F.   R. Jonathan b. Joseph said, "It is anyone who has sons and does not raise them to study Torah."

    G.   Others say, "Even if one recites Scripture and repeats Mishnah sayings, but has not attended upon a disciple of sages, such a one is an am haares.

H.   "If he has learned to recite Scripture but has not repeated Mishnah traditions, lo, such a one is a boor.

I.   "If he has neither learned to recite Scripture nor to repeat Mishnah traditions, concerning him Scripture says, 'I will sow the house of Israel and the house of Judah with the seed of man and with the seed of beast' (Jer. 31:27)."

In this passage, Scripture supplies a proof text alone. It does not define a principal component either of the content of the unit of discourse or even of its rhetoric. The principle of conglomeration of the materials at hand bears no relationship whatsoever to the contents of Scripture. From our perspective Scripture provides mere pretexts and from the compositors' perspective supplies probative proof texts, for what is to be said. In other words, these types of compositions treat Scripture as a collection of miscellanies. In the foregoing example, the function of the verse of Scripture is hardly to make the main point of the passage. The verse is tangential; it is included because it is a convention to insert texts in this way. Let us proceed to our catalogs of more consequential facts.

1. A sequence of verses is subjected to systematic discussion, or a single scriptural topic or event is amplified. The principle of conglomeration rests upon Scripture's presentation of the verses as a group. The passage then is organized around Scripture's sequence of verses. Here is a simple example of a sequence of units of discourse devoted to the exposition of a set of verses, in rough order and sequence. The principle of conglomeration therefore derives from Scripture.

Y. Sotah 1:8.II.

A.   It is written, "[Then Samson went down with his father and mother to Timnah,] and he came to the vineyards of Timnah" (Judg. 14:5).

B.   Said R. Samuel bar R. Isaac, "This teaches that his father and his mother showed him the vineyards of Timnah, sewn in mixed seeds, and they said to him, 'Child! Just as [17b] their vineyards are sewn with mixed seeds, so their daughters are sewn with mixed seeds.'"

C.   "His father and mother did not know that it was from the Lord; for he was seeking an occasion against the Philistines" (Judg. 14:4).

D.   Said R. Eleazar, "In seven places it is written, 'You should not intermarry with them.'"

E.   Said R. Abin, "This is to prohibit intermarriage with the seven peoples [of the land].

F.   "And here why does it say [that Samson was punished for marrying a Philistine woman, when there is no prohibition in the Torah against marrying Philistines]?"

G. Said R. Isaac, " 'Toward the scorners he is scornful, [but to the humble he shows favor]' (Prov. 3:34). [Since Samson got involved with scornful people, he was punished.]"

Y. Sotah 1:8.III.

A. It is written, "And the spirit of the Lord began to stir him in Mahaneh-dan, between Zorah and Eshtaol" (Judg. 13:25).

B. There are two Amoraim who interpret this passage.

C. One of them said, "When the Holy Spirit rested upon him, his footsteps were as if from Zorah and Eshtaol."

D. The other one said, "When the Holy Spirit rested on him, his hair grew stiff like a bell, and the sound went as between Zorah and Eshtaol."

Y. Sotah 1:8.IV.

A. "[And the woman bore a son, and called his name Samson; and the boy grew] and the Lord blessed him" (Judg. 13:24).

B. R. Huna in the name of R. Yose: "For [despite his great strength,] his sexual capacities were like those of any other man [and so he could enjoy sexual relations with a normal woman]."

Y. Sotah 1:8.V.

A. It is written, "[Then Samson called out to the Lord and said, 'O Lord God, remember me, I pray thee, and strengthen me, I pray thee, only this once, O God,] that I may be avenged upon the Philistines for one of my two eyes'" (Judg. 16:28).

B. Said R. Aha, "He said before Him, 'Lord of the world! Give me the reward of one of my eyes in this world, and let the reward for the other eye be readied for me in the world to come.'"

Y. Sotah 1:8.VI.

A. One verse of Scripture states, "He judged Israel forty years." [This verse is not in the present version.]

B. And yet another verse of Scripture says, "He had judged Israel twenty years" (Judg. 16:31).

C. Said R. Aha, "It teaches that the Philistines feared him for twenty years after his death just as they feared him for twenty years when he was alive."

Sotah	Yerushalmi	Sotah	Bavli
1:8	II, III, IV, V, VI, VIII	1:8–9	III, XIV, XVII, XVIII–XXVI,
1:10	V, VI, VIII		XXVIII–XXIX, XXXI–LXXI

Sotah	Yerushalmi	Sotah	Bavli
8:3	I	7:1–5	XIII, XV
		8:1	VI–VIII
		9:5–6	XVII–XIX
10/319	3%	53/411	12.8%

Sukkah	Yerushalmi	Sukkah	Bavli
0/139	0.0%	0/237	0.0%

Sanhedrin	Yerushalmi	Sanhedrin	Bavli
2:5	III–IV	1:1–6	XXX, LXXXV–LXXXVI
		2:1–2	XIII
		2:5	II–III
		3:1	XI
		4:3–4	III–IV
		4:5	VIII
		6:2	I–XI
		7:10–11	VIII, X
		10:5–6	X
		11:1–2	CXC–CXCIV, CXCVI–CCIII, CCXIV–CCXIX, CCXXI, CCXXIII–CCXXXVII
		11:3A–CC	IV–X, XXI–XXIII, XXXVI–XL
2/322	0.6%	63/909	6.9%

2. A common theme, independent of a single scriptural passage, is illustrated by scriptural verses. In this type of Scripture unit of discourse, the introduction of scriptural verses is central to the rhetoric of the passage. The principle of conglomeration therefore derives from the subject matter, that is to say, the point that the framer wishes to make about a given topic or the exposition of that topic from a variety of perspectives. Materials are joined together because they are relevant to that common topic. Here is an example of the use of Scripture to deal with a problem distinct from the verses at hand, yet closely related to them.

Y. Sotah 5 :6.I.

A. When did Job live?

B. R. Simeon b. Laqish in the name of Bar Qappara: "In the days of Abraham, our father, did he live.

C. "This is in line with that which is written, 'There was a man in the land of Uz, whose name was Job, [and that man was blameless and upright, one who feared God, and turned away from evil]' (Job 1 :1).

D. "And it is written, '[Now after these things it was told to Abraham, 'Behold, Milcah also has born children to your brother Nahor:] Uz the first born, [Buz his brother, Kemuel the father of

Amram, Chesed, Hazo, Pildash, Jidlaph, and Bethuel]'" (Gen. 22:20–21).

E.   R. Abba said, "It was in the days of our father, Jacob, and his wife was Dinah.

F.   "This is in line with that which is written, '[But he said to her,] You speak as one of the foolish women would speak' (Job 2:10).

G.   "And it is written, '[The sons of Jacob came in from the field when they heard of it; and the men were indignant and very angry,] because he had wrought folly in Israel [by laying with Jacob's daughter, for such a thing ought not to be done]'" (Gen. 34:7).

H.   R. Levi said, "It was in the time of the tribes that he lived.

I.   "That is in line with that which is written, '[I will show you, hear me; and what I have seen I will declare,] what wise men have told, and their fathers have not hidden'" (Job 15:17–18).

J.   R. Yose b. Halafta said, "He was among those who went down to Egypt, and when they came up, he died.

K.   "It may be compared to a shepherd, to whose flock a shepherd came along and joined up. What did he do? He set up the bell-wether against him.

L.   "That is in line with the following verse of Scripture, 'God gives me up to the ungodly, and casts me into the hands of the wicked'" (Job 16:11).

M.   R. Ishmael taught, "Job was one of the servants of Pharaoh. He was one of the great members of his retinue.

N.   "That is in line with the following verse of Scripture: 'Then he who feared the word of the Lord among the servants of Pharaoh made his slaves and his cattle flee into the houses' (Exod. 9:20).

O.   "And concerning him it is written, 'And the Lord said to Satan, Have you considered my servant Job, [that there is none like him on the earth,] a blameless and upright man, who fears God and turns away from evil?'" (Job 1:8).

P.   R. Yose bar Judah says, "He was in the time in which the judges ruled Israel.

Q.   "That is indicated in the following verse of Scripture: 'Behold, all of you have seen it yourselves; why then have you become so vain?' (Job 27:12).

R.   "You have seen the deeds of my generation.

S.   "For they collected tithes at the threshing floors: '[Rejoice not, O Israel! Exult not like the peoples; for you have played the harlot, forsaking your God.] You have loved a harlot's hire upon all the threshing floors'" (Hos. 9:1).

T.   R. Samuel bar Nahman in the name of R. Jonathan: "He lived in the time of the kingdom of the Sabeans, for it is said, 'And the Sabeans fell upon them and took them, [and slew the servants with the edge of the sword; and I alone escaped to tell you]'" (Job 1:15).

U. R. Nathan said, "He lived in the time of the Chaldeans, for it is said, '[While he was yet speaking, there came another, and said,] The Chaldeans formed three companies, [and made a raid upon the camels and took them, and slew the servants with the edge of the sword; and I alone have escaped to tell you]'" (Job 1:17).

V. R. Joshua b. Qorha said, "He lived in the days of Ahasueros, for it is said, '[Then the king's servants said,] Let beautiful young virgins be sought out for the king' (Esther 2:2).

W. "And it is written, 'And in all the land there were no women so fair as Job's daughters; [and their father gave them inheritance among their brothers]'" (Job 42:15).

X. R. Joshua b. Levi said, "He was among those who came up from the Exile."

Y. R. Yohanan said, "He was among those who came up from the Exile, but he was an Israelite."

Z. On that account R. Yohanan derived, from his behavior, rules governing conduct in the time of mourning.

AA. "Then Job arose, and rent his robe, [and shaved his head, and fell upon the ground, and worshipped]" (Job 1:20).

BB. R. Judah b. Pazzi in the name of R. Yohanan, "On the basis of the cited verse we learn that a mourner has to tear his garment while standing up."

CC. R. Hiyya taught, "In my realm [?] there was a righteous gentile [such as Job, who was not an Israelite], and I paid him his wage, and I dismissed him from my realm."

DD. R. Simeon b. Laqish said, "Job never existed and never will exist."

EE. The opinions attributed to R. Simeon b. Laqish are at variance with one another.

FF. There R. Simeon b. Laqish said in the name of Bar Qappara, "He lived in the time of Abraham, our father," and here has he said this?

GG. But he really did exist, while the sufferings ascribed to him never really took place.

HH. And why were these sufferings ascribed to him? It is to indicate that if such sufferings had come to him, he would have been able to endure them.

Sotah	Yerushalmi	Sotah	Bavli
1:4	III	1:1-2	XI, XVI, XVII, XVIII-XXIX
5:6	I, II, III	1:7	III
7:1	II	1:8-9	XV-XVI, LXXIII-LXXIV, LXXXI-

Sotah	Yerushalmi	Sotah	Bavli
			LXXXIII, LXXXVI–LXXXVII
		3:3–4	VI
		7:1–5	XX–XXII
		7:6	IX–XVI
		7:8	VI–VII
		8:1	XIII
		9:5–6	X–XXV [XVII–XIX]
		9:11–13	III, XI–XIII
7/319	2.1%	48/411	11.6%

Sukkah	Yerushalmi	Sukkah	Bavli
4:3	V	4:5–7	IV
		4:9–10	II, XV
1/139	0.7%	3/237	1.2%

Sanhedrin	Yerushalmi	Sanhedrin	Bavli
1:4	V–VI	1:1–6	XVIII, XX, XXI, XXV, XXIX
2:3	V	2:5	IV, VIII
2:4	III	3:3	XI
2:6	II		
4:1–2	XXII		
4:2	I	4:5	IV, VI, IX–XIII, XV–XXIII,
4:9	II		XXX–XXXV
6:3	I	6:1H–J	III
6:7	II	6:2	XII
10:1	II, III, V, VI, VII	6:4N–6	VI–VIII, XVI–XVII
10:2	III	7:5	XIII–XVI, XIX
11:4	I	7:6	XI–XV
11:5	I, III, IV	8:1	VI
		8:2	IV–VIII
		9:6	VII–X
		10:5–6	VIII
		11:1–2	II–X, XXII–LIII, LXXXVIII–LXXXIX, XCIII–CI, CVI–CVII, CIX–CXV, CXVII, CXIX–CXXIV, CXXVIII–CXXIX, CXXXII–CXXXIII, CXLIV, CXLVIII, CLIII–CLX, CLXVII–CLXXI, CLXXX, CLXXXIX, CCVII–CCIX, CCXXXVIII–CCLI, CCLII–CCLVI
		11:3A–CC	XI–XIX, XXIV, XXVII–XXVIII, XLI–XLVII
		11:3DD–FF	II–VIII
		11:4–6	XX–XXII
19/322	5.9%	194/909	21.3%

3. *Here is an example of interpretation of a single verse in its own terms or as an illustration of some theme distinct from the verse at hand.*

B. Sukkah 48B, 4:9–10.III.

A.   A heretic named Joy said to R. Abbahu, "You are destined to draw water for me in the world to come, for it is written, 'Therefore with joy you shall draw water' (Isa. 12:3)."

B.   He said to him, "If it were written, 'for joy,' matters would have you been as you maintain. But since it is written 'with joy,' the sense is that with the skin of that man [you] people will make a water bucket and will draw water with it."

Sotah	Yerushalmi	Sotah	Bavli	
0/319	0.0%	0/411	0.0%	

Sukkah	Yerushalmi	Sukkah	Bavli	
		4:9–10	III, VIII, XII–XIII	
0/130	0.0%	4/237	1.6%	

Sanhedrin	Yerushalmi	Sanhedrin	Bavli
		1:1–6	XXIII, XXVI
		2:3	III
		2:4A–D	IV
		2:4E–I	III
		5:1–5	XVII
		11:1–2	CLXXVI–CLXXVII, CCXLIX–CCL
		11:3A–CC	XXX, XXXII
0/322	0.0%	12/909	1.3%

The figures at hand prove surprisingly one sided. Yerushalmi contains a negligible proportion of Scripture units of discourse composed around sequences of verse. The Yerushalmi's compositors clearly neglected units of discourse that find cogency in Scripture, not in the Mishnah, on the one side, or in some well-established value or virtue, on the other. The Bavli's framers made use of units of discourse of this type in which Scripture, as much as the Mishnah, defines a principle of redactional cogency and rhetorical coherence. The Bavli finds itself entirely at home in the utilization of such units of discourse, which, we recognize, can as readily have served the purposes of the redactors of exegeses of Scripture (midrashim), such as Genesis Rabbah or Lamentations Rabbah. In the third and final catalog the results are meagre but again quite one sided. We find no examples of the Yerushalmi's inclusion of units of discourse built up around the exposition of a single verse of Scripture. That result runs parallel to the one attained in the first catalog.

We see a remarkably satisfying correlation with the first taxonomy. Just as the Yerushalmi's redactors composed large-scale discourse on a principle of law rather than on a Mishnah paragraph in particular, so they put together equivalently sizable units of discourse in which a single theme, topic, value,

or ideal formed the focus, which then is amplified, illustrated, or validated by
scriptural verses. The framers of the Yerushalmi in the tractates surveyed did
not resort to Scripture in search of principles of cogency and coherence of
discourse. Those of the Bavli did. And that has made all the difference.

Alike and Not Alike

What the Bavli's framers accomplished in organizing and composing units of
discourse was to form a synthesis of two of the available components of the
canon, the Mishnah and Scripture. First, they made far more ample use than
did the authors of the Yerushalmi of units of discourse focused upon Scripture
rather than upon the Mishnah. Second, they drew upon the redactional structure supplied by Scripture, as much as upon that provided by the Mishnah,
when they went about organizing their units of discourse into large-scale compositions. That is why the Bavli's more sizable stretches of exposition are
made up of two quite distinct types of materials—first, those focused upon
the Mishnah paragraph; second, others centered upon verses of Scripture.
While the Yerushalmi's authors built their Scripture units of·discourse around
one or the other of those two sources of cogency, the Bavli's had yet a third. In
selecting as a redactional principle the order of the Mishnah, the framers of
the Bavli followed the example of the authors of the Yerushalmi. In asking
Scripture to dictate the sequence of discourse, they followed the example of
the authors of Genesis Rabbah and Leviticus Rabbah, not to mention Sifra,
the two Sifres, and Lamentations Rabbah.

Viewed from a literary angle, as compositors and redactors of large-scale
compositions the authors of the Bavli constructed a vast synthesis of the two
principles of composition and redaction employed prior to their time in available and distinct types of literature. These were Mishnah exegesis in the
Yerushalmi and Scripture exegesis in the collection of scriptural exegeses
(midrashim). The Bavli differs from the Yerushalmi in the clear and self-
evident program of its compositors and redactors. Specifically, these compositors and redactors synthesized the two formerly distinct principles of,
first, redaction of completed units of discourse concerning the Mishnah and,
second, composition or conglomeration of cogent units of discourse using
Scripture. Their Talmud is not like the one that had come before specifically
because it appealed to two components of the available tripartite canon, not
only for law and theology but also for the logic and rhetoric of cogent discourse. So, to state the result in one sentence, Scripture as much as the Mishnah told the Bavli's, but not the Yerushalmi's, authors and compositors how to
organize completed thoughts, on the one side, and how to hold together the
components of completed thoughts and make of them a cogent statement of
size and consequence, on the other.

5

The Talmuds and the Sages

Differentiating Documents

The third component of Judaism is the figure of the sage, shown in chapter 1 to be equal in standing to the Mishnah and Scripture. In the ultimate formulation of the mythic system at hand, "God revealed one whole Torah in two media, written and oral, to Moses, our master. It was up to Moses to transmit the oral part through the memory and mind of his disciple, Joshua, and so on down." Accordingly, the sage in the model of Moses, "our master," took a central place in the work of revealing the Torah, the will of God. To complete our analysis of the relationship of the Bavli to the Yerushalmi, therefore, we turn now to this final constituent of the canonical myth of Torah as the myth was revealed at the end of its development.

We ask, in particular, about the literary expression of the matter. We want to know whether, where, and how the two Talmuds made use of units of discourse devoted to stories about and sayings attributed to sages in particular. So I raise literary questions. For example, we inquire whether sages—their lives, sayings, names—provided a mode of organizing discourse in the way in which, in the Yerushalmi, the Mishnah does, and the way in which, in the Bavli, the Mishnah and Scripture do. As before, we ask whether one Talmud made proportionately greater use than the other of such sage units of discourse.

The character of a sage unit of discourse requires careful definition. It is one in which what is imputed to a sage forms the center of discussion and precipitant of analysis. The name, saying, or deed of a sage in a sage unit provides the principle of coherence and cogency to the unit of discourse as a whole.

Since nearly all units of discourse in both Talmuds feature names of sages, the reader will wonder what characterizes a sage unit of discourse that we do not find in a Mishnah or a Scripture unit of discourse. The answer is in two parts. In a sage unit of discourse we find a story, told about a sage, in which what the sage says or does defines the purpose of putting the passage together. If we are told that, while sitting before such and such a master, a given sage raised a question, with the substance of the question and its answer filling up the rest of the unit of discourse, that would *not* constitute a sage unit of discourse. If we are told what the sage said and did, and if the substance of the message or deed centers upon the sage's personal opinions or individual deeds, that does constitute a sage unit of discourse.

A second type of unit of discourse falls within the present classification as well. It is one in which the redactional principle derives from the sage's name in particular. A sequence of sayings in which a given tradent tells us what a given master said two or three or ten times over—thus, *R. Judah said Rab said*—may or may not fall into the classification of a sage unit of discourse. If all of the collected sayings of tradent and master take shape around the exegesis of a statement of the Mishnah or a legal rule, then the pericope remains in the category of a legal unit of discourse, generally a Mishnah unit of discourse. The reason is that the law, or the Mishnah in particular, tells us why what is contained in the unit of discourse forms a cogent and distinct statement. But if the sayings take shape around the names alone, with diverse sayings, exhibiting no shared topic or common inner logical point of cogency assigned to the names, then the unit of discourse at hand has been bonded solely around the names of tradent and authority. That construction attains cogency only or mainly because of the sage's name, not because of the inner coherence of what the sage says. That would constitute a sage unit of discourse, different from a Mishnah or a Scripture unit of discourse.

Let us briefly consider examples of this second type of sage unit of discourse—one from the Yerushalmi, the other from the Bavli.

Y. San. 8:2.IV.

    A.   Said R. Yohanan, "If your name is mentioned for service on the council, let the Jordan be your border."

    B.   Said R. Yohanan, "People appeal to the government to be rid of the duty of serving on the council."

    C.   Said R. Yohanan, "People may lend on interest to an association formed for a religious duty and for sanctifying the new moon."

    D.   R. Yohanan would go up to the synagogue in the morning, and he would gather crumbs and eat them, and he said, "Let my lot be with him who sanctifies the month here evenings [because they have such a fine meal]."

A and B relate, but C and D are totally miscellaneous. Only Yohanan's name explains their presence. The same phenomenon occurs in the Bavli's much larger construction, which follows.

B. Sanhedrin 92A, 11:1–2.XXXIII.

A.   Said R. Eleazar, "Every authority who leads the community se-renely will have the merit of leading them in the world to come, as it is said, 'For he who has mercy on them shall lead them, even by springs of water shall he guide them' (Isa. 49:10)."

B.   And said R. Eleazar, "Great is knowledge, for it is set between two letters of the divine name, as it is written, 'For a God of knowledge is the Lord' (1 Sam. 2:3)."

C.   And said R. Eleazar, "Great is the sanctuary, for it is set between two letters of the divine name, as it is written, 'You have made for yourself, O Lord, a sanctuary, O Lord, your hands have estab-lished it' (Exod. 15:17)."

D.   To this view R. Ada Qarhinaah objected, "Then how about the following: Great is vengeance, for it is set between two letters of the divine name, as it is written, 'O God of vengeance, O Lord, O God of vengeance, appear' (Ps. 94:1)."

E.   He said to him, "In context, that is quite so, in line with what Ulla said."

F.   For Ulla said, "What purpose is served by these two references to 'appear'? One speaks of the measure of good, the other, the mea-sure of punishment."

G.   And said R. Eleazar, "In the case of any man who has knowledge it is as if the house of the sanctuary had been built in his own time, for this [knowledge] is set between two letters of the divine name, and that [the Temple] likewise is set between two letters of the divine name."

H.   And said R. Eleazar, "Any man in whom there is knowledge in the end will be rich, for it is said, 'And by knowledge shall the chambers be filled with all precious and pleasant riches' (Prov. 24:4)."

I.   And said R. Eleazar, "It is forbidden to have pity on any man in whom there is no knowledge, as it is said, 'For it is a people of no understanding; therefore he that made them will not have mercy upon them, and he that formed them will show them no favor' (Isa. 27:11)."

J.   And said R. Eleazar, "Whoever gives his bread to someone who does not have knowledge in the end will be afflicted with suffer-ings, for it is said, 'They who eat your bread have laid a wound under you, there is no understanding in him' (Obad. 1:7), and the word for 'wound' can mean only suffering, as it is written, 'When Ephraim saw his sickness and Judah his suffering' [using the same word] (Hos. 5:13)."

K.   And said R. Eleazar, "Any man who has no knowledge in the end will go into exile, as it is said, 'Therefore my people have gone into exile, because they have no knowledge' (Isa. 5:13)."

L.   And said R. Eleazar, "Any house in which words of Torah are not heard by night will be eaten up by fire, as it is said, 'All darkness is hid in his secret places; a fire not blown shall consume him; he grudges him that is left in his tabernacle' (Job 20:26).

M.   "The word for 'grudges' means only a disciple of a sage, as it is written, 'And in those left [using the same root] whom the Lord shall call' (Joel 3:5)." [H. Freedman, trans. (London, 1945), p. 616, n. 12: "The first part of the verse, 'all darkness is hid . . . ,' is interpreted as, his secret places are not illumined by the study of the law; the last part, 'he grudges . . . ,' as, he looks with disfavor upon any student who enters his house for a meal."]

N.   And said R. Eleazar, "Whoever does not give a benefit to disciples of sages from his property will see no blessing ever, as it is said, 'There is none who remains to eat it, therefore shall he not hope for prosperity' (Job 20:21).

O.   "The word for 'remain' refers only to a disciple of a sage, as it is written, 'And in those left whom the Lord shall call' (Joel 3:5)."

P.   And said R. Eleazar, "Anyone who does not leave a piece of bread on his table will never a sign of blessing, as it is said, 'There be none of his food left, therefore shall he not hope for his prosperity'(Job 20:21)."

Q.   But has not R. Eleazar said, "Whoever leaves pieces of bread on his table is as if he worships an idol, as it is said, 'That prepare a table for God and that furnish the drink offering to Meni' (Isa. 65:11)"?

R.   There is no contradiction, in the one case [the latter] a complete loaf is left alongside, and in the other case [the former], no complete loaf is left [with the crumbs].

S.   And said R. Eleazar, "Whoever goes back on what he has said is as if he worships an idol.

T.   "Here it is written, 'And I seem to him as a deceiver' (Gen. 27:12), and elsewhere it is written, 'They [idols] are vanity and the work of deceivers' (Jer. 10:15)."

U.   And said R. Eleazar, "Whoever stares at a woman's sexual parts will find that his 'bow' is emptied out, as it is said, 'Shame shall empty your bow [of strength]' (Hab. 3:9)."

V.   And said R. Eleazar, "One should always accept [things] and so endure."

W.   Said R. Zira, "We too also have learned on Tannaite authority:

X.   *"As to a room without windows, people are not to open windows for it to examine whether or not it is afflicted with a plague sign*

[M. Neg. 2:3]. [Thus the possible signs will be missed because of the obscurity of the room. Likewise humility protects one's life.]"

Y. That makes the case.

The definitive trait of the foregoing is obvious. This second type of sage unit of discourse occurs too seldom in the three tractates that serve as our sample. The statistical sample therefore proves not significant, and I did not catalog the items. It suffices for the present purpose to note that in both Talmuds we find such materials. That tells us that, in the circles of compositors of units of discourse, the name of a sage, as much as a sentence of the Mishnah or a verse of Scripture or a legal problem served to form the framework of a sustained discussion. But the meager results also warn that the ultimate compositors, at least of the three tractates before us, did not commonly resort to the inclusion of sage units of discourse of this second type. My best guess at the reason is that the intent of the compositors was to make use of units of discourse organized around cogent subjects or problems, not names. Diverse sayings set up around the names of a common tradent and master contradicted that intent. As we see, the subject matter proves too diverse for sustained and systematic analysis, which is why the present type of sage unit of discourse did not serve.

These, then, are the types of units of discourse treated here. Where the sage forms the center of interest, on the one side, or supplies the point of composition and proportion, on the other, then the sage as an autonomous figure and a source of Torah teaching correlative with the written Torah, Scriptures, and the oral Torah, the Mishnah, defines, in literary terms, the type of discourse at hand. Here once more our interest encompasses two matters. First, on the basis of proportions of use and type of sage units of discourse in each of the two Talmuds, are we able to differentiate one from the other? Second, does a single taxonomy serve both Talmuds or does the second of the two, the Bavli, demand for itself a fresh taxonomic structure?

Stories about Sages and Collections of Sages' Sayings in the Talmuds

The first of our two exercises of taxonomy compiles sage units of discourse in each of the two Talmuds and compares the proportions of such units in the one Talmud against that in the other.

Sotah	Yerushalmi		Sotah	Bavli	
1:1	—	(0/10)	1:1–2	—	(0/31)
1:2	—	(0/9)	1:3A–D	—	(0/1)
1:3	—	(0/4)	1:3E–G	—	(0/3)
1:4	II	(1/3)	1:4–6	—	(0/13)
1:5	—	(0/5)	1:7	—	(0/4)

Sotah	Yerushalmi		Sotah	Bavli	
1:6	—	(0/3)	1:8–9	—	(0/87)
1:7	—	(0/4)			
1:8	—	(0/9)			
1:10	—	(0/8)			
2:1	—	(0/7)	2:1	—	(0/19)
2:2	—	(0/8)	2:2	—	(0/8)
2:3	—	(0/1)	2:3	—	(0/2)
2:4	—	(0/5)	2:4	—	(0/3)
2:5	—	(0/10)	2:5–6	—	(0/5)
2:6	—	(0/1)			
3:1	—	(0/6)	3:1–2	—	(0/5)
3:2	—	(0/1)	3:3–4	—	(0/14)
3:3	—	(0/4)	3:5–8	—	(0/13)
3:4	VII, XI	(2/12)			
3:5	—	(0/3)			
3:6	—	(0/4)			
3:7	—	(0/4)			
3:8	—	(0/7)			
4:1	—	(0/6)	4:1–5	—	(0/18)
4:2	—	(0/1)			
4:3	—	(0/3)			
4:4	—	(0/3)			
4:5	—	(0/2)			
5:1	—	(0/2)	5:1–5	—	(0/14)
5:2	—	(0/8)			
5:3	—	(04)			
5:4	—	(0/2)			
5:5	IV	(1/4)			
5:6	—	(0/3)			
6:1	—	(0/3)	6:1–4	—	(0/2)
6:2	—	(0/3)			
6:3	—	(0/1)			
6:4	—	(0/6)			
7:1	—	(0/6)	7:1–5	—	(0/26)
7:2	—	(0/3)	7:6	XXIV (2x)	(2/27)
7:3	—	(0/4)	7:7	—	(0/6)
7:4	—	(0/5)	7:8	—	(0/7)
8:1	—	(0/3)	8:1	—	(0/13)
8:2	—	(0/1)	8:2–4	—	(0/17)
8:3	—	(0/9)	8:5–7	—	(0/3)
8:4	—	(0/4)			
8:5	—	(0/5)			
8:6	—	(0/2)			
8:7	—	(0/2)			
8:8	—	(0/2)			
8:9	—	(0/2)			
8:10	—	(0/4)			
9:1	—	(0/8)	9:1–2	—	(0/10)
9:2	—	(0/8)	9:2G–4	—	(0/5)
9:3	—	(0/1)	9:5–6	—	(0/25)
9:4	—	(0/1)	9:7–10	—	(0/12)
9:5	—	(0/12)	9:11–13	XV	(1/15)

Sotah	Yerushalmi		Sotah		Bavli
9:6	—	(0/6)	9:14–15	—	(0/8)
9:7	—	(0/2)			
9:8	—	(0/1)			
9:9	—	(0/1)			
9:10	—	(0/2)			
9:11	—	(0/10)			
9:12	—	(0/3)			
9:13	—	(0/6)			
9:14	—	(0/4)			
9:15	III	(1/6)			
9:16	II (3x)	(3/2)			
	8/319	2.5%		3/411	0/7%

Sukkah	Yerushalmi		Sukkah		Bavli
1:1	—	(0/12)	1:1	—	(0/20)
1:2	—	(0/3)	1:2	—	(0/2)
1:3	—	(0/2)	1:3	—	(0/3)
1:4	—	(0/1)	1:4	—	(0/6)
1:5	—	(0/3)	1:5	—	(0/2)
			1:6	—	
1:6	—	(0/3)	1:7	—	(0/1)
1:7	—	(0/2)	1:8	—	(0/4)
1:8	—	(0/1)	1:9	—	(0/3)
1:9	—	(0/2)	1:10	—	(0/9)
1:10	—	(0/1)	1:11	—	(0/2)
1:11	—	(0/3)	1:12	—	(0/3)
1:12	—	(0/2)			
2:1	—	(0/3)	2:1	—	(0/3)
2:2	—	(0/1)	2:2A–B	—	(0/1)
2:3	—	(0/2)	2:2C–H	—	(0/3)
2:4	—	(0/3)	2:3	—	(0/8)
2:5	I	(1/4)	2:4	—	(0/11)
2:6	—	(0/1)	2:5	—	(0/2)
2:7	—	(0/3)	2:6	VI, VII	(2/8)
2:8	—	(0/3)	2:7–8	—	(0/4)
2:9	—	(0/1)	2:9	—	(0/8)
2:10	—	(0/3)			
3:1	—	(0/12)	3:1	—	(0/14)
3:2	—	(0/2)	3:2	—	(0/10)
3:3	—	(0/1)	3:3	—	(0/5)
3:4	II	(1/4)	3:4	—	(0/4)
3:5	—	(0/2)	3:5–7	—	(0/19)
3:6	—	(0/3)	3:8	—	(0/3)
3:7	—	(0/3)	3:9A–D	—	(0/2)
3:8	—	(0/3)	3:9E–H	—	(0/1)
3:9	—	(0/1)	3:10–11D	—	(0/6)
3:10	VI	(1/8)	3:11E–F	—	(0/4)
3:11	—	(0/3)	3:12	—	(0/2)
3:12	—	(0/1)	3:13–14	—	(0/5)
			3:15	—	(0/2)
4:1	—	(0/3)	4:1–4	—	(0/15)
4:2	—	(0/1)	4:5–7	—	(0/15)

Sukkah	Yerushalmi		Sukkah	Bavli	
4:3	—	(0/5)	4:8A–B	—	(0/1)
4:4	—	(0/1)	4:8C–F	—	(0/1)
4:5	—	(0/3)	4:9–10	—	(0/17)
4:6	—	(0/9)			
4:7	—	(0/3)			
5:1	—	(0/6)	5:1A–C	—	(0/3)
5:2	—	(0/4)	5:1D–4	IX	(1/31)
5:3	—	(0/4)	5:5	—	(0/10)
5:4	—	(0/5)	5:6	—	(0/2)
5:5	—	(0/3)	5:7A–D	—	(0/6)
5:6	—	(0/5)	5:7E–8	—	(0/5)
5:7	—	(0/1)			
5:8	—	(0/7)			
	3/139	2%		3/237	1.2%

Sanhedrin	Yerushalmi		Sanhedrin	Bavli	
1:1	—	(0/7)	1:1–6	X.CC-HH, XXXVIII (x3),	(5/91)
1:2	V, VI, X, XIII	(4/19)		LIV	
1:3	—	(0/8)			
1:4	—	(0/6)			
2:1	III	(1/7)	2:1–2	IX	(1/13)
2:2	—	(0/3)	2:3	—	(0/3)
2:3	—	(0/5)	2:4A–D	—	(0/5)
2:4	—	(0/3)	2:4E–I	—	(0/5)
2:5	—	(0/4)	2:4J–N	—	(0/6)
2:6	IV, V VI	(3/6)	2:5	—	(0/11)
3:1	—	(0/1)	3:1	—	(0/11)
3:2	—	(0/2)	3:2	—	(0/3)
3:3	—	(0/2)	3:3	X	(1/17)
3:4	—	(0/3)	3:4–5	—	(0/16)
3:5	II	(1/3)	3:6–7	XXI	(1/27)
3:6	—	(0/6)	3:8	—	(0/7)
3:7	—	(0/10)			
3:8	—	(0/4)			
3:9	—	(0/6)			
3:10	—	(0/1)			
3:11	—	(0/1)			
3:12	—	(0/3)			
4:1	—	(0/4)	4:1–2	—	(0/27)
4:2	—	(0/1)	4:3–4	V	(1/6)
4:3	—	(0/2)	4:5	V, XVIII–XXVII	(11/35)
4:4	—	(0/1)			
4:5	—	(0/1)			
4:6	—	(0/2)			
4:7	—	(0/5)			
4:8	—	(0/2)			
4:9	—	(0/2)			
5:1	—	(0/6)	5:1–5	—	(0/22)
5:2	—	(0/2)			
5:3	—	(0/2)			
5:4	—	(0/2)			

Sanhedrin	Yerushalmi		Sanhedrin	Bavli	
5:5	—	(0/3)			
6:1	—	(0/2)	6:1A–G	—	(0/8)
6:2	—	(0/1)	6:1H–J	—	(0/3)
6:3	III	(1/3)	6:2	—	(0/16)
6:4	—	(0/1)	6:3	—	(0/2)
6:5	—	(0/3)	6:4A–G	—	(0/5)
6:6	II (2x)	(2/2)	6:4H–M	—	(0/4)
6:7	—	(023)	6:4N–6	—	(0/17)
6:8	—	(0/1)			
6:9	—	(0/1)			
6:10	III	(1/3)			
7:1	—	(0/4)	7:1	—	(0/15)
7:2	—	(0/4)	7:2	—	(0/6)
7:3	—	(0/3)	7:3A–F	—	(0/2)
7:4	—	(0/2)	7:3G–J	—	(0/2)
7:5	—	(0/4)	7:4A–R	—	(0/3)
7:6	—	(0/5)	7:4S–V)	—	(0/10)
7:7	—	(0/5)	7:5	XIX.EE–II	(1/26)
		(1/7)	7:6	XV	(1/18)
7:8	VII	(1/7)	7:7A–E	—	(0/6)
7:9	—	(0/5)	7:7F–I	—	(0/6)
7:10	—	(0/10)	7:8	—	(0/4)
7:11	—	(0/4)	7:9	—	(0/3)
7:12	—	(0/4)	7:10	IX, XI	(2/13)
7:13	III, IV, V, VI	(4/7)			
8:1	—	(0/2)	8:1	—	(0/7)
8:2	—	(0/5)	8:2	—	(0/15)
8:3	—	(0/3)	8:3	—	(0/2)
8:4	—	(0/2)	8:4	—	(0/6)
8:5	—	(0/2)	8:5	—	(0/1)
8:6	—	(0/2)	8:6	—	(0/7)
8:7	—	(0/2)	8:7	—	(0/11)
8:8	—	(0/3)			
8:9	—	(0/4)			
9:1	—	(0/8)	9:1A–C	—	(0/11)
9:2	—	(0/3)	9:1D–M	—	(0/13)
9:3	—	(0/5)	9:1N–T	—	(0/2)
9:4	—	(0/2)	9:2	—	(0/4)
9:5	—	(0/1)	9:3	—	(0/4)
9:6	—	(0/3)	9:4	—	(0/4)
9:7	—	(0/4)	9:5	—	(0/5)
			9:6	IV	(1/13)
10:1	—	(0/11)	10:1	—	(0/18)
10:2	—	(0/12)	10:2	—	(0/6)
10:3	—	(0/2)	10:3	—	(0/1)
10:4	—	(0/2)	10:4	—	(0/1)
10:5	II	(1/4)	10:5–6	—	(0/13)
10:6	—	(0/3)			
10:7	—	(0/2)			
10:8	—	(0/1)			
11:1	—	(0/2)	11:1–2	V–VI, X–XI, XIII–XIV	
11:2	—	(0/4)		XV–XVII, XVIII–XXI,	
11:3	—	(0/3)		LXXXV, CIII, CXL,	

Sanhedrin	Yerushalmi		Sanhedrin	Bavli	
11:4	—	(0/2)		CXLII, CXLIII, CLXI,	
11:5	—	(0/4)		CLXII, CXCVI, CCXIX,	
11:6	—	(0/2)		CCLIV	(28/256)
			11:3A–CC	XXV	(1/48)
			11:3DD–FF	V	(1/8)
			11:4–6	XXII	(1/24)
	19/322	5.9%		41/909	4.5%

The results do not seem to me significant. The total number as well as the proportion of sage units of discourse in both Talmuds' versions of the three tractates prove negligible. True, the Yerushalmi consistently presents us with higher proportions of such units than does the Bavli. But the raw numbers are so slight that, standing by itself, the present result does not sustain any proposition whatsoever. For example, we surely cannot conclude that the compositors of the Yerushalmi exhibited a marked preference for using sage units of discourse, while those of the Bavli did not. A comparison to the numbers and proportions presented in the foregoing chapter suffices to show that on the basis of the sample at hand we cannot sustain such a thesis. Indeed, if the sample of three tractates suffices, we may conclude that the compositors of the two Talmuds made only episodic use of sage units of discourse, though it is clear such units were available and in circulation.

The Talmuds and Stories about Sages and Collections of Sages' Sayings

We turn to the more important question: When the authors used the present type of unit of discourse, what purpose did they have in mind? In the following taxonomy, I have undertaken two complementary and, in some measure, repetitive exercises.

In the first I ask the questions: Does a sage unit of discourse fit into the larger context in which it appears? Or is such a unit of discourse parachuted down, out of all relationship to the place at which, in the Talmud before us, it has landed? In this way we find out whether one Talmud differs from the other in its approach to the use of a sage unit of discourse. The matter of distinguishing contextual from noncontextual use depends upon a simple criterion. If the theme or main idea of a sage unit of discourse relates to something that has gone before or that follows, then the unit belongs in its larger redactional context. If we discern no connection, however remote, between the unit and its redactional context, then the unit is noncontextual. For each entry I list the principal theme or polemic of a given item so that, if they choose, readers can see for themselves what seems to me an adequate connection to the context at hand.

1. Used in context, for example, as precedent or illustration of a law or value.

Sotah	Yerushalmi	Sotah	Bavli
1:4	I. Blot out divine name to make peace between husband and wife.	7:6 9:11–13	XXIV/40A. Humility. XV. Fruit lost taste after 70.
3:4	VII. Not teach Torah to women. XI. Not give advice to disadvantage of a widow.		
5:5	IV. Serve God with all one's might.		
9:15	III. Torah study.		
9:16	II A–C. Copying master. II D–G. Modesty. II H–K. Modesty.		

Sukkah	Yerushalmi	Sukkah	Bavli
2:5	I. Precedents and examples of law as it is kept.	2:6	VI. Never say what master and not say first. VII. As above.
3:4	II. As above.	5:1D–4	IX. Sage has greater evil
3:10	VI. Saying blessings.		impulse than do others.

Sanhedrin	Yerushalmi	Sanhedrin	Bavli
1:2	V. Precedence. VI. Intercalating in Galilee. X. Intercalating abroad. XIII. Ordination.	1:1–6 2:1–2	X.CC–HH. Disciple must pronounce words might. XXXVIII. Humility and shame. LIV. Ordination in emergency. IX. Cowardice of sages, bravery
2:1	III. Removing a ruler who sinned.	3:3	of Simeon. X. As above.
2:6	IV. Honor owing to officers. [V. Criticism of patriarch.] VI. Samaritan polemic.	3:6–7 4:3–4 4:5	XXI. Ordination. V. Repentance and sage's merit. V. Drink is bad. XVIII–XXVII. Disputes with Min.
3:5	II. Resist idolator's oppression.	7:5 7:6	XIX.EE–II. Meat comes down from heaven. XV. Idolator remains loyal to idolatry.
6:3	III. Perjurer punished when victim is killed.	7:10–11	IX. Rabbinical magic. XI. Death of Eliezer.
6:6	II. Status of Simeon II b. Shatah, mentioned in the Mishnah.	9:6 11:1–2	IV. Burial rite. V–VI, X–XI, XIII–XIV.
6:10	III. Accept divine decree.		Resurrection of dead.
7:8	VII. Encounter with Samaritan.		XV–XVII. Disputes with gentiles.
7:13	III. Magic of rabbis. IV. As above. V. As above.		XVIII–XXI. Antolinus and rabbi. LXXXV. Truth. CIII. Messiah.
10:5	II. Rabbi and Antolinus.		CXL. Magic. CXLII, CLXIII. Death of rabbi CLXI, CLXII. Rabbis and biblical kings.

Sanhedrin	Yerushalmi	Sanhedrin	Bavli
			CXCVI. Rabbis share peoples' grief.
			CCXIX. Rabbis and Min.
			CCLIV. Simeon and Jesus.
		11:3A–CC	Trust in God.
		11:3DD–FF	Dispute with Egyptian.
		11:4–6	Elijah and rabbi.

2. Used not in context, as a story told "for its own sake."

Yerushalmi	Bavli
Sotah—	Sotah—
Sukkah—	Sukkah—
Sanhedrin—	Sanhedrin—

So far as I can tell, not a single sage unit of discourse fails to establish for itself a connection to the larger context in which it occurs. This concurrence that, when sage units occur, they must serve a redactional purpose distinct from their own point of interest and inner cogency, is important. For the Bavli's redactors inserted numerous Scripture units of discourse formed around their own principle of conglomeration and without any connection whatsoever to the redactional framework defined by the Mishnah and its analysis. In that regard the Bavli's authors differed from those of the Yerushalmi. In the present setting, they followed the example of their precursors. So solely in regard to Scripture units of discourse do we differentiate redactional policies of the Bavli's compositors and organizers from those of the Yerushalmi. So the framers of the Bavli concur with those of the Yerushalmi that, when we tell stories about sages, we must have a purpose connected to the exposition of matters deemed primary and more fundamental, specifically, the articulation and amplification of a matter of either Scripture or Mishnah (as these were already in hand).

Among the original authors of sage units of discourse, by contrast, the figure of the sage alone served to form a principle of internal cogency and inner coherence in the composition of a unit of discourse. That is why we have such units to begin with. The redactors who succeeded, the ones who received the completed compositions, however, did not concur that the figure of a sage alone might serve to form a principle of cogency and coherence in the conglomeration of several such units of discourse. A "Talmud," that is to say, what we now see as a sustained exposition of either a verse or theme of Scripture or a sentence or paragraph of the Mishnah, in no instance took shape around the name of a sage alone.

That result is important for two reasons. First, it tells us that, when the framers of the Yerushalmi went about their work, they indeed had access to stories told "for their own sake." That is, they had in hand a record of what a man said or did, preserved because the record, by itself, mattered. Second, we learn that they and, all the more so, their successors in the Bavli rarely, if ever, regarded such stories as supplying an ample basis for a sustained essay, a sequence of units of discourse, a cogent discussion of some dimensions. They did not build their large compositions—two or more units of discourse—around lives of sages.

These two results will now find reinforcement in the second taxonomy. In the following I review the sage units of discourse so as to divide them into three classifications.

In the first I list those stories that are told to illustrate a value or rule. In stories such as these a shared and common ideal, trait, characteristic, or concern finds concrete exemplification in a given sage's deeds. The sage is an exemplary hero, not an individual. Why? Because the purpose of the narrative itself is to exemplify either a value or a position on the law at hand. Individuation contradicts such a purpose. This list, of course, corresponds to the one given first in the foregoing pair. That is to say, a story told in (redactional) context (list 1 above) also treats the hero as contextual and not individual (list 1 here).

In the second list, I catalog stories told with some interest in the distinctive traits of an individual, stories we may claim were narrated in some measure "for their own sake." Here we find the heroes of stories treated as individuals, not mere exemplifications in flesh and blood of common values and personifications of objective traits.

In the third catalog I distinguish stories that are not narratives in any meaningful sense. Why not? Here a narrative setting serves to encapsulate a conventional dialogue. This third list is an appendix to the first. Now, as before, the names of sages serve only as pegs on which to hang stunning repartee. All such cases are located in polemical settings. I list these items only because of the superficially narrative character of the composition, not because I regard them as stories in the sense in which a story tells us things people not only said but did and indicates the circumstances and consequences of what they said and did.

1. Story told to illustrate a common value or rule.

Sotah		Yerushalmi	Sotah		Bavli
1:4	II		7:6	XXIV/40A	
5:5	IV		9:11–13	IV	
9:15	III				
9:16	II				

Sukkah	Yerushalmi	Sukkah	Bavli
2:5	I	2:6	VI, VII
3:4	II	5:1D–4	IX

Sanhedrin	Yerushalmi	Sanhedrin	Bavli
1:2	V, VI, X, XIII	1:1–6	X.CC–HH, XXXVIII, LIV
[2:1	III]	2:1–2	IX
2:6	IV	3:3	X
3:5	II	3:6–7	XXI
6:3	III	4:3–4	V
6:10	III	4:5	V, XVIII–XXVII
7:8	VII	7:5	XIX.EE–II
7:13	III, IV, V	7:10–11	IX, XI
		9:6	IV (relevant to detail in context)
		11:1–2	LXXXV, CIII, CXL, CXLII, CXLIII, CLXI, CLXII, CXCVI, CCXIX, CCLIV
		11:3A–CC	XXV
		11:3DD–FF	V
		11:4–6	XXII

2. Story told because of interest in the character or personality of the hero of the story.

	Yerushalmi	Bavli
Sotah—		Sotah—
Sukkah—		Sukkah—
Sanhedrin		Sanhedrin—
2:1	IV. The story of Simeon b. Laqish and the patriarch treats the heroes as individuals.	
2:6	V. Individuals well characterized here.	
6:6	II. Story has a plot line, no mere tableau.	

3. Story told to convey a polemic or dispute in dramatic setting.

	Yerushalmi	Bavli
Sotah		Sotah —
3:4	VII. Eliezer against teaching women Torah.	
Sukkah		Sukkah —
3:10	VI	

Yerushalmi		Bavli	
Sanhedrin		Sanhedrin	
2:6	VI. Samaritan.	4:5	XVIII–XXVII
7:8	VII. Samaritan.	11:1–2	V–VI, X–XI, XIII–XIV,
			XVI–XVII, XVIII–XXIV
10:5	II		

The results may be stated briefly. The Talmuds share the powerful preference for stories that serve a larger purpose at hand. The Yerushalmi presents us with three exceptions. Only a far larger sample (I should say, both Talmuds reviewed from beginning to end) will tell us whether the present result bears any consequences at all for the comparison of the two Talmuds.

Alike and Not Alike

The Talmuds prove remarkably alike when they take up sage units of discourse. The framers of both documents utilized such stories mainly when the stories fit into the larger purpose of the composite of units of discourse under construction. Nearly all stories in our sample, moreover, were told to serve the purpose of exemplifying an ideal, value, law, or point under dispute. A single taxonomy, moreover, serves both Talmuds' sage units of discourse. First, as we saw, when we distinguished tales told in context from those told not in context, we saw that the authors of both Talmuds insisted that whatever available materials were to be used would serve the compositors', not the authors', purposes. Nothing in either Talmud stood entirely out of context, even though in a few cases the context or connection did not prove paramount in shaping the narrative and making its point. Second, when we then divided up the stories, distinguishing those that permitted individuals to stand out from those that treated individuals as exemplifications of virtues to be held in common, the sage as exemplar vastly predominated. Characterization of individuals proved rare in our sample. We may safely surmise that individuation is rare in the two Talmuds, though not entirely absent.

Further research may indicate that the Yerushalmi's framers exhibited a greater willingness to allow a sage to present himself as an individual, and that the Bavli's authors imposed with greater rigor a single standard for the inclusion of tales about sages—a story's power of exemplification and absence of substantial traits of individuation. To investigate the present hypothesis, we ask two questions. First, as is obvious, we need to know how many tales about heroes as individuals, not only as good examples, the two Talmuds present, and in what proportions these sorts of stories occur in each Talmud. Second, if we find that the Bavli takes over stories already available in the Yerushalmi, we should compare the versions of these stories and look for evidence of a pronounced tendency, in the Bavli, to remove traits of individuation and impose lessons of an exemplary character. While such a study would substantially assist in the differentiation of one Talmud from the other, the results seem not urgent for our present purpose.

The statistical sample for our tractates is so slight, and the main results so one sided, that, for the moment, we may reach a simple, if tentative, conclusion. It is that, when the writers of the Bavli came to the third component of the canon of Rabbinical Judaism, that is to say, when they determined how they would receive and give written form to the Torah as the sage presents it, they skimped. That is, the sage as a medium of Torah and a vehicle of God's will for Israel and the world is not a principal source of narrative interest. What did they do? They did pretty much what their predecessors had done, which, from the viewpoint of large-scale composition and redaction, is very little. They made use of what served their larger purposes of exposition and analysis. But they seldom built sustained expositions or purposeful, penetrating analyses around lives and teachings of sages viewed as distinctive sources of Torah. The way in which, in redactional context, these authors built enormous constructions around the Mishnah or, in the Bavli, the Mishnah and Scripture in no way found a counterpart when it came to sages.

Sage units of tradition always turned out to be subordinate and contingent. The reason, I maintain, is not difficult to find. When sages writing the Talmuds looked for individuals to serve as heroes and exemplars, they found them in two places but took them in hand in only one. They found their heroes, first, in their own circles, past and present, and second, also in Scripture. But for purposes of sustained narrative, on the one side, and for equally ambitious and sustained composition of large-scale discourse, on the other, they clearly invested their best energies into compositions of discourses on Scripture's heroes. That alone is where we see their narrative powers, their fresh and ingenious modes of storytelling for a purpose. That also—and in context, predictably—is where we see their redactional skills, their capacity to build compelling and remarkably sustained discourse about persons as much as about legal problems and theses.

Scripture's rabbis and the Talmuds' contemporary rabbis lived in a single age and bore identical authority for the Torah that they taught and exemplified. But while contemporary sages served to exemplify common values and to make points in acutely current debates, stories about scriptural rabbis—Moses, David—allowed for freer expression. Inner motivation and other traits of individuation occur commonly in stories about scriptural rabbis, David or Job for instance, but rarely in the others. When sages of the Mishnah's and the Talmuds' age do occur, it is to teach in a vivid way lessons for all to learn equally.

That fact underlines and explains the failure of the present taxonomies to allow us to distinguish the two Talmuds from one another. Why have these classifications failed? It is because the sages who composed the units of discourse as well as those who, in the aftermath, built those units of discourse into large-scale talmudic discussions did not make the distinction that we have made, between heroes of the Scripture and heroes of the sages' world itself. The reason is that the Torah was one. So heroes of the written Torah, as much as heroes of the oral Torah, formed a single community of sanctity. For the purpose of the present exercise in differentiating the two Talmuds and showing how the Bavli stands by itself, the reason that the taxonomies show no difference hardly matters. We now have found out what we needed to know, which is that, when the authors of the Bavli made up and used sage units of discourse, the authors did not materially differ from their predecessors. But I should be the first to concede that the fact at hand, important for our inquiry, generates more questions than it settles.

Part Three

The Bavli at the End

6

What the Bavli Contributes

The Bavli relates not only to the Yerushalmi, with which the Bavli's authors shared the Mishnah and the Tosefta. Its lines of transmission reach back to other compilations and compositions in the larger canon of Judaism completed before the Bavli's own closure. Defining the Bavli in particular, therefore, demands that we show how the Bavli relates to these other compositions and compilations as well as to the Yerushalmi. Just as, when we compared the Bavli to the Yerushalmi, we began by asking what they have in common and used that shared common denominator as the baseline for comparisons, so we seek points in common among diverse documents. These we find in sayings and stories that circulate from document to document—the peripatetic saying, the thrice-told tale. How they relate in general will permit us to ask for traits of the Bavli's authors and their preferences and viewpoints in particular.

Since the Bavli organizes its materials around the Mishnah, by definition the Bavli stands autonomous of all documents that do not. The sole exception, the Yerushalmi, has already given its testimony in this exercise of definition. We may proceed forthwith to the more complex question of the Bavli's connection and continuity with numerous other documents of the canon. In the present part of the study we take up the issue of connection, and in part 4, that of continuity.

What links both Talmuds to the rest of the compositions of the rabbinic canon—the peripatetic saying and the thrice-told tale—has so impressed prior students of the literature as to obliterate what distinguishes each document from all others. That is to say, until the studies inaugurated by me, the important point of interest focused not upon the definition of essentially distinct documents and the discovery of the complex relationships among them. Rather, people sought the law shared among the documents or, later on, their theology. That is, they looked for the torah, contained everywhere and equally, in essentially neutral carriers of indifferent components of a uniform Torah. Why *not* ask about the traits of each vehicle and its viewpoint? People did not look at that problem because they did not find it important. If they were traditionalists, as most were, they took for granted the essential continuity of all documents as part of one whole Torah of Moses, our rabbi. If they were not traditionalists but Reform or Conservative historian-theologians, their search for sayings relevant to a given topic of interest—an idea, a sage, an event— led them throughout the literature. They scarcely thought they had to discriminate or stop at the boundaries between one document and another. So a study of "rabbinic Judaism" or "rabbinic theology" would draw freely upon sayings relevant to a given topic, without distinction as to where and when those sayings made their original appearance. No one cared how what was said in a given document related to other things important in the statement of that same document. Everybody accordingly knew that the literature emerged essentially uniform in viewpoint and outlook and conveyed an entirely coherent system and doctrine. That supposition, necessary and dominant in legal studies, never found doubters among those who carried on theological (including historical) ones as well.

Along these same lines, those who took an interest in historical questions, wanting to trace the development and history of rabbinic Judaism and of the Jews in late antiquity (which they called, significantly, the "period of the Mishnah and the Talmud"), worked on the foundation of exactly the same premise. Translating into a judgment on sources the old dictum that temporal categories do not apply to the Torah, they made up their history by collecting relevant data from all sources and joining those data into a single portrait. In consequence, sayings from documents of the third century in historical literature about the "Talmudic period" stood side by side with sayings from documents of the thirteenth and eighteenth centuries. All sayings testified not to the mind of their (diverse) makers but to the events of which they (uniformly and accurately) spoke.

The complete homogenization of sources therefore characterized all three approaches—legal, theological, historical—to the study of the Jews and Judaism in the period of which the documents speak and also in the period out of which the documents emerge. From the established perspective, therefore, issues of autonomy of, and connection among, documents cannot arise. Why not? "Moses, our rabbi," speaking in God's name, had settled them long ago. Whether framed in that mythic language or in categories more appropriate to the nineteenth- and twentieth-century Jewish seminary, the premise remained the same and produced identical suppositions of research. The sole dimension was that of continuity, which in itself measured autonomy and connection alike.

But we now know otherwise. No one who has studied the obvious polemic of the Sifra can doubt that its framers proposed to raise and settle a particular question. None who has taken seriously the systemic philosophical and uniform rhetorical character of the Mishnah, seeing the document whole and not merely as a collection of discrete sayings, can miss the distinctive and particular address of the Mishnah's authors to their own time and circumstance. The odd redactional preferences of the organizers of the Tosefta testify to the problem they took for themselves. The literary and rhetorical program of the writers of the Yerushalmi and of Leviticus Rabbah, viewed as systematic and cogent enterprises, likewise provides ample testimony on the same matter. Those writers produced cogent documents, compositions and not merely amorphous collections of unrelated observations about this and that. Once we merely look, we can uncover recurrent points of emphasis. We readily discern points of inner tension, generative of a single coherent statement, repeated in innumerable forms and addressed to a broader world beyond. Even the part of this book now concluded, in which we have shown that the authors of the Bavli did some things differently from the way the authors of the Yerushalmi did, leaves no doubt as to the facts. Each document, examined by itself, yields its method and therefore also its message. So each document is examined by itself, read in the perspective of its own rhetoric and logic, and understood and interpreted in the framework of its own context.

But documents are not only autonomous or connected. Both the traditionalists and their modern epigones also speak of inescapable facts. The documents all together flow together. They constitute a canon and not merely a library. They define *a* Judaism (though the traditionalists would stake much against the insertion of the indefinite article just now used). The same names recur throughout. The same basic values find exemplification and advocacy everywhere. Thus, as I just said, the message of the components of the canon so coheres that we may, after all, speak of a canon, not merely a library. That is to say, were the main constitutive documents of the rabbinic canon to have reached us the way the scrolls of the Essene community of Qumran did—all together yet totally out of any context, continuous with ourselves and our own world—we should understand them not as a library, assembled accidentally by a collector of congenial materials. Rather, I insist they form a single canon, the authoritative and harmonious statement of the theology and law of a coherent religious group. That the Essene library constituted a library, while the rabbinic documents form a canon, seems to me self-evident. We deal with not a collection but a canon, not books but torah. But it is a continuity to be discerned with effort, not merely assumed in a facile and gullible spirit.

If it seems so self-evident that the various documents form a canon and constitute a Judaism, then how in fact do the documents, seen separately, actually relate in detail when viewed all together? How do we discern the marks of continuity among books we have carefully distinguished from one another? These questions define the critical issues of the next phase of research into the rabbinic canon. In the present context, however, we deal with only one aspect: the Bavli in particular, in relation to antecedent compositions.

This brings us back to the peripatetic saying and the thrice-told tale. What in fact sustains the claim that the Bavli stands within a larger canonical context than merely that defined by the Mishnah and the Tosefta for the Bavli and the Yerushalmi alike? Why shall I claim that the Bavli comes in conclusion as a summa? It is not general points of concurrence but the detailed occurrence, in other rabbinic documents of late antiquity, of sayings and stories that may wend their way from one composition to the next but commonly end up in the Bavli. Examples of these shared units of discourse already have attracted our attention in the simplest way. How so? The paragraphs of the Mishnah and many of the paragraphs of the Tosefta fall into the classification of peripatetic sayings. They move, in bits and pieces, here and there.

The Mishnah assuredly emerged as a single whole statement, not merely a composite of this and that. But in the two Talmuds, the Mishnah's paragraphs circulate in parts and never as a component of a single, whole document, autonomous and distinct on its own. They always occur, rather, as components of a single Torah, everywhere continuous within itself and cogent throughout. When we look at the pages of the two Talmuds, we find numerous other units of discourse shared both between the two Talmuds and among diverse other rabbinic compositions. These other shared units of discourse do not compare to the Mishnah and elements of the Tosefta. The Mishnah recurs in the two Talmuds but far less commonly elsewhere, the Tosefta still less. The peripatetic units of discourse occurring in collections of scriptural exegeses (midrashim) and various other sorts of rabbinic writings, by contrast, make an appearance more or less randomly (so it now appears), but in any case far more promiscuously among the diverse constituents of the rabbinic corpus.

The work of tracing materials as they move from book to book occupied the scholarly life of the great Israeli talmudist, E. Z. Melammed, who collected and organized them in such works (all in Hebrew) as *Tannaite Exegetical Works in the Babylonian Talmud* (1943), *The Relationship between the Legal Exegetical Works and the Mishnah and Tosefta* (1967), and *Introduction to Talmudic Literature* (1973), among others. Lesser scholars undertook aspects of the same inquiry, for instance H. Albeck, *Studies in Baraita and Tosefta and Their Relationship to the Talmud* (1954), and Benjamin DeFries, *History of Talmudic Law* (1966) and *Studies in the Literature of the Talmud* (1968). The enormous catalogs collected by Melammed, however, provide the definitive picture of the state of the question.

I find matters confused for one simple reason. I am not able to locate in these available works general theories to account for how one document borrows from another or to explain when and why a given composition will use one already-used saying or story and not use some other. What does one set of editors commonly do to, and with, what it takes from some other set? The principal focus of research has been on how diverse documents testify to a common "tradition." In general people have wanted to find out the basic or original "form" or version or wording of a given "tradition." The purpose of collections of sayings shared among a number of compositions has been to guide students of the literature in their search for these original versions. I put quotation marks around *form* and *tradition* because I am not clear on the premises of research. I cannot point to a lucid statement of what people expect to find or to prove when they have recovered all of the various ways in which a given statement occurs in the entirety of the rabbinic canon (which then extends far beyond the limits of late antiquity).

Rather than explain other peoples' work, let me turn back to the task at hand. What is this task? It is to define the Bavli and explain for ourselves its position in the formation of Judaism, analyzed as a problem presented by literary sources of the canon of Judaism. To repeat: we seek a theory of the Bavli so as to grasp the Bavli's position in the end of the formation of the canon, that is, of Judaism. We want to define that position so as to understand how the Bavli forms the seal of Judaism. In what ways is the Bavli the full and complete statement of the Torah of Moses, our rabbi, the authority, the final judgment, the summa? For Judaism, from the Bavli onward, always looked to the Bavli as the ultimate statement of affairs. It is our task to understand whether that perspective matched the reality of the document and, if it did (as I believe it did), how and why that was the case.

We therefore ask a far more circumscribed question than how, in general, stories circulate across the far frontiers of the realm of the rabbinic canon. We want only to know what ordinarily or characteristically happens when sayings or stories that occur in documents closed earlier than the Bavli take up a place and a position in the composition of the Bavli as well. If we are able to point to some gross, recurrent, and general traits—things that are likely to appear in a number of different cases—we shall have made such progress as serves the larger purposes of this book. But the work of relating one document to the next, whether the Sifra to the Mishnah or the Fathers according to Rabbi Nathan to the two Talmuds, begins and cannot end when we have listed what each document shares with the other. A theory of a given document seen whole will ultimately tell us why that document uses what it does out of the antecedent heritage at hand. Still more important, a theory should explain what a given document's authors ordinarily will choose to do with what they have borrowed, for example, in adding to or changing the wording, and what they will refrain from doing. The great and pioneering work of Melammed and his contemporaries will serve this comparative inquiry. But not one line any of them ever wrote can tell us anything serviceable for the study at hand. So, in full recognition of the excellence of what has gone before, let us begin afresh.

7

The Matter of Topic

The Fundamental Questions

As we contemplate the fundamental questions before us, we discern two—
one dealing with topic, the other with rhetorical formulation. By *topic* I mean
simply what subjects occur in one document and what in another. By *rhetorical formulation* I refer to traits in framing, or reframing and revising and amplifying, sayings or stories as these stories pass from one document to another.
Specifically, in the setting of the Bavli, do we find subjects treated that rarely
occur in a systematic way in earlier compositions? And, again in the setting of
the Bavli, do we find a pronounced tendency of rhetoric, for example, to treat
in a single way or to cut or to add a saying or a story that has already occurred
in a document redacted earlier than the Bavli? These are the two indicators of
what the Bavli contributes and how it does so.

I can think of no more basic issue, first, than whether a given composition
coming later in the formation of the canon takes up topics not dealt with in an
earlier one. Such a matter leaves no room for subjective impressions or guess-
work. Either a subject occurs or it does not occur.

The second question is whether a traveling saying or story occurring in a
later document is changed in rhetoric from its version appearing in an earlier
one and, if it is, what changes consistently occur in the later document. Either
a story or saying is copied without substantial revision or it is cut down or
built up, losing or gaining weight of detail as it makes its journey down the
path from document to document. Here too the facts make their own statement. When we discern changes of a single classification, consistently revealed in the versions of stories or sayings occurring in a later document in the
canon, we may impute to the authors of that document a reasonably consistent
policy about receiving and revising what they got from earlier hands. We may,
conversely, take the position that such changes as we do discern represent
matters of decision and policy effected by the framers of the document (at
whatever stage in the formulation and the formation of the materials in that
document).

If we can show consistent patterns particular to the Bavli's framers, we may dismiss the possibility that diverse versions circulated at random, with one version chosen here, the other chosen there. We can demonstrate that the larger traits in matters of topic and rhetoric characteristic of the authors of a given document do make a difference in detail. To the contrary, if I can show that the editors of the Bavli take a special interest in a set of topics uncommonly treated in earlier documents, and if I can demonstrate that what they do with received materials—those occurring in earlier compositions—they do consistently and as a matter, therefore, of policy, I once more am able to describe the Bavli in particular—a document, a statement, a judgment on its own. Then the Bavli will be shown to stand in conclusion, placing the mark of its makers' mind upon all that had gone before—and, as we now know, therefore also upon all that would follow. We then need not entertain the unlikely view that if we have three versions of a given saying or story, all of them stand for three separate occasions on which the saying was said ("He would often say . . .") or on which the story actually took place ("One time . . . and then again . . ."). That position surely has to be sent down the path of the Sermon on the Mount and the Sermon on the Plain, not to mention the literal creation of the world in six days and other legacies of ages of excessive credulity.

These two matters—topical preference, rhetorical pattern—take up the remainder of this part of the book. In the present chapter we ask about the topical program of the Talmuds together, then about that of the Bavli in particular. In the next chapter we turn to the rhetorical patterns recurrently presented to us by the Bavli in particular as it takes up antecedent materials and reworks them for its own purposes.

The Issue of Topic

When we seek to classify the sayings and stories in the rabbinic canon as a whole, we begin with the issue of subject matter or topic. To state the issue simply: What sorts of themes or subjects do sayings and stories address? The broadest and encompassing categories prove to be three: legal, scriptural, and biographical topics. How so? The three sources of Torah, as we noted at the beginning, encompass the Mishnah, Scripture, and the sage. It is hardly surprising, therefore, that we can categorize all units of discourse in one of three consequent classifications: discourse on the Mishnah in particular or the law generated by the Mishnah in general; discourse on Scripture, its teachings and its heroes; discourse on the sage, his sayings and doings. Let me then make the simple claim that no complete unit of discourse in all of the rabbinic corpus falls entirely outside the boundaries of one of these three categories.

Some units may demand inclusion within more than one classification. For example, Scripture is cited nearly everywhere. But Scripture units of discourse already have found a suitable definition. Another instance of some fuzziness at the fringes comes to us from "historical tales." These prove mainly biographical, for example, what happened to a given sage on a specified occasion. But in some instances they also exhibit traits of scriptural-exegetical discourse in that the historical tale speaks of an event in the biblical record. Yet in other instances they treat the sage as tangential, with a figure other than a sage, such as Alexander the Great or Pharaoh, or the emperor, presented as primary. The instances just now listed constitute problems within the classification scheme, not precipitants of the definition of yet another classification; they are few, marginal, and not wholly exceptional to the proposed scheme.

Now at issue in the present context in which we address the matter of topic is a simple question: At what point in the unfolding of the canonical documents of Judaism do we find substantial representation of the several classifications of material? We want to know whether all three types of units of discourse occur in the several successive documents of the rabbinic canon, or whether one type predominates at one layer while another type makes an appearance only at a later layer. Let me spell out what is at stake for the study at hand.

We want to know whether we can differentiate the Bavli (or, as we shall see, both Talmuds) on the basis of types of topics amply represented in that document in particular. If we can show that, in the unfolding of materials, the Bavli encompasses all three classifications of units of discourse while earlier compositions do not, then we may reasonably claim that by its compendious character the Bavli is to be distinguished from the other components of the rabbinic canon. Since our goal is to see the Bavli as a document on its own and to ask whether and how it stands as a conclusion to the canonical history of Judaism, such an exercise takes a crucial step in the argument. So the issue of topical preference, framed in the simple taxonomy just now explained, requires attention.

Once the taxonomy has laid forth the vertical lines of structure—the sequence of documents, in the order conventionally assigned to them, from the Mishnah down to the Bavli with a number of compositions scaled in between—we turn to the next question. It is the horizontal lines of the taxonomy at hand. What sort of subject permits us to ask questions about the provenance and distribution of units of discourse among the three topical divisions I have established? We require a subject that encompasses law, Scripture, and sage, the three components of the canon. Equally obvious, we should in theory be able to turn our taxa into subjects. For instance, we should be able to show how a law of the Mishnah relates to scriptural exegesis, on the one side, and to a given sage and his views, on the other. A given scriptural passage should serve as the base of relative comparison to a law, on the one side, and a given sage's sayings, on the other. A given sage and what he says about law and scripture, on the one side, as well as what is said about his history—his biography—on the other, likewise should be subject to study.

Among the three possible taxa, I choose as my subject the figure of the sage. It is the only horizontal taxon, among the three, that will by definition find substantial representation in all three vertical (canonical) taxa. Clearly, to a sage many sayings are attributed. About him many stories are told. All important sages who occur in the Mishnah are given statements about the law of the Mishnah—by definition. To most Mishnah sages are assigned sayings about Scripture, in the context of legal exegesis of the Mishnah as well as in the context of exegesis of other-than-legal scriptural passages. So we turn forthwith to the subject of a sage.

Once the sage defines the horizontal for our taxonomical exercise, and the vertical lines of structure—the sequence of documents—are established, we return to our original topical division: Mishnah (and law in general), Scripture, sage. We divide sayings by their subcategory within the larger classification at hand. That is to say, we classify everything associated with a given sage: sayings about the Mishnah and its law, sayings about Scripture, and biographical stories. In doing so, to repeat, our interest is to ask whether a given classification of units of discourse appears wholly or primarily within a given constituent of the rabbinic canon.

We shall now take up six names or name sets—five whose names or name sets are supposed to have lived before A.D. 70 and one who flourished shortly afterward—specifically, Simeon the Righteous, Hillel, Shammai, Shammai and Hillel, Gamaliel I, and Eliezer b. Hyrcanus. In all cases, we propose to trace whether, and where, materials of each of the three classifications predominate.

The method and argument for which the exercises are adduced in evidence are as follows: When we take up the entire corpus of sayings imputed to, and stories told about, a given authority, we investigate how a sequence of topics unfolds. That sequence will tell us which topics make their appearance in one book or set of books, which ones first occur only in another, and later, book or set of books. We wish to find out whether the Talmuds, or the Bavli in particular, bear distinctive topical interests. The order of the books themselves derives from what I take to be the consensus that places the Mishnah first in line beyond Scripture, and the Bavli last in line, after the formation of the bulk of the compilations of scriptural exegeses generally thought to have reached closure in late antiquity, down to the seventh century. The relationships among collections in between the Mishnah and the Bavli have yet to find a settled consensus. For example, some would place the Sifra and the two Sifres in the third century, others would put them in the fourth. Since the two Sifres and Sifra cite the Mishnah verbatim as well as out of their own distinctive rhetorical context, we need not doubt that they reached closure after the completion of the Mishnah. In any event, for our purpose we shall treat the Mishnah, carrying the Tosefta in its wake, as the beginning and set the Bavli at the end. We then ask whether there are topics, important to the two Talmuds or only to the Bavli, that fall into classifications of data absent mostly or entirely absent in the Mishnah. If there are, then we may say that the two Talmuds take up topics neglected in the earlier documents and so find definition in that fact.

All the charts that follow arrange the sources in the same order. First come items in the Mishnah (I.i), then those in the Tosefta (I.ii). The third vertical line (II) presents items that occur in collections of exegeses of legal materials conventionally attributed to the authorship of Mishnah's authorities. These collections are distinguished in that they contain names only of Mishnaic (that is, Tannaite) figures. The fourth and fifth categories go over materials in the two Talmuds. The fourth, subdivided between the Yerushalmi (III.i), then the Bavli (III.ii), distinguishes materials attributed to Tannaite authority but first occurring in the Talmuds. The fifth (IV.i; IV.ii) then goes over all other materials about a given sage first found in the Talmuds. The penultimate category treats materials that first occur in the Fathers according to Rabbi Nathan (V), and the last, later compilations of exegeses (VI).

Five Names of Sages before A.D. 70

We begin with six charts, covering the names of five authorities assumed to have lived before A.D. 70: Simeon the Righteous, first named sage; Shammai by himself; Hillel by himself; then Shammai and Hillel; and Gamaliel. In each case we ask only about the documentary order in which sayings of the three categories made their appearance.

The Case of the Corpus of Materials Concerning Eliezer ben Hyrcanus

The traditions that impute sayings to Eliezer b. Hyrcanus or contain stories about him provide a more suitable sample than any of the ones surveyed earlier. The result now is quite one sided. Most legal traditions begin in the Mishnah and the Tosefta (here treated as a single entry). Most biographical and exegetical traditions begin in the two Talmuds and or in the exegetical compilations (midrashim), respectively. It is hardly remarkable that the exegetical compilations should introduce into Eliezer's corpus of units of discourse a sizable number of fresh items. Nor are we surprised to find that the Bavli provides the vast predominance of those exegetical units that first occur in the Talmuds' stratum. That fact confirms the results already attained in the preceding part. What is important is that the Bavli also contributes the greater part of the biographical-historical items, though in this aspect the Yerushalmi runs a close second. That is to say, from no. 238, at which the earlier stratum peters out, the number of items original to the Yerushalmi is seven; the number of items shared among both Talmuds is two; the number of items original to the Bavli is nine.

Simeon the Just

	I.i Mishnah	I.ii Tosefta	II Tannaitic Midrashim	III.i Tannaitic Materials in Palestinian Gemara	III.ii Tannaitic Materials in Babylonian Gemara	IV.i Amoraic Materials in Palestinian Gemara	IV.ii Amoraic Materials in Babylonian Gemara	V ARN	VI Later Compilations of Midrashim
1. Prepared red heifer	M. Parah 3:5 (Meir)			y. Sheq. 4:2 (Ulla)					Pes. R. Kah. Pes. Rab.
2. Heard decree was annulled		Tos. Sot. 13:7a (2d century)			b. Sot. 33a (Yohanah-Judah; 3d century)				
3. Change in supernatural after death		Tos. Sot. 13:7b		[y. Yoma 6:3]	b. Yoma 39a-b	y. Yoma 6:3			
4. World stands on three things	M. Avot 1:3			y. Ta. 4:2 y. Meg. 3:6 (Jacob b. Aha)					Pes. R. Kah.
5. Ate guilt offering of worthy Nazirite		Tos. Nez. 4:7	Sifre Num. 22	y. Ned. 1:1 y. Naz. 1:5	b. Naz. 4b b. Ned. 9b (Judah + Simeon)		b. Ned. 10a (Abayye)		Num. R. 10:7
6. Met Alexander and saved temple					b. Yoma 69a				Lev. R. 13:5 Pes. R. Kah. Pes. Rab.
7. Served forty years as high priest (see no. 3)						y. Yoma 1:1 y. Yoma 5:2 (R. Abbahu)	b. Yoma 9a (Yohanan; 3d century)		

Simeon the Just

	I.i	I.ii	II	III.i	III.ii	IV.i	IV.ii	V	VI
	Mishnah	Tosefta	Tannaitic Midrashim	Tannaitic Materials in Palestinian Gemara	Tannaitic Materials in Babylonian Gemara	Amoraic Materials in Palestinian Gemara	Amoraic Materials in Babylonian Gemara	ARN	Later Compilations of Midrashim
8. Raised up to meet Greek threat							b. Meg. 11a (Samuel; 3d century)		
9. Predicted own deaths					b. Sot. 39b b. Men. 109b	y. Yoma 6:3			
10. Onias					b. Men. 109b				

Note: Simeon's materials are mainly in the category of sages' biographies. They occur in the Talmudic stratum. Since there is no legal stratum to speak of, however, the result is of marginal interest.

Shammai

	I.i	I.ii	II	III.i	III.ii	IV.i	IV.ii	V	VI
	Mishnah	Tosefta	Tannaitic Midrashim	Tannaitic Materials in Palestinian Gemara	Tannaitic Materials in Babylonian Gemara	Amoraic Materials in Palestinian Gemara	Amoraic Materials in Babylonian Gemara	ARN	Later Compilations of Midrashim
1. Heave-offering vetches eaten dry	M. M.S. 2:4 M. Ed. 1:8								
2. Changing sela of second-tithe money in Jerusalem	M. M.S. 2:9 M. Ed. 1:10	Tos. M.S. 2:10				y. M.S. 2:4			
3. What conveys flavor can	M. Oriah 2:5								

#	Item	Mishnah	Tosefta	Midrash	Bavli	Yerushalmi
3.	...				b. Yev. 13a	
4.	Made sukkah for infant	M. Suk. 2:8				
5.	Uncleanness of stools	M. Kel. 22:4				
6.	Ploughing in seventh year		Tos. Shev. 3:10			
7.	Remember Sabbath (see no. 2)			Mekh. deR Simeon, p. 148 1.29-30		
8.	Three rules re siege, trip before Sabbath		Tos. Eruv. 3:7 (re siege)	Sifre Deut. 203 (weigh anchor)	b. Shab. 19a (re siege)	
9.	Phylacteries of my grandfather			Mekh. deR Ishmael Pisha IV.209-16		
10.	Would not add food to be eaten with one hand				b. Yoma 77b / b. Hul. 107b	
11.	Shammai and Jonathan b. Uzziel				b. B.B. 133b-134a	y. Ned. 5:6
12.	Even a single bone from the backbone defiles by overshadowing	M. Ed. 1:7			b. Naz. 52b	
13.	Sender is liable				b. Qid. 43a	
14.	White of egg contracts				b. Git. 57a	
15.	Three sayings	M. Avot. 1:15				

Note: Where there are biographical materials on Shammai, they pertain to legal issues and fall into the category of law, for example, at nos. 4, 9, 10. The one point of interest is at no. 11 (an item to which we return in the next chapter). Here the biographical unit of discourse makes its original appearance in the talmudic stratum. But once more, the result is based on inconsequential evidence.

Hillel

	I.i Mishnah	I.ii Tosefta	II Tannaitic Midrashim	III.i Tannaitic Materials in Palestinian Gemara	III.ii Tannaitic Materials in Babylonian Gemara	IV.i Amoraic Materials in Palestinian Gemara	IV.ii Amoraic Materials in Babylonian Gemara	V ARN	VI Later Compilations of Midrashim
1. Forbade interest in kind	M. B.M. 5:9	Tos. B.M. 6:10			b. Shab. 148b		b. B.M. 75a		
2. Apophthegms and sayings	M. Avot 1:12-14; 2:5-7				b. Suk. 53a (skull)			ARN chap. 28 (the more . . . the more)	
3. Hillel would fold together massah, bitter herbs, etc.		Tos. Pisha 2:22	Mekh. deR. Simeon b. Yohai, p. 13 l.12	y. Hal. 1:1	b. Pes. 115a				
4. Whoever touches insect is unclean—even if in a ritual pool			Sifra Shemini 9:5			(Compare y. Pes. 6:1)			
5. Itch within itch: On this account Hillel came up from Babylonia		Tos. Neg. 1:16	Sifra Tazria 9:16			(Compare y. Pes. 6:1)			
6. Redeem property at end of year	M. Arakh 9:4		Sifra Behar 4:8		b. Git. 74b				
7. Stimulated students		Tos. Ahilot 16:8; Tos. Parah 4:7	Sifre Num. 123						
8. Prozbul	M. Shev. 10:3; M. Git. 4:3		Sifre Deut. 113; Mid. Tan., p. 80	y. Shev. 10:2	b. Git. 36a				
9. Lived one-hundred-			Sifre Deut. 357; Mid.						Gen. R. 100:24

	Avot. 4:5	Tos.	y.	b.			
	crown shall perish						
11.	Six moral sayings	Tos. Ber. 2:21, 6:24	y. Ber. 9:5 (scatter/gather)	b. Ber. 63a (scatter/gather)			
12.	Bought horse and slave for poor man	Tos. Peah 4:10	y. Peah 8:7				b. Ket. 67b
13.	Reliability for tithes	Tos. Maaserot 3:2-4=Tos. Ed. 2:4					
14.	Pesah overrides Sabbath	Tos. Pisha 4:13; Tos. Sanh. 7:11	y. Shab. 19:1; y. Pes. 6:1	b. Pes. 66a-b		(b. B.M. 85a)	ARN chap. 37=Tos. Sanh. 7:11
15.	If you will come to my house	Tos. Suk. 4:3		b. Suk. 53a	y. Suk. 5:4		ARN chap. 12
16.	Expounded Alexandrian ketuvah	Tos. Ket. 4:9	y. Yev. 15:3; y. Ket. 4:8	b. B.M. 104a			
17.	Was worthy of the Holy Spirit	Tos. Sot. 13:3	y. Sot. 9:13	b. Sanh. 11a; b. Sot. 48b	y. A.Z. 3:1=y. Hor. 3:5	b. Sot. 48b	
18.	Do not fear report		y. Ber. 9:3	b. Ber. 60a			
19.	Had eighty (pair) of disciples		y. Ned. 5:6	b. Suk. 28a; b. B.B. 134a			
20.	Man crushed in Temple court in days of Hillel			b. Pes. 64b			
21.	Studied as a poor man			b. Yoma 35b			
22.	Ten genealogical classes (?)			b. Yev. 37a; b. Qid. 75a			

Hillel

	I.i Mishnah	I.ii Tosefta	II Tannaitic Midrashim	III.i Tannaitic Materials in Palestinian Gemara	III.ii Tannaitic Materials in Babylonian Gemara	IV.i Amoraic Materials in Palestinian Gemara	IV.ii Amoraic Materials in Babylonian Gemara	V ARN	VI Later Com- pilations of Midrashim
23. No one trespassed through burnt offering					b. Ned. 9b; b. Pes. 66b				
24. These are my grandfather's tefillin						y. Eruv. 10:1 [=Shammai; Mekh. Pisha III.209-16]			
25. For three things did Hillel migrate (nos. 4-5)						y. Pes. 6:1			
26. Hillel from David						y. Ta. 4:2			Gen. R. 98:8
27. Two disciples before Hillel							b. Pes. 3b		
28. Ezra, Hillel, and Hiyya restored Torah							b. Suk. 20a		
29. Ben He He							b. Hag. 9b		
30. Hillel and Shebna							b. Sot. 21a		
31. How much wheat per seah									
32. My self-abasement is my exaltation								ARN Chap. 12	Lev. R. 1:5
33. To wash is a religious duty									Lev. R. 34:4

Shammai and Hillel

	I.i	I.ii	II	III.i	III.ii	IV.i	IV.ii	V	VI
	Mishnah	Tosefta	Tannaitic Midrashim	Tannaitic Materials in Palestinian Gemara	Tannaitic Materials in Babylonian Gemara	Amoraic Materials in Palestinian Gemara	Amoraic Materials in Babylonian Gemara	ARN	Later Compilations of Midrashim
1. Retroactive uncleanness of menstruant	M. Ed. 1:1; M. Nid. 1:1				b. Shab. 15a	y. Nid. 1:1	b. Nid. 2a–4b; b. Nid. 15a		
2. Liability of loaf for hallah	M. Ed. 1:2	Tos. Ed. 1:1			b. Shab. 15a				
3. Drawn water in immersion pool	M. Ed. 1:3	Tos. Ed. 1:3			b. Shab. 15a				(Mid. Ps. 17A)
4. Dispute for the sake of heaven	M. Avot 15:17								
5. Source of disputes is inadequate study with Shammai-Hillel		Tos. Hag. 2:9; Tos. Sot. 14:9; Tos. Sanh. 7:1		y. Hag. 2:12; y. Sanh. 1:4			b. Sot. 47b; b. Sanh. 88b		
6. Lay on hands; Hillel's vs. Shammai's students	M. Hag. 2:2	Tos. Hag. 2:11		y. Hag. 2:3; y. Bes. 2:4	b. Bes. 20a; (b. Pes. 66b) (b. Ned. 9b)				
7. Hillel and Shammai decreed uncleanness of hands		y. Shab. 1:4; y. Pes. 1:6; y. Ket. 8:11		b. Shab. 14b–15a					

Shammai and Hillel

	I.i	I.ii	II	III.i	III.ii	IV.i	IV.ii	V	VI
	Mishnah	Tosefta	Tannaitic Midrashim	Tannaitic Materials in Palestinian Gemara	Tannaitic Materials in Babylonian Gemara	Amoraic Materials in Palestinian Gemara	Amoraic Materials in Babylonian Gemara	ARN	Later Compilations of Midrashim
8. Uncleanness of vintaging grapes for the vat					b. Shab. 15a; b. Shab. 17a		b. A.Z. 39b; b. Hul. 36b		
9. Hillel + Simeon; Gamaliel + Simeon					b. Shab. 15a				
10. Gentle like Hillel, not impatient like Shammai					b. Shab. 30b-31a			ARN chap. 15	

Note: Here too what is important is simply that the legal materials cluster at the Mishnah's side of the table; the very (few) biographical materials—nos. 9, 10—at the Talmud's side.

Gamaliel the Elder

	I.i	I.ii	II	III.i	III.ii	IV.i	IV.ii	V	VI
	Mishnah	Tosefta	Tannaitic Midrashim	Tannaitic Materials in Palestinian Gemara	Tannaitic Materials in Babylonian Gemara	Amoraic Materials in Palestinian Gemara	Amoraic Materials in Babylonian Gemara	ARN	Later Compilations of Midrashim
1. Woman remarries on testimony of one witness	M. Yev. 16:7				b. Yev. 115a				
2. Simeon asks Gamaliel re peah	M. Peah 2:6								

	M.	Tos.	y.	b.
...house gave Terumah				
5. How his house prostrated selves in Temple	M. Sheq. 6:1			
6. Ordinance re witnesses	M. R.H. 2:5			
7. Approved Admon's decisions	M. Ket. 13:3-5; M. B.B. 9:1 =M. Ket. 13:3	Tos. Ket. 12:4 [=M. Ket. 13:5]	y. Ket. 13:5	b. Ket. 109a
8. When Gamaliel died, glory of Torah ceased	M. Sot. 9:15		(b. Meg. 21a)	
9. Ordinance re annulling divorce	M. Git. 4:2a		y. B.B. 10:4	
10. Ordinance re listing nicknames in divorce	M. Git. 4:2b			
11. Ordinance re collecting ketuvah	M. Git. 4:3			
12. Banned Targum of Job		Tos. Shab. 13:2	y. Shab. 16:1	b. Shab. 115a
13. Letters re leap year		Tos. Sanh 2:6	y. M.S. 5:4; y. Sanh. 1:2	b. Sanh. 11a
14. Married daughter to Simeon b. Netanel		Tos. A.Z. 3:10		
15. Permitted drinking from vessels used for gentile wine		Tos. A.Z. 4:9		

Gamaliel the Elder

	I.i Mishnah	I.ii Tosefta	II Tannaitic Midrashim	III.i Tannaitic Materials in Palestinian Gemara	III.ii Tannaitic Materials in Babylonian Gemara	IV.i Amoraic Materials in Palestinian Gemara	IV.ii Amoraic Materials in Babylonian Gemara	V ARN	VI Later Compilations of Midrashim
16. Hanina healed his son					b. Ber. 34b				
17. Instructed king and queen re Pesah, etc.					b. Pes. 88b				
18. After death, men studied Torah sitting down					b. Meg. 21a				
19. Hillel's proselyte named one of sons Gamaliel								ARN chap. 15	
20. Four kinds of disciples								ARN chap. 40	
21. Blessed beautiful gentile						y. A.Z. 1:9	(b. A.Z. 20a: Simeon b. Gamaliel)		

Note: I have omitted from the table all items that may belong to a Gamaliel other than the Gamaliel who flourished before A.D. 70. Here again our attention is drawn to two questions. First, where do we find the preponderance of biographical materials? The answer is at nos. 16, 18, 19, 20, and 21. Legal sayings, whether cast in the form of sayings or stories, are paramount in the Mishnah. The only solely biographical unit of discourse not in the talmudic stratus is at no. 14.

Item		Mishnah-Tosefta	Tannaitic Midrashim	Baraita-Stratum in the Talmuds	Amoraic Materials in the Talmuds	Later Compilations
			I. Legal Units			
1.	Read Shema in evening	M. Ber. 1:1			b. Ber. 26	
2.	Read Shema in morning	M. Ber. 1:2				
3.	Night has three watches			b. Ber. 3a		
4.	Shema requires intention		Mid. Tan Deut. 6:6	b. Ber. 13a		
5.	No fixed text for prayer	M. Ber. 4:5				
6.	Short prayer		Mekh. I, p. 216; II, p. 9-72; Mekh. R. Sim., p. 57, 103; Sifre Num., p. 105	b. Ber. 29b; b. Ber. 34a		
7.	Say Havdalah in thanksgiving	M. Ber. 5:2				
7A.	Say Sanctification of the day in thanksgiving	Tos. Ber. 3:10, 3:11				
8.	Who is am haares?			b. Ber. 47b		
9.	Why wipe with left hand?			b. Ber. 62a		
10.	Ground liable for peah	M. Peah 3:6				
11.	Vineyard entirely composed of defective clusters	M. Peah 7:7	Mid. Tan. Deut. 24:2; Sifra Qed. 3:1; Sifre Deut. 285			
12.	First fruits in valley re demai	Tos. Dem. 1:3		y. Dem. 1:1		
13.	Thorns in vineyard	M. Kil. 5:8	Sifre Deut. 230	y. Kil. 1:1, 5:7		
14.	Handkerchiefs, etc., re Kilaim	M. Kil. 9:3; Tos. Kil. 5:18				
15.	Arum after seventh year	M. Shev. 5:3; Tos. Shev. 4:3		y. Shev. 5:2		
16.	Hide anointed with seventh-year oil	M. Shev. 8:9-10			y. Shev. 8:8	
17.	Three vegetables in jar	M. Shev. 9:5	Sifra Behar 3:4	y. Shev. 9:4		
18.	Seventh-year fruits as gift	M. Shev. 9:9				
19.	Heave offering from clean for unclean	M. Ter. 2:1; Tos. Ter. 3:18			y. Ter. 2:1	

	abroad—re hallah	
36.	Dough in qavs re hallah	M. Hal. 2:4
37.	Dough offering clean for unclean (= no. 19)	M. Hal. 2:8
38.	Israelite farmers in Syria	M. Hal. 4:7
39.	Cakes of thanks offering of Nazir	Tos. Hal. 1:6 [= M. Hal. 1:6; Anonymous]
40.	Curdle milk with sap of oriah	M. Orl. 1:7
41.	Etrog-like tree	M. Bik. 2:6
42.	Not kill vermin on Sabbath		b. Shab. 12a, 107b
43.	Baking before Sabbath	M. Shab. 1:10
44.	Wick for Sabbath lamp	M. Shab. 2:3
45.	Weapons on Sabbath	M. Shab. 6:4
46.	Tiara on Sabbath	Tos. Shab. 4:6
47.	Spice box on Sabbath	Tos. Shab. 4:11
48.	Scratch on flesh on Sabbath	M. Shab. 12:4; Tos. Shab. 11:15	y. Shab. 12:4; b. Shab. 104b
49.	Weave threads on Sabbath	M. Shab. 13:1; Tos. Shab. 12:1
50-50A.	Window shutter [add to building] + spread out filter	M. Shab. 17:7, 20:1	y. Shab. 20:1
51.	Circumcision on Sabbath	M. Shab. 19:1; Tos. Shab. 15:16	y. Shab. 19:1; b. Shab. 131a-b
52.	Erred by circumcising wrong child on Sabbath	M. Shab. 19:4; Tos. Shab. 15:10	b. Shab. 137b
53.	Rendering alleyway valid	M. Eruv. 1:2; Tos. Eruv. 1:2	y. Eruv. 1:2; b. Eruv. 11b-12a

Item	I Mishnah-Tosefta	II Tannaitic Midrashim	III Baraita-Stratum in the Talmuds	IV Amoraic Materials in the Talmuds	V Later Compilations
54-56.	Carry in garden; hart's tongue; not prepare eruv	M. Eruv. 2:6; Tos. Eruv. 2:7-8			
57.	Two eruvs for Sabbath + festival	M. Eruv. 3:6; Tos. Eruv. 4:1-2			
58.	Eruv with any food	M. Eruv. 7:10			
59.	Buy eruv with coins	M. Eruv. 7:11			
60.	Breach between courtyard and public domain	M. Eruv. 9:2			
61.	Repeat lesson four times			b. Eruv. 54b		
62.	Burn unclean homes sepa- rately from clean	M. Pes. 1:7			
63.	Make massah with fruit juice			b. Pes. 36a; y. Pes. 2:7		
64.	Do not designate dough offering on 15th of Nisan un- til dough is baked	M. Pes. 3:3; Tos. Pis. 3:7			
65.	Measure of dough	Tos. Pis. 3:8			
66-67.	Passover overrides Sabbath in all respects	M. Pes. 3:8; Tos. Pis.			
68.	Study on festival		Sifre Zutta 9:2	b. Pes. 68b		
69.	Offerings eligible as Passover slaughtered under other des- ignation	M. Pes. 6:5; Tos. Pis. 5:4			
70.	Anyone not in temple keeps second Passover	M. Pes. 9:2; Tos. Pis. 8:2	Sifre Num. 69			
71.	Passover not from tithes		Simeon, p. b. Men. 82a-b 39, Isa. 7-14	Mekh. deR. b. Yev. 46a		
72.	Barbecue Passover [may not be our Eliezar]		Mekh. Ishmael, Lau- terbach, I, p. 50			
73.	Sacrifice Passover in evening		Sifre Deut. 133	b. Ber. 9a		
74.	Sanctified property including cattle—disposition	M. Sheq. 4:7; Tos. Sheq. 2:10				

No.				
77.	High priest counts sprinklings	Tos. Kip. 2:16		
78.	High priest sprinkled in place	M. Yoma 5:5		
79.	If goat fell ill	Tos. Kip. 3:14; M. Yoma 7:3		b. Yoma 66b
80.	Lambs offered in morning	M. Yoma 7:3; Tos. Kip. 3:19		
81.	Sukkah-like cone-shaped hut	M. Suk. 1:11; Tos. Suk. 1:10		
82.	Spreading cloth over sukkah	Tos. Suk. 1:9		
83.	Bake for Sabbath + festival		Mekh. Ishmael; Lauterbach, II, p. 118	
84.	Sweeping chips, etc., on festival	M. Bes. 4:6-7; Tos. Y.T. 3:18; Tos. Y.T. 3:2		
85.	Animal and offspring in pit	Tos. Y.T. 3:2		
86.	When to say rain prayer	M. Ta. 1:1		
87.	Rained before fast was done	M. Ta. 3:9		
88.	Asseret-like Sabbath	M. M.Q. 3:6		
89.	Mourners + tefillin			y. M.Q. 3:5
89A.	Mourners overturn beds			y. M.Q. 3:5; b. M.Q. 21a
90.	Leper + tefillin		Sifra Tazria 12:6	
91.	Mourners re festival			b. M.Q. 20a
92.	Eunuch re halisah	M. Yev. 8:4		
93.	Halisah at night	M. Yev. 12:2		
94.	Said words but did not spit at halisah	M. Yev. 12:3; Tos. Yev. 12:11	Sifre Deut. 291	
95.	Deed of female minor is nothing	M. Yev. 13:2; Tos. Yev. 13:3-5; 12:12		
96.	Divorce wife + remarry her—she cannot marry levir	M. Yev. 13:6		
97.	Minor told to exercise rite of refusal	M. Yev. 13:7		Story: y. Yev. 13:2

Item		I Mishnah-Tosefta	II Tannaitic Midrashim	III Baraita-Stratum in the Talmuds	IV Amoraic Materials in the Talmuds	V Later Compilations
98.	Permitted to deceased Levirs = permitted to all	M. Yev. 16:2; Tos. Yev. 14:3				
99.	Widow may not remarry on evidence of one witness	M. Yev. 16:7				
100.	One offering for each act of sin (see no. 158)	Tos. Yev. 11:14				
101.	Uncircumcized priest may not eat heave offering				b. Yev. 70a	
102.	Proselyte does not have to immerse			b. Yev. 46a		
103-6.	Claims of virginity, etc.— rules of evidence	M. Ket. 1:6-9; Tos. Ket. 1:6				
107.	Orphan has right to usufruct	Tos. Ket. 11:4				
108.	Nurse for 24 months	Tos. Nid. 2:3		b. Yev. 34b, 60b; y. Ket. 5:6; y. Nid. 1:4		
109-10.	Releasing vows	M. Ned. 9:1-2				
111.	Husband annuls vows of bogeret	M. Ned. 10:5				
112.	Levir annuls vows	M. Ned. 10:6				
113.	Annul vow in advance	M. Ned. 10:7; M. Ned. 6:5				

Item	Mishnah-Tosefta	Tannaitic Midrashim	Baraita-Stratum in the Talmuds	Amoraic Materials in the Talmuds	Later Compilations
114-16.	Unclean Nazir loses 7/30 days	M. Naz. 3:3-5; Tos. Naz. 2:2-13, 4:8			
117.	Nazir unclean during sacrifices loses all	M. Naz. 6:11; Tos. Naz. 4:9-10			
118.	High priest and Nazir re neglected corpse	M. Naz. 7:1			
119.	Warn wife before two	M. Sot. 1:1			
120.	Do not teach daughter Torah	M. Sot. 3:4		(Num. R. 9:48)	
121.	Evidence against wife	M. Sot. 6:1			
122-24.	Neglected corpse	M. Sot. 9:2-4			
125.	Testify re get	M. Git. 1:1			
126.	Exception in divorce	M. Git. 9:1; Tos. Git. 9:1-5			
127.	New-produce taboo applies abroad	M. Qid. 1:9			
128.	Purify mamzer	M. Qid. 3:13			
129.	Guilt offering subject to rule of sin offering	M. Zev. 1:1			
130.	Other animal sacrificed on 14th of Nisan offered for Passover	Tos. Pis. 4:5-6			
131.	Slaughter with wrong intention	M. Zev. 3:3; Tos. Zev. 2:16			
132.	If no blood, no flesh; but if no flesh, there is blood	Tos. Zev. 4:1-2			
133.	Whole offering of bird offered below line subject to	M. Zev. 7:4; Tos. Zev. 7:16-20		b. Zev. 67a (Joshua wins)	
134.	Limbs of sin offering mixed with those of whole offering	M. Zev. 8:4; Tos. Zev. 8:15			
135-40.	Mixture of limbs, bloods, etc.	M. Zev. 8:5, 7, 8, 9, 10, 11, 12; Tos. Zev. 8:19, 20, 21, 23, 24			

	I	II	III	IV	V
Item	Mishnah-Tosefta	Tannaitic Midrashim	Baraita-Stratum in the Talmuds	Amoraic Materials in the Talmuds	Later Compilations
141.	Meal offering with wrong intention	M. Men. 3:1; Tos. Men. 2:16			
142.	Residue of meal offering contracted uncleanness—sacrifice is valid	M. Men. 3:4; Tos. Men. 4:2, 5, 6			
143.	Bread is sanctified even if thanks offering is blemished	M. Men. 7:3; Tos. Men. 8:19			
144.	Date of Pentecost			b. Men. 65b	
145.	Slaughter dying animal	M. Hul. 2:6; Tos. Hul. 2:11			
146.	Cock partridge	M. Hul. 12:2			
147.	Redeem firstling with hybrid	M. Bekh. 1:5			
148.	Liability for redemption money set aside for firstling	M. Bekh. 1:6; M. Ed. 7:1			
149.	Slit ear of firstling	M. Bekh. 5:3			
150.	Dedicated goods—re divorce	M. Ar. 6:1			
151.	No pledge of utensils of one's livelihood	M. Ar. 6:3; Tos. Ar. 4:6			
152.	Cannot dedicate to temple all of one's goods	M. Ar. 8:4; Tos. Ar. 4:24			
153.	Progeny of peace offerings may not be offered as peace offerings	M. Tem. 3:1			
154.	Progeny of guilt offering	M. Tem. 3:3C–E			
155.	Guilt offering whose owner has died	M. Tem. 3:3F–H			
156.	Progeny of terefah	M. Tem. 6:3			

mitted

159.	Suspensive guilt offering offered any time	M. Ker. 6:1, 3; Tos. Ker. 4:4	
160-62.	Flesh of Most Holy Things which went out before sprinkling of blood are subject to law of sacrilege, etc.	M. Me. 1:2-3; Tos. Me. 1:4, 6; Tos. Men. 4:10, 4:14-15; Tos. Zev. 4:5, 8	
163.	Fire in own property	M. B.Q. 6:4; Tos. B.Q. 6:22	
164.	Acquire property by walking [?]	Tos. B.B. 2:11	
165.	Verbal division of property	M. B.B. 9:7; Tos. B.B. 10:12	
166.	No trial for wild animals	M. Sanh. 1:4; Tos. Sanh. 3:1	
167.	Hang those stoned to death	M. Sanh. 6:4 Tos. Sanh. 9:6	Sifre Deut. 221
168.	Liability for unawareness of creeping thing + temple	M. Shav. 2:5; Tos. Shav. 1:6	
169.	Comb of watercooler unclean	M. Kel. 2:8; Tos. Kel. B.Q. 2:8; Tos. Ed. 2:1	
170.	Size of hole to render lamp insusceptible to uncleanness—perutah	M. Kel. 3:2	
171.	Oven of Akhnai	M. Kel. 5:10; Tos. Ed. 2:1; M. Ed. 7:7	b. B.M. 59b
172.	Insect in divided oven does not render food unclean	M. Kel. 8:1; Tos. Kel. B.M. 6:4	
172A.	Metal vessel = no. 170 B.M. 4:2	M. Kel. 14:1; Tos. Kel.	
173.	Clean broken metal vessel	M. Kel. 14:7; Tos. Kel. B.M. 4:14	

Item	I Mishnah-Tosefta	II Tannaitic Midrashim	III Baraita-Stratum in the Talmuds	IV Amoraic Materials in the Talmuds	V Later Compilations
174.	Baker's shelf attached to wall is clean	M. Kel. 15:2; M. Ed. 7:7; Tos. Ed. 2:1, 3:1; M. Ed. 7:7			
175.	Wooden vessel = no. 170	M. Kel. 17:1			
176.	Money pouch is unclean	M. Kel. 26:2; Tos. Kel. B.B. 4:3			
177.	Shoe on last is clean	M. Kel. 26:4; Tos. Kel. B.B. 4:7; Tos. Ed. 2:1			
178.	Throwing away piece of new cloth does not make it cloth	M. Kel. 27:2			
179.	Small cloth used as rag is clean	M. Kel. 28:2			
180.	Worm from corpse is unclean	M. Oh. 2:2F			
181.	Ashes of cremated corpse	M. Oh. 2:21			
182.	Gravestone renders unclean by carrying	M. Oh. 2:4; Tos. Ah. 3:7			
183.	Vessels under bier are clean	M. Oh. 6:1; Tos. Ah. 7:1			
184.	Uncleanness of tomb	M. Oh. 9:15			
185.	Projecting windowsill does not bring in uncleanness	M. Oh. 12:3; Tos. Ah. 13:3			
186.	Olive's bulk of corpse on threshold makes house unclean	M. Oh. 12:8; Tos. Oh. 13:10			
187-88.	Wall projection house unclean (= nos. 185-86)	M. Oh. 14:4-5; Tos. Ah. 13:12			
189.	Grave area makes grave area	M. Oh. 17:2			
190-91.	One who intentionally removed signs of uncleanness—signs of purification	M. Neg. 7:4-5			

Item	I Mishnah-Tosefta	II Tannaitic Midrashim	III Baraita-Stratum in the Talmuds	IV Amoraic Materials in the Talmuds	V Later Compilations
214.	Quarter log of drawn water at the outset invalidates ritual pool	M. Miq. 2:4; Tos. Miq. 3:1			
215.	Using water collected in pot in ritual pool	M. Miq. 2:8			
216.	May not immerse in ritual pool	M. Miq. 2:10			
217.	Four types of women rely on normal period in determining cleanness	M. Nid. 1:3			
218.	Also a woman past menopause	M. Nid. 1:5			
219.	Hard labor three days out of eleven + 24 hrs. of relief = she is one who gives birth while in flux	M. Nid. 4:4			
220.	Hard labor during eighty days of female purification produces unclean blood	M. Nid. 4:6			
221.	Zab who examined first and seventh day is presumed to have been clean throughout intervening days	M. Nid. 10:3; Tos. Nid. 9:13			
222.	Zab's semen does not render susceptible to uncleanness	M. Maksh. 6:6			
223.	He who carries carrion is unclean	M. Zab. 5:3			
224.	He who carries flux of Zab, etc., is unclean	M. Zab. 5:7; Tos. Zab. 5:2			
225.	Beehive is like real estate	M. Shev. 10:7 = M. Uqs. 3:10; Tos. Uqs. 3:15			

Item	Mishnah-Tosefta	Tannaitic Midrashim	Baraita-Stratum in the Talmuds	Amoraic Materials in the Talmuds	Later Compilations
226. Woman may wear tiara on Sabbath	M. Ed. 2:7 (M. Shab. 6:1); Tos. Ed. 1:10				
227. Pigeon racers are eligible to give testimony	M. Ed. 2:7 (M. Sanh. 3:3—Anonymous); Tos. Ed. 1:10				
228. Limb from a living being even less than olive's bulk is unclean	M. Ed. 6:2-3				

II. Biographical Units

Item	Mishnah-Tosefta	Tannaitic Midrashim	Baraita-Stratum in the Talmuds	Amoraic Materials in the Talmuds	Later Compilations
229. Destruction of temple marked decline sages (Tos.: When Eliezer died)	M. Sot. 9:15; Tos. Sot. 15:3				
230. Three sayings	M. Avot. 2:10			b. Shab. 153a	ARN chap. 15, etc.
231. Built temple walls outside curtains	M. Ed. 8:6				
232. Gathering cucumbers by sorcery	Tos. Sanh. 11:5 (Aqiba)		y. Sanh. 7:13 (Joshua)		
233. Eliezer arrested for minut	Tos. Hul. 2:24		b. A.Z. 16b-17a		
234. Ammon and Moab pay poorman's tithe	M. Yad. 4:3; Tos. Yad. 2:16		(b. Yev. 16a = Dosa)		
235. Eliezer sick + Tarfon, Joshua, Eleazar b. Azariah, Aqiba visit him		Mekh. Bahodesh 10:58-86			
236. Eliezer at wedding of Gamaliel's son		Sifre Deut. 38			
237. Eliezer's court is a good one		Sifre Deut. 144	b. Sanh. 32a		
238. Death scenes (various types)			y. Shab. 2:7; b. Sanh. 68a, etc.	y. Sot. 9:16; y. A.Z. 3:1	
239. Whoever has a scrap of bread and fears for the morrow has no faith			b. Sot. 48b		
240. Oven of Akhnai			b. B.M. 59b		

Item	I Mishnah-Tosefta	II Tannaitic Midrashim	III Baraita-Stratum in the Talmuds	IV Amoraic Materials in the Talmuds	V Later Compilations
241.	Eye of Leviathan		b. B.B. 74b		
242.	On 15th of Av wood no longer cut		b. B.B. 121b		
243.	Tefillin at all times			y. Ber. 2:3	
244.	Onqelos's Targum on the au- thority of Eliezer + Joshua			y. Meg. 1:9	
245.	Eliezer + Joshua at home of Abbuya re circumcision of Elisha			y. Hag. 2:1	
246.	Aqiba studied with Eliezer + Joshua			y. Naz. 7:1; b. Ned. 50a	
247.	Yohanan b. Zakkai ordained Eliezer + Joshua			y. Sanh. 1:2	
248.	Collected funds with Joshua + Aqiba			y. Hor. 3:4	
249.	Elizer and Joshua helped Yohanan escape from Jerusalem			b. Git. 56a	ARN chap. 4
250.	Honor father before mother			b. Qid. 31a	(Num. R. 1:15)
251.	To have sons, give to the poor, etc.			b. B.B. 10a	Kallah R. 52b
252.	Had intercourse at midnight			b. Ned. 20b	
253.	Children born with defects because women refuse intercourse				Kallah R. 1:1, 51b
254.	Mamzer is boldfaced				Kallah R. 2:1, 52a
255.	Eliezer knew seventy lan- guages			b. Sanh. 17b	
256.	The origins of Eliezer				ARN chap. 6, Gen. R. 42:1, Tanhuma, Buber I, 34b-35a, PRE chaps. 1-2

III. Exegetical Units

260-62.	Generation of wilderness have share in world to come; Qorah will be forgiven; Ten Tribes will return, etc.	M. Sanh. 10:3; Tos. Sanh. 13:10		b. Sanh. 110b	
263.	Gentiles have no share in world to come	Tos. Sanh. 13:2		b. Sanh. 105a	Mid. Ps. 9:5
264.	Men of Sodom have no portion in world to come				ARN chap. 3:6
265.	Exod. 12:1		Mekh. Pisha 1:114		
266.	Sukkoth was place where they built booths		Mekh. Pisha 14:11-22; Sifra Emor 17:11		
267.	Idol crossed sea with Israelites		Mekh. Pisha 14:95; Sifre Num. 84		
268.	Redemption will come in Tishri, not Nisan		Mekh. Pisha 14:113; Mekh. deR. Simeon to Exod. 12:42		
(268A.	World created in Tishri)			b. R.H. 10b-12a	
269.	Exod. 13:18		Mekh. Beshallah 1:57-69		
270.	Exod. 14:2: What were Hirot?		Mekh. Beshallah 2:8-15		
271.	Two hundred plagues at sea		Mekh. Beshallah 7:109-21		
272.	Taste of manna		Mekh. Vayassa 6:27-29		
273.	Exod. 15:2		Mekh. Vayasa 1:1-12		
274.	Exod. 17:16		Mekh. Amalek 2:186-92		
275.	Exod. 17:13		Mekh. Amalek 1:173-75		Mid. Ps. 9:10
276.	Blot out memory of Amalek				Lam. R. 3:66

Item	I Mishnah-Tosefta	II Tannaitic Midrashim	III Baraita-Stratum in the Talmuds	IV Amoraic Materials in the Talmuds	V Later Compilations
277.	Rephidim and shittim		b. Bekh. 5b; b. Sanh. 106a		
278.	How God saved Moses at Pharaoh's court	Mekh. Amalek 3:127-40			
279.	Exod. 19:5—What is covenant?	Mekh. Bahodesh 2:43-45; Mekh. deR Simeon to Exod. 13:10, 19:5			Pes. R. 23 Aggad. Ber. 17:2
280.	Exod. 19:19	Mekh. Bahodesh 4:36-44			
281.	God revealed self in bush to show redemption follows degradation	Mekh. deR. Simeon, p. 1; Isa. 12-18			
282.	Milk + honey	Mekh. deR. Simeon to Exod. 13:5			
283.	Aaron's sons died outside tent	Sifra Mekh. deMil. 2:35			
284.	God warns before punishing people	Sifra Beh. 5:1			
285.	Deut. 3:26	Sifre Deut. 29 Mid. Tan. to Deut. 3:26			
286.	With all your soul vs. might	Sifre Deut. 32			
287.	Moses saw whole land	Sifre Num. 136; Sifre Deut. 338			
288.	Serving temple brings man to study Torah	Mid. Tan. to Deut. 14:22			

289.	Man's agent is like himself			
290.	Isa. 1:18	y. Shab. 9:3		
291.	Redemption depends on repentence	y. Ta. 1:1, b. Sanh. 97a–98a		
292.	Deut. 28:10 refers to tefillin	b. Ber. 6a		
293.	Gen. 49:4 re Reuben	b. Shab. 55b	b. Eruv. 40b	Pes. R. Kah., p. 419; Isa. 10-13
294.	Qoh. R. 11:2 refers to creation, circumcision			
295.	Psalms refer to David himself	b. Pes. 117a		
296.	World draws water from ocean	b. Ta. 9b		Gen. R. 13:9-10
297.	Ezekiel's dead sang I Sam. 2:6	b. Sanh. 92b		
298.	World is lik exedra	b. B.B. 25a-b		
299.	World created from center	b. Yoma 54b		
300.	Earth created from earth, heaven from heaven	b. Yoma 54b		Gen. R. 12:11
301.	Job sought to turn the dish upside down	b. B.B. 16a		
302.	Patriarchs could not stand before diving reproof	b. Ar. 17a		
303.	Reprove until beaten	b. Ar. 16b		
304.	Gen. 40:10 refers to patriarchs	b. Hul. 92a		
305.	Prov. 14:34		b. B.B. 10b	Pes. deR. Kah., p. 20; Isa. 6-11, etc.
306.	Divine names in reference to Naboth are sacred		b. Shav. 35b	

Item	I Mishnah-Tosefta	II Tannaitic Midrashim	III Baraita-Stratum in the Talmuds	IV Amoraic Materials in the Talmuds	V Later Compilations
307.	Solomon built gates for bridegrooms and mourners				Soferim 42b
308.	Sea absorbed waters—Ps. 93:3				Gen. R. 5:3
309.	Planets functioned during flood				Gen. R. 25:2
310.	Sow early and late				Gen. R. 61:3
311.	Gen. 49:3				Gen. R. 98:4
312.	Wickedness of court—Qoh. 3:16				Lev. R. 4:1
313.	Job. 38:8 + Lev. 12:2				Lev. R. 14:4
314.	Song of Sol. 5:11				Lev. R. 19:1
315.	Reuben—Gen. 37:29				Pes. deR. Kah., p. 356; Isa. 6-11
316.	Ps. 139:16				Pes. Rab. 23:1; Tanh. Ber. 28
317.	Recompense for woman falsely accused (Num. 5:28)				Num. R. 9:25
318.	Angel spoke through Balaam				Num. R. 20:18
319.	Ruth 4:1				Ruth R. 7:7
320.	Song of Sol. 6:10				Mid. Ps. 22:12
321.	Ps. 90:15				Ps. 90:4

The Talmuds' Contribution and the Bavli's Contribution

Clearly, the Bavli's contribution to the formation of the topical repertoire of units-of-discourse categories by the name of a sage shares traits both with the Yerushalmi and the collections of scriptural exegeses. As in the Yerushalmi so in the Bavli we observe a strong tendency for biographical materials to make their first appearance only in the talmudic stratum. Hence the two Talmuds cannot be differentiated in this aspect. Like the collections of exegetical scriptural exegeses, on the other hand, the Bavli makes its share of contributions of scriptural exegeses to the formation of the larger corpus of units of traditions distinguished by the occurrence of a given sage's name. This result, as noted, confirms the earlier one, which showed us a far more pronounced tendency in the Bavli than in the Yerushalmi to organize large-scale discourse around biblical heroes and topics.

Our purpose in the present exercise has now been fully realized. We wanted to know about the topical preferences of the Bavli in particular. We have found out about topical preference traits that the Bavli shares with the Yerushalmi, on the one side, and with the collections of scriptural exegeses, on the other. The upshot is that Bavli stands in conclusion and at the end in two respects. It shares the powerful interest, exhibited (by definition) by compilations of scriptural exegeses, in organizing materials around verses of Scripture. It also shares with the Yerushalmi the pronounced trait of contributing sage units, materials framed around biographical (or broader historical) topics. But, it goes without saying, the Yerushalmi does not exhibit as a principal trait the topical program of introducing scriptural exegeses. The compilations of scriptural exegeses obviously do not compare to the Yerushalmi in their principal topical program. Since as to topic, the two Talmuds are alike in what they contribute, the urgent question now becomes whether we can distinguish the Bavli from the Yerushalmi in the dimension of rhetoric—for that is all that remains as a criterion for distinguishing the one Talmud from the other.

8

The Matter of Rhetoric

Differentiating among Documents by Parsing Stories

Differentiating one document from another by a taxonomy of topics leads us to the striking facts that in some ways the Bavli is like the Yerushalmi and in some ways unlike it; in some ways the Bavli is like collections of scriptural exegeses, and in some ways unlike them. The former of the two results defines the logical next step in the inquiry, since, as we recall, our principal problem to begin with was how the Bavli differs from the Yerushalmi and how it is like the Yerushalmi. Accordingly, we turn to further analysis of that aspect in which the Yerushalmi and the Bavli intersect, namely, their shared interest in contributing to the unfolding canonical corpus of Judaism, stories about sages in particular. That interest, as we just saw, marks the two Talmuds as sharply distinct from the Mishnah, more than marginally distinct from the Tosefta, and quite different from the collections of scriptural exegeses.

But how do the two Talmuds in this aspect relate to one another? The answer obviously derives from the data on how, when dealing with sayings and stories, the Bavli differs from the Yerushalmi and how it is like the Yerushalmi. Since we are focusing on the Bavli, we have to see whether the relationships we discern between the Yerushalmi's treatment of sayings and stories and the Bavli's disposal of these same materials also characterize the Bavli's relationships to other prior compilations now in the larger canon.

I phrase matters in terms of rhetoric because the issue of rhetoric encompasses how materials are worked over so as to win their audience. In the present context we therefore ask about the rhetorical policies of framers of materials located in the Bavli as compared to the policies of the authors of the same materials located in earlier documents. We ask what changes the Bavli's authors consistently introduced into received materials. When we discern a consistent policy of revision, we reasonably suppose that the authors assumed the story in hand would attain greater credibility or interest, and hence persuasive power, on account of the addition.

What the comparisons that follow show, therefore, is the rhetorical power consistently displayed by the Bavli's writers. How so? They revise, augment, amplify, and rework earlier materials to heighten their effect, to underline their main point, to give larger meaning to a simple statement or to an unadorned saying. The rhetoricians before us consistently and ubiquitously reworked everything they received from earlier authors, except for what they got from the Mishnah. They operated within the restraints imposed by the original wording of other-than-Mishnah materials, but then exercised unlimited freedom to add and, through the effects of these additions, to change much of everything else.

If, then, we ask how the rhetoric of the Bavli serves to impose a conclusion upon what had gone before, we find a simple answer. The Bavli's writers made certain that the conclusions implied earlier were made explicit. The stories earlier told in bare-bones fashion now were fully exposed in rich detail. All things in their hands reached ample and complete expression. The task of completing the inherited corpus and giving it its definitive form demanded provision of that last, missing but ineluctable detail. It required patient polishing and securely fastening upon the pedestal the tableaux and icons made of words that had come down from earlier components of that canon.

To identify the distinctive rhetorical preferences of the Bavli's writers, therefore, we compare what had come before with what they produced. Where we find elements of a composition given in word-for-word correspondences between what is given in prior compositions and what occurs in the Bavli, we conclude that the Bavli's authors received and revised these earlier compositions. Then the new points that appear in the version of the matter given by the Bavli accrue to the credit of the Bavli's authors. These additions are what testify to their larger tendencies. Tendencies in rhetoric, as much as the ones we discern in their redactional work, convey the intent of the Bavli's authorities.

To introduce the exercises that follow, let me begin with a comparison of a single passage as it makes its way from Mekhilta, generally thought to be an early composition of exegeses of Scripture, to the Tosefta, thence to the Yerushalmi, and finally to the Bavli. Here we see precisely how the sages who received a piece of composition proposed to preserve the given but also to transmit something new. The passage at hand complements M. Hag. 2:1-2, which refers to a corpus of doctrine connected to Ezekiel's vision of the chariot (Ezek. chap. 1). In the left-hand column I present the matter as it occurs in the Mekhilta attributed to R. Simeon. In the next, I give the Tosefta's version, in the third, the Yerushalmi's, and in the fourth, the Bavli's.

Mekhilta de R. Simeon	Tos. Hag 2:1-2	y. Hag. 2:1	b. Hag. 14b
And the story is told that Yohanan was	*(See Mekhilta de R. Simeon.)*	*(See Mekhilta de R. Simeon.)* going	*Teno rabbanan.* The story is told that

Mekhilta de R. Simeon	Tos. Hag 2:1–2	y. Hag. 2:1	b. Hag. 14b
riding on an ass and going out of Jerusalem.		on the way riding on an ass	Yohanan was riding an ass and going on the way, and Eleazar was driving the ass.
Eleazar b. Arakh his disciple was going behind him. Eleazar: Teach me a chapter in the Merkavah.	Driving the ass *(See Mekhilta de R. Simeon.)*	going *(See Mekhilta de R. Simeon.)*	*(See Mekhilta de R. Simeon.)*
Yohanan: Have I not *taught* you. Not of the Merkavah . . . understand of his own knowledge.	told	*(See Mekhilta de R. Simeon.)*	taught
If not, give me permission to speak before you.	*(See Mekhilta de R. Simeon.)*	*(See Mekhilta de R. Simeon.)*	before you *something you taught me*
	Yohanan descended from the ass, covered self with cloak; both sat on a stone under an olive tree.	Yohanan descended saying, It is not lawful that I should hear the glory of my creator and be riding on an ass. They went and sat under the tree.	Forthwith Yohanan descended from the ass, covered himself, and sat on the *stone* under the olive tree. He said to him, Rabbi, why did you descend. He said to him, Is it possible that you should expound the chariot, and the Shekhinah be with us, and the ministering angels accompany us, and I should ride an ass?
Eleazar expounded until flames licked around about.	He lectured before him.	Forthwith all the trees broke out in song and said Ps. 96.	Eleazar opened on the chariot and expounded, and fire went down from heaven and encompassed all the trees roundabout. What song did the trees sing? Ps. 145. An angel answered from the fire and said, These, these are the works of the chariot.
When Yohanan saw the flames, he got	He stood and kissed him and said,	When Eleazar finished the works of	Yohanan stood up and kissed him on

Mekhilta de R. Simeon	Tos. Hag 2:1–2	y. Hag. 2:1	b. Hag. 14b
off the ass, kissed him, and said. Eleazar, Happy she that bore you. Happy Abraham our father that such has come forth from his loins.	Blessed is the Lord God of Israel who gave a son to Abraham our Father who knows how to understand and expound the flory of his father in heaven. Some expound well but do not fulfill well, and vice versa, but Eleazar does both well.	the chariot, Yohanan stood and kissed him on his head and said, Blessed is the Lord, God of Abraham. Jacob who gave to Abraham a son wise and knowing how to expound the glory of our father in heaven. Some preach well . . . Eleazar does both well.	his head and said Blessed is the Lord, God *of Israel* who gave a son to Abraham our father who knows how to understand and *to investigate,* and to expound the chariot. Some preach well, etc. Happy are you Abraham our father that Eleazar has come forth from your loins.
	Happy are you, Abraham our father that Eleazar b. Arakh has come forth from your loins, who knows how to understand and expound the glory of his father in heaven.	Happy are you, Abraham our father, that Eleazar has come forth from your loins.	
He would say, If all sages were on one side of the scale and Eleazar on the other, he would outweigh them all.	R. Yose b. Judah: Joshua lectured before Yohanan, Aqiba before Joshua, Hananiah b. Hakhinai before ʿAqiba.	When Joseph the priest and Simeon b. Natanel heard, they too opened a discourse on the chariot. They said, it was the first day of summer, and the earth trembled, and a rainbow appeared, and an echo came and said to them, Behold the place is ready for you and your disciples are slated for the third class.	And when these things were told to Joshua, he and Yose the priest were walking on the way. They said Let us also expound the chariot. Joshua opened and expounded. That day was the first day of summer, but the heavens clouded over and a kind of a rainbow appeared, and the angels gathered and came to hear like men running to a wedding. Joshua and Yose the priest went and told these things to Yohanan, who said, Happy are you, and happy are those who bore you. Happy are my eyes who have seen such.

And also you and I in my dream were reclining on Mount Sinai and an echo came forth to us from heaven, "Come up hither, come up hither. Your disciples are slated for the third class."

Is this so? And is it not taught? (TNY'):

Joshua laid out matters before Yohanan, Aqiba before Joshua, Hananiah b. Hakhinai before ʿAqiba.

And Eleazar is not mentioned.

It would be difficult to invent a better example of the development of a tradition from simplicity to complexity, from being relatively unadorned to being fully articulated, and from earlier to later versions. In the earliest document the story is shortest and simplest. The Tosefta represents an obvious expansion. The Palestinian talmudic account is still further enriched with details and entirely new components. And the Babylonian version, last of all and youngest in the age of the document in which it appears, clearly is most fully, carefully worked out. The Mekhilta's components are as follows:

1. Yohanan riding an ass
2. Eleazar with him
3. Teach me—it is illegal
4. Then let me speak
5. Eleazar expounded and flames licked round about
6. Then Yohanan blessed him, Your mother and Abraham are happy
7. Scale

The concluding element (no. 7) is a separate and unrelated saying. It plays no integral part whatever in the Merkabah tradition.

The Tosefta's version is close to the foregoing, but it adds that Yohanan ceremoniously descended from the ass before the lecture began. Only then did Eleazar say his sermon. The detail about the flames, on the other hand, is absent. But the blessing is greatly expanded. The praise is now extended to Eleazar's ability to achieve a fully realized mystic experience; he does not merely describe the Merkabah but presumably is able to go down in it. Then a second, and separate, blessing is repeated from Mekhilta beginning, "Happy are you." This clearly indicates dependence, for the first blessing would be sufficient in an independent account. But the second blessing is augmented with reference to the Mekhilta's: Abraham should be happy because you expound well and fulfill well. Thus the narrator tied in the duplicated blessing of the original version. The most important omission is the praise of Eleazar. This is replaced by the story that Joshua did the same before Yohanan, Aqiba afterward, and so forth. The later version thus emphasizes that despite the excellence of Eleazar, which no one denied, the true line of transmission extended through Joshua, not through Eleazar. We may assume the first and simplest version derives from Eleazar's school, and the second has been altered, then handed on in the Joshua-Aqiba line.

The Palestinian version begins as do the early ones. But it adds a careful explanation of why Yohanan got off the ass. This explanation is itself rather fulsome. Only afterward do the master and disciple sit down—under a tree, the olive is lost. Then fire comes down, but this detail, from the Mekhilta version, is greatly embellished. Angels dance as at a wedding. They even praise Eleazar's sermon before Yohanan has a chance to say anything. He plays no part in the proliferating details. Then the trees sing a Psalm. Only after the expanded element has been completed do we return to the matter of Yohanan. He then kisses Eleazar and gives the double blessing. "Blessed is the Lord . . . , Happy are you, Abraham." Then Joseph/Yose the priest and Simeon are introduced, with further supernatural events accompanying their never-recorded sermon. The echo invites them to the third level of the heavens.

The Babylonian version is augmented in almost every detail. Eleazar is not merely walking but driving the ass. He wants to teach something he has already heard. Not only does Yohanan descend, but Eleazar asks why he did so. This is clearly a point at which the Babylonian version has expanded on a mute detail in the immediately preceding account. Yohanan then develops his earlier saying. It is not merely the glory of the creator, but rather both the Shekhinah and the ministering angels are present. Eleazar speaks, and fire pours from heaven. The trees sing a psalm, this time Ps. 145. An angel repeats the message of the Palestinian version. The order of the trees' psalm and the angels message is therefore reversed. Then comes the kiss—now on his head—and the blessing is expanded to include *to investigate* after *to understand* and *to expound*. The "Some preach well" formula comes verbatim, then the second blessing. Joshua is now the link. The story is drawn from the earlier version. The rainbow is not enough; now the angels come to a wedding—a detail presumably borrowed from the Palestinian dance of the ministering angels. Then Yose told Yohanan, who expressed approval. The heavenly echo of the Palestinian version becomes the whole dream about the circle of

Yohanan on Mount Sinai, with a direct invitation to heaven, both elements based upon and developments of *Behold the place is ready for you.*

As I said, I can think of no better demonstration of the fact that versions of a single story appearing in documents of successive age normally proceed from the simpler to the more complex formulation as they pass from an earlier document to a later one. Since the versions clearly depend on one another, there can be no question as to which comes first, which later, in time of formulation. Let me now generalize on the basis of the demonstration at hand. The framers of the Bavli clearly proposed to contribute their own original ideas to a received tradition. What they wished to do, it further is clear, is to rewrite and revise to suit their tastes about what a full and conclusive account of the matter required.

A single example does not constitute a proof, of course. I cannot say precisely what sort of sample of the whole would be required to establish the simple but critical claim at hand concerning the Bavli's editorial policies and program. One important aspect is whether the same relationship that the Bavli's authors establish to the materials presented to them in the Yerushalmi characterizes their approach to other documents. A second is to see the somewhat more complex interplay among three documents, one of them the Bavli. A third is to ask whether the Bavli's authors find themselves constrained by the details of what the Yerushalmi's authors in particular set down or whether they were prepared to make fundamental changes in the received materials. A fourth is to inquire about whether attribution to Tannaite authority in one of the Talmuds means that a passage enjoyed more protection from the hands of the artists of the Bavli than the absence of such an attribution. We proceed to take up examples pertinent to each of these questions in turn.

From the Yerushalmi to the Fathers according to Rabbi Nathan to the Bavli

In the following exercise, we take up four versions of the death scene of Yohanan ben Zakkai—two occurring in the Yerushalmi, one in the Fathers according to Rabbi Nathan, a document secondary to Mishnah tractate Abot (the "Fathers"), and, finally, the Bavli's version of the same matter.

Y. A.Z. 3:1	Y. Sot 9:16	ARNa Ch. 25	B. Ber. 28b
R. Jacob b. Idi in the name of R. Joshua b. Levi	(see y. A.Z. 3:1)	—	Teno rabbanan. When Eleazar was dying, his disciples came to visit . . .
When Yohanan was dying, he said	commanded and said	—	And when Yohanan fell ill, his disciples came to visit. When he saw them, he wept.

Y. A.Z. 3:1	Y. Sot 9:16	ARNa Ch. 25	B. Ber. 28b
—	—	When Yohanan was dying, he raised his voice and wept.	
—	—	Disciples said, Tall pillar, light of the world, mighty hammer why weep?	Disciples said Light of Israel, right-hand pillar, mighty hammer why weep?
—	—	Do I go to judgment before a mortal kind, who dies and can be bribed? I go before king of kings and don't know his decision. Ps. 22:30	If I were going before mortal king who may be bribed, I'd weep. Now that I go before immortal God, and do not know his decision, should I not weep?
—	—	—	They said, Bless us. He said, May you fear heaven as much as you fear men.
Clear the house because of uncleanness	clear the courtyard	—	When he died, he said, Clear out the vessels and prepare a chair for Hezekiah who comes.
And give a chair for Hezekiah king of Judah.	ordain		
Rabbi Eliezer when dying said	—	—	—
Clear the house because of uncleanness.	—	—	—
And set a chair for Rabban Yohanan ben Zakkai	—	—	—

The two Palestinian talmudic versions are simple and unadorned. That in Y. A.Z. 3:1 includes the death scene of Eliezer, but in proper chronological order, that is, first Yohanan, then Eliezer. The reference to a chair for Yohanan is omitted in the corresponding death scene in B. Ber. 28b, which is as different for Eliezer as it is for Yohanan. Y. Sot. 9:16 omits all reference to Eliezer's death scene. It is otherwise close to the account of Jacob b. Idi in Joshua's name in Y. A.Z. and is given the same attribution. The long beraita in B. Ber. 28b involves an extended account of Eliezer's death, followed by a similarly long version of Yohanan's. The *clear out the vessels,* which is the point of the Palestinian versions, is rather awkwardly tacked on at the end by the device of having the long sermon introduced by *When he was sick,* and the dying words by *In the hour of his death.* The final blessing is included, parallel to that of Eliezer, but of different content. The ARNa version omits all reference to Eliezer. It begins with Yohanan's weeping; the disciples play a less important role, and they do not get a blessing at the end. *Light of Israel* becomes *of the world; right-hand pillar* becomes *tall pillar;* that is, the Babylonian version is more specific and alludes to concrete images. The actual homilies require closer comparison:

ARNa	B. Ber. 28b
Do I go before a king of flesh and blood — whose anger is of this world — whose punishment is of this world — whose death penalty is of this world — who can be bribed with words or money?	If I went before a king of flesh and blood, who is here today and in the grave tomorrow — whose anger is not eternal — whose imprisonment is not eternal — whose death penalty is not eternal And I can bribe him with words or money
I go before King of Kings — whose anger is eternal — who cannot be bribed with words or money	Even so would I weep. I go before the eternal God — whose anger is eternal — whose imprisonment is eternal — whose death penalty is eternal.
Before me are two roads, one to Paradise, one to Gehenna And I do not know to which he will sentence me. And of this the verse says—Ps. 22:30.	And before me are two roads, one to Paradise, one to Gehenna And I do not know to which one he will sentence me. Should I not weep? They said to him, Master, bless us? [As above.]

The homilies are practically identical, certainly close enough to show dependence on one another. It is therefore striking that the concluding blessing is absent in ARNa. The additional clause in the Bavli's version was added so that Yohanan's death scene would be symmetrical to Eliezer's. The same factor accounts for the importance of the disciples in the beraita's death scene, by contrast to their role as mere bystanders in ARNa.

It seems clear that the primary Palestinian version is Y. A.Z. 3:1, for it is unlikely that Jacob b. Idi in Joshua's name would have handed on two separate versions, one long, the other short. Rather the Y. Sot. 9:16 version has merely been shortened by the omission of reference to Eliezer. It is otherwise so close as to be completely dependent on the longer version. There can be no question of relative age. Both appear in the name of the same master and cannot be thought to come from different schools or periods.

The Babylonian and ARNa versions are another matter. I should imagine, following the former analogy, that B. Ber. 28b is the older, more complete version, shaped along the lines of Eliezer's death scene, as I said. ARNa afterward omits the details involving masters other than Yohanan, introduces the exegesis of Ps. 22:30, and concludes with the (probably) famous, "Clear the house . . ."

What are the primary elements of Yohanan's death scene? Clearly they began with "Clear the house . . . prepare a chair," which appears throughout, even to the point of being awkwardly tacked on in B. Ber. 28b and ARNa. In the Palestinian accounts, by contrast, the twofold message fits together without strain. In the ARNa and B. Ber. versions, we thus find five further, certainly later elements:

1. He wept as he was sick/dying,
2. Disciples [came to visit and] asked why,
3. And heaped on him encomia,
4. He replied saying he was going to eternal judgment and did not know the likely decision
5. [They asked to be blessed].

I see no reason to suppose all these elements are not late inventions, coming long after the very simple account of Joshua b. Levi. They cannot be called "expansions" of Joshua's account; indeed they bear little or no relationship to it. Rather they make use of some of the same materials as Joshua, particularly the *Clear the house . . . set a chair.* These may not have been original with Joshua. We do not have to imagine the Bavli's version was shaped by masters who had never heard Joshua's version. Indeed, I doubt they did.

To conclude: The death scene went from the simple to the complex, and from the Palestinian Talmud's attribution by Jacob b. Idi to R. Joshua, on the one hand, to the fully articulated beraita-form *(Teno rabbanan)* on the other. ARNa again seems closer to the Babylonian beraita than to the simpler Palestinian version. It seems possible that the question of the date of the ARNa will have to be restudied, for it sometimes conforms not to the earlier Palestinian versions but to the substantially later Babylonian ones. Even though all authorities derive from the third century or earlier, the forms of important sayings that do exhibit Babylonian parallels normally adhere to those Babylonian parallels, hence to later, Babylonian developments of Palestinian materials or to materials invented to begin with in the Babylonian schools.

We once again see clearly that a passage frequently shows development and elaboration when it appears in later documents, with the Bavli at the end of the line more often than not. Details are added later on. As we follow stories through several recensions, we find that passages are normally developed, details are added, and, as I said, the Bavli's version commonly is the fullest and best elaborated.

From the Sifre on Deuteronomy to the Bavli

Sifre Deut. 144	B. San. 32b
Righteousness . . . shall pursue.	*Teno rabbanan.*
Go after a good court.	Righteousness . . . shall pursue.
After the court of Yohanan.	Go after a good court.
After the court of Eliezer.	After the court of Eliezer in Lud.
	After the court Yohanan in Beror Hayil.
	Teno rabbanan.
	Righteousness . . . shall pursue.
	Go after the sages to the academy [yeshivah].
	After Eliezer to Lud.
	After Yohanan to Beror Hayil.
	After Joshua to Peqiin.
	After Gamaliel to Yavneh.
	After Aqiva to Bnei Beraq.
	After Matthew to Rome.
	After Hananiah b. Teradion to Sikhnin.
	After Yose to Sepphoris.
	After Judah b. Bathyra to Nisibis.
	After Hananiah nephew of R. Joshua to the Exile.
	After Rabbi [Judah] to Beth Shearim.
	After the sages to the hewn stone chamber.

The two versions appear in sequence in the Babylonian Talmud. The latter of the two obviously is an expansion of the former, the brief and simple version of Sifre Deut. It adds the details of where their courts were. I think it unlikely that, had those details been at first included, they would later on have been suppressed. It would have deprived the disciples of useful information, and there was no good reason to do so. The longer entry cannot date from earlier than the first third of the third century. We see the immense expansion of the Sifre. Eliezer and Yohanan keep their places. Then follows the first generation of Yavneh, that is, Joshua and Gamaliel; then the generation of Aqiba; then the one immediately following the Bar Kokhba War; finally Judah; and at the end, the sages to the (eschatological?) hewn stone chamber. It is again noteworthy that the version appearing in the later document is elaborated and clearly later than the version appearing in the earlier document.

From the Yerushalmi to Bavli

We come now to two simple instances in which materials occur in the Yerushalmi and then in the Bavli, with no intervening stage (if that is what the Fathers according to Rabbi Nathan represents) and little complexity.

The Mishnah (M. Ber. 9:3) states that if one is coming along the way and hears an outcry and says, "May it be his will that this does not come from my house," that is a false prayer. We then find the following:

> He was coming from the way, what does he say? "I am sure that these are not in my house."
> Hillel the Elder says, "From a bad report he does not fear" (Ps. 112:7).

The next version is attributed to Tannaim, with the redactional superscription. Our rabbis taught *(Teno rabbanan)*, then given a duplicated superscription, story about (Maaseh b). It follows:

> Hillel the Elder was coming from a journey, and he heard the sound of an outcry in the city. He said, "I am sure this is not my house."
> And of him Scripture says, "From a bad report he does not fear: his heart is steadfast, trusting in the Lord (Ps. 112:7)."

Hillel's "exegesis" of Ps. 112:7 thus is turned into a story. The verse of Scripture cited concerning Hillel is made to say in the second story what anyone is supposed to say according to the first version. I take it for granted that the Bavli's version comes later than, and is based upon, the Palestinian talmudic version (which is not given a Tannaitic attribution). The word-for-word correspondences make this virtually certain, and the movement from an anonymous to a named teaching seems to me decisive evidence that the Babylonian version depends upon the Palestinian.

The second story bears attribution, in the Bavli's version, to Tannaite authority. While such an attribution is commonly interpreted to mean that the story derives from authorities who occur, also, in the Mishnah and hence from the second century or before, the example at hand will not sustain that theory of the matter. From the present perspective that is a tangential point. The main thing, once more, is simply to see what the Bavli is prepared to do with materials first used in the Yerushalmi. In the present exercise, however, I list the Bavli first, then the Yerushalmi, to show that the result remains the same, however we arrange the sources. We begin with the texts under study.

A.   Our rabbis taught (TNW RBNN): The story is told about (M'SH B) a certain man whose sons did not conduct themselves in a proper manner. He arose and wrote his estate over to Jonathan b. Uzziel. What did Jonathan b. Uzziel do? He sold a third, consecrated a third, and returned a third to his sons [of the man].

B.   Shammai came upon him with his staff and bag.
     He said to him, "Shammai, if you can take back what I have sold and what I have consecrated, you can also take back what I have returned. But if not, neither can you take back what I have returned."

C.   He exclaimed, "The son of Uzziel has confounded me, the son of
     Uzziel has confounded me."
     —B. Baba Batra 133b–134a; trans. I. W. Slotki, 562

The setting is supplied by a saying of Samuel to Judah not to transfer in-
heritances even from bad sons to good ones. What is even more interesting is
the following story, which concerns the disciples of Hillel: The greatest of
them was Jonathan, the least was Yohanan ben Zakkai. So the framework is a
set of pericopes on the greatness of Jonathan b. Uzziel, and the above story is,
with interruptions and glosses, in fact part of a small Jonathan b. Uzziel
tractate.

The story seems to be a unity, but only if it depends on Y. Ned. 5:6, which
follows. Otherwise, part B is certainly separate, for we have no hint of Shammai's involvement in part A. Here is the Yerushalmi's version:

A.   Said Rabbi Yose b. Rabbi Bun, "Thus was the case ['BD']:
     Jonathan b. Uzziel's father foreswore him from his property, and
     arose and wrote them over to Shammai.
B.   "What did Shammai do? He sold part, sanctified part, and gave
     the rest to him [Jonathan] as a gift, and said, 'Whoever will come
     and complain against this gift, let him remove the property from
     the purchasers and from the sanctuary and afterward he may re-
     move the property from him too.'"
     —Y. Nedarim 5:6

The Palestinian version of the Jonathan story is strikingly different from the
Babylonian beraita. Here the gift is to Shammai, who acts on behalf of
Jonathan by saving for him part of the father's property. Shammai's presence is
now comprehensible. This is the whole pericope. The story certainly is a unitary composition. No element comes as a surprise; nothing is intruded. Now
to the comparison:

B. B.B. 133b–134a	Y. Ned. 5:6
1. TNW RBNN	1. R. Yose b. R. Bun said
2. *Ma'aseh b-*	2. Thus was the thing ('BD')
3. One man whose sons did not behave according to rule.	3. —
4. He rose and wrote his property to Jonathan b. Uzziel.	4. Jonathan b. Uzziel's father prevented him by vow from his property and rose and wrote them to Shammai.
5. What did Jonathan b. Uzziel do?	5. What did Shammai do?
6. He sold a third	6. He sold part
7. consecrated a third	7. consecrated part
8. and returned a third to his sons.	8. and gave him the rest as a gift.

B. B.B. 133b–134a	Y. Ned. 5:6
9. Shammai came to him in his staff and bag.	9. —
10. He said to him, Shammai, if you can take away what I have sold and what I have consecrated, you can take away what I have returned.	10. He [Shammai] said, Whoever will come and complain against this gift, let him retrieve the property from the sanctuary, and afterward let him remove it from this one.
11. If not, you cannot take away what I have returned.	11. [As above]
12. He said, Ben Uzziel has confounded me [twice].	12. —

One version completely reverses the account of the other. The first question is Which comes first? It seems to me that the Palestinian version absolutely must precede the Babylonian beraita and that the latter certainly had to have been shaped in complete dependency upon it. Why so sure? The decisive fact is the intrusion of Shammai into the Babylonian version in no. 9. Who mentioned his name? Only in the Palestinian version is Shammai integral to the story. One could certainly divide the beraita into fragments of two independent stories, one in which Jonathan b. Uzziel plays the major and affirmative role, the other in which Shammai somehow is brought into play. But that theoretical division seems unlikely since the Palestinian account supplies a complete and unitary story. Both parties there play a part from the outset. No one has to be intruded afterward.

The Babylonian version has translated 'BD' into its conventional superscription, *ma'aseh b.* It has supplied the reason for the disinheritance. In the Palestinian version we understand at the very outset why Jonathan was included—it was his own father. In the Babylonian, we are as mystified by the flight to Jonathan as by the intrusion of Shammai.

The Babylonian concretizes *part* to *third,* obvious but still an improvement. The action of Shammai in the Palestinian version is now copied by Jonathan in the other. Since Shammai is involved in the Palestinian one, the Babylonians have to invent a dramatic encounter to bring in Shammai. Now "whoever will come" is turned into "Shammai, if you." The elements of no. 10 are otherwise not much different. The beraita is somewhat more fluent: if you can do this, you can do that and if you cannot do this, you cannot do that. The Palestinian has thus been improved by the division into affirmative and negative clauses, thus making a binding condition, and the references to purchasers/sanctuary are turned into active verbs. The absence of no. 12 in the Palestinian version is for obvious reasons. So the Babylonian version is certainly later than the Palestinian one.

From Josephus to the Bavli

Since Josephus wrote his works in Aramaic and then had them translated into Greek, we may hardly be surprised to find in rabbinic documents familiarity with materials also known to us in the writings of Josephus. To begin with, let us deal with the relevant passages as they occur in the rabbinic canon, then turn to Josephus' version of the same matters. There are two important passages, one in the Tosefta, the other in the Bavli. The former serves to establish the fact that exactly the same words occur in both a rabbinic composition and Josephus' narrative. The latter then shows clear and unmistakable dependence of the talmudic version of a story upon Josephus' version of the same story.

Yohanan the high priest heard from the house of the Holy of Holies, *"The young men who went out to make war against Antioch have conquered* and they noted that hour, and it tallied that they had conquered at that very hour." The italicized words are in Aramaic, the rest in Hebrew. The point of the pericope is a miraculous revelation to Yohanan, another indication of the high favor he enjoyed in rabbinical circles. The kernel of the pericope is the Aramaic passage, in which case the point must be as given, that Yohanan was vouchsafed a heavenly revelation. The Bavli's story of importance in our inquiry is as follows:

A. Abbaye said, "How do I know it [that the silence of a husband in a case in which the wife is charged with committing adultery by one witness only means that the husband must divorce the wife]?"

B. DTNY': The story is told that (M^cSH B) Yannai the king went to Kohalit in the wilderness and there conquered sixty towns. When he returned, he rejoiced greatly and invited all the sages of Israel.

C. He said to them, "Our forefathers would eat salt fish when they were engaged in the building of the holy house. Let us also eat salt fish as a memorial to our forefathers."

D. So they brought up salt fish on golden trays, and they ate.

E. There was there a certain scoffer, evil hearted and empty headed, and Eleazar ben Poirah was his name.

F. Eleazar b. Poirah said to Yannai the king, "O King Yannai, the hearts of the Pharisees are [set] against you."

G. "What shall I do?"

H. "Test them by the plate that is between your eyes."

I. He tested them by the plate that was between his eyes.

J. There was there a certain sage, and Judah b. Gedidiah was his name. Judah b. Gedidiah said to Yannai the king, "O King Yannai, Let suffice for you the crown of sovereignty [kingship]. Leave the crown of the [high] priesthood for the seed of Aaron."

K. For people said that his [Yannai's] mother had been taken captive in Modiim. The charge was investigated and not found [sustained]. The sages of Israel departed in anger.

L. Eleazar b. Poirah then said to Yannai the king, "O King Yannai, That is the law [not here specified as the punishment inflicted on Judah] even for the ordinary folk in Israel. But you are king and high priest—should that be your law too?"

M. "What should I do?"

N. "If you take my advice, you will trample them down."

O. "But what will become of the Torah?"

P. "Lo, it is rolled up and lying in the corner. Whoever wants to learn, let him come and learn."

Q. R. Nahman b. Isaac said [in Aramaic], *"Forthwith Epicureanism ['PYQWRSWT] was instilled in him [Yannai], for he should have said, 'That is well and good for the written Torah, but what will become of the oral Torah?' "*

R. The evil blossomed through Eleazar b. Poirah. All the sages of Israel were killed.

S. The world was desolate until Simeon b. Shetah came and restored the Torah to its place.

—b. Qid.66a

A persistent tradition on a falling out between the Pharisees and Alexander Jannaeus evidently circulated in later times. One form of that tradition placed the origin of the whole difficulty at the feet of Simeon b. Shetah himself, holding that the king believed he had been cheated; therefore Simeon fled for a time but later on returned. A second, and different, set of traditions, of which the above is one exemplum, held that difficulties between Yannai and the Pharisees (rabbis) as a group led to the flight of many of them, including Judah b. Tabbai and/or Joshua b. Perahiah to Alexandria. Simeon managed to patch things up—we do not know how—and therefore summoned the refugees to return. But the two traditions cannot be reconciled or translated into historical language, nor can we profitably speculate on what kernel of historical truth underlay either or both of them. All we do know is that Simeon b. Shetah was believed to have played a role in either the difficulty or the reconciliation or both. This brings us to Josephus' versions of both items. They occur in the account of John Hyrcanus (135–104 B.C.), first in *War* I:54ff. He succeeded his murdered brothers as high priest and led the state for thirty-one years (1:68). He enjoyed the "three highest privileges: the supreme command of the nation, the high priesthood, and the gift of prophecy. He could invariably predict the future." In the pertinent materials in the *War,* Josephus makes no mention of Pharisees. In *Antiquities* XIII, Josephus vastly expands his account. He credits John Hyrcanus with the destruction of the Gerizim temple and the conversion of Idumaea (13:2524; trans. L. H. Feldman). The heavenly message now appears as follows:

Now about the high priest Hyrcanus an extraordinary story is told, how the Deity communicated with him, for they say that on the very day on which his sons fought with Cyzicenus, Hyrcanus, who was alone in the temple, burning incense as high priest, heard a voice saying *that his sons had just defeated Antiochus.* And on coming out of the temple, he revealed this to the entire multitude, and so it actually happened.

The message here preserved in indirect discourse is presented in direct discourse in the rabbinic materials: "The youths who have made war on Antioch have conquered." But the message is nearly identical, and so is the setting. Josephus now introduces the story of the Pharisees and Hyrcanus (13:288ff.; trans. L. H. Feldman):

As for Hyrcanus, the envy of the Jews was aroused against him by his own successes, and those of his sons. Particularly hostile to him were the Pharisees, who are one of the Jewish schools . . . . And so great is their influence with the masses that even when they speak against a high or high priest, they immediately gain credence.

Hyrcanus too was a disciple of theirs, and was greatly loved by them. And once he invited them to a feast and entertained them hospitably, and when he saw that they were having a very good time, he began by saying that they knew he wished to be righteous and in everything he did tried to please God and them—for the Pharisees profess such beliefs; at the same time he begged them, if they observed him doing anything wrong or straying from the right path, to lead him back to it and correct him. But they testified to his being altogether virtuous, and he was delighted with their praise.

However, one of his guests, named Eleazar, who had an evil nature and took pleasure in dissension, said, "Since you have asked to be told the truth, if you wish to be righteous give up the high priesthood and be content with governing the people."

And when Hyrcanus asked him for what reason he should give up the high priesthood, he replied, "Because we have heard from our elders that your mother was a captive in the reign of Antiochus Epiphanes."

But the story was false, and Hyrcanus was furious with the man, while all the Pharisees were very indignant.

Then a certain Jonathan, one of Hyrcanus' close friends, belonging to the school of Sadducees, who hold opinions opposed to those of the Pharisees, said that it had been with general approval of all the Pharisees that Eleazar had made his slanderous statement; and this, he added, would be clear to Hyrcanus if he inquired of them what punishment Eleazar deserved for what he had said.

Hyrcanus did so, and the Pharisees replied: Eleazar deserved stripes and chains; for they did not think it right to sentence a man to death for calumny, and the Pharisees are naturally lenient in the matter of punishments.

Hyrcanus was outraged, and Jonathan in particular inflamed his anger, and so worked upon him that he brought him to join the Sadducean party and desert the Pharisees and to abrogate the regulations which they had established for the people and punish those who observed them.

At this point, Josephus explains who the Pharisees are and alleges that everyone listens to them, while the Sadducees are followed only by the wealthy (etc.). Then Josephus returns to the account of *War.* Hyrcanus lived happily ever after and had the three greatest privileges, etc.

Clearly, the rabbis' tradition of Alexander Jannaeus at b. Qid. 66a and Josephus' story of John Hyrcanus in *Antiquities* exhibit remarkable affinities. On Abbaye's theory that Yannai and Yohanan were one and the same, we have no difficulties whatever, and it is Abbaye who cites the materials in b. Qid. 66a.

I am impressed by the near identity of the miracle story with the rabbinical one, even more impressed by the antiquity of the language attributed to the heavenly echo, and would be inclined to imagine that to both Josephus and the rabbis was available a single, brief logion in Aramaic. The parallels certainly are too close to be accidental.

The long story about Hyrcanus (= b. Qid.'s Jannaeus) and the Pharisees is another matter. It is long, well developed, and involves not a single short phrase but a complex narrative. Josephus has inserted it whole into his larger setting. He does not account for Pharisaic hostility but takes it for granted; then he makes Hyrcanus a Pharisee, so their hostility is even more incredible. Now comes the famous banquet, with Eleazar (= Judah b. Gedidiah of the Talmud) as the troublemaker, described with much the same adjectives, and his message is identical in substance. Everyone "leaves indignant" in both versions. Then Jonathan (the Talmud's Eleazar b. Poirah) tells the king to let the Pharisees show their true feelings. They impose the normal punishment. This detail is absent in b. Qid. 66a. But it is there taken for granted, which is striking indeed. "That is the law even for the most humble . . . shall that be your law too?" follows the departure of the sages. Let me state with appropriate emphasis: *The version in b. Qid. 66a, if not garbled or defective, is simply incomprehensible without the details supplied in Josephus' story.* Now Josephus explains how Hyrcanus left the Pharisees and joined the Sadducees, after which he lived happily. This detail ignores the foregoing narrative. For the rabbis the break came on the threshold of his death and is left unexplained. Then Simeon b. Shetah comes along and restores the Pharisees to power.

I find it impossible to imagine how the two versions could have been shaped independently of one another. Two facts seem to me decisive. The first is the length and complexity of the narrative; the second, the constant parallels of theme, development, and detail between the two versions. The two cannot be thought entirely separate traditions but, on the contrary, may be best accounted for within one of three theories: either Josephus here cites an ancient prerabbinic, Pharisaic story (highly unlikely); or both refer in common to a third, independent source; or the rabbis cite Josephus. This third seems most probable, if in fact rabbis knew Josephus' writings in the original Aramaic. However we explain matters, the upshot is that the Bavli's authors took over and shaped in their own framework materials of a quite elaborate character.

The Bavli at the End

The Bavli's authors imposed the mark of their own minds upon received materials. They did so in such a way as to revise everything that had gone before. They placed upon the whole heritage of the past the indelible and distinct, unmistakable stamp of their own minds. The reason is that the Bavli's authorities did not confuse respect with servility. They carefully nurtured critical and creative faculties. Gibbon said (probably unfairly) of the Byzantine schools, "Not a single composition of history, philosophy, or literature has been saved from oblivion by the intrinsic beauties of style, or sentiment, or original fancy, or even of successful imitation." By contrast, the Bavli is the product not of servility to the past or of dogmatism in the present but of an exceptionally critical, autonomous rationalism and an utterly independent spirit. The authority of the received materials was set aside by the critical judgment of the newest generation. In the fullest sense, the Bavli's authors were not traditionalists. They took traditions of the early generations into their care, respectfully learning them, reverently handing them on. But these they thoroughly digested and made their own. Their minds were filled with the learning of the ancients. But their unrelenting criticism was wholly their own, which is why they added, changed, and rewrote nearly everything they received from, hence shared with, earlier compositions.

Part Four

Judaism in Conclusion

9

The Yerushalmi
Partial Evidence of a Complete System

Judaism

The form of Judaism that the Talmuds defined predominated from late antiquity to our own day and continues to flourish. Its principal verbal symbol is the word *torah,* which stands for God's will. Its central religious authority is the sage, called by the honorific *rabbi,* qualified by mastery of torah attained through discipleship to a prior sage. Its primary religious document is "the one whole Torah of Moses, our rabbi," consisting of the written Torah (the "Old Testament" more or less) and the oral Torah. The oral half now is represented by the canon beginning with the Mishnah and moving onward through the compilations of scriptural exegeses and the Talmuds.

These three—torah as the symbol, the sage as the ideal type, the dual Torah as the definitive and authoritative holy book—together define the Judaism at hand. Any book that finds a place within the system of sage and dual Torah and expresses the notion that Israel, the Jewish people, is to live a holy way of life defined by the model of the rabbi and the message of the Torah, constitutes a canonical document within the type of Judaism at hand. And any book that does not, finds its place within some system other than the Judaism of torah, the generic, and of the dual Torah. From the Middle East of late antiquity to the West in medieval and modern times, this is the symbolic system, with its consequent way of life, worldview, and set of ideal types, that predominated.

Clearly, at some specific point, in some one document, we may hope to see the system just now adumbrated emerge whole and complete. That is to say, we may legitimately expect that a system of Judaism will attain comprehensive expression in one or more of its writings. No one will be surprised to discover that such system will enjoy in one aspect or another partial testimony in all of the books that said system deems authoritative or holy. That fact seems self-evident. Every document of the canon of the Judaism of the dual Torah in some aspect or other expresses that Judaism, and every detail fundamentally—and by definition—must form part of the whole and point to the whole. It also is obvious that all books taken into a system, wherever they originate, will be read within their values by the authorities of that system. A fair amount of eisegesis serves to encompass, to naturalize within the state of the faith, whatever to begin with had stood outside. The obvious example is the Hebrew Scriptures themselves, taken in, in part or in toto, by all forms of Judaism of late antiquity, all forms of Christianity, and, in substantial part, Islam as well. But no one would look to the Hebrew Scriptures (the "Old Testament," the "written Torah") for a distinctive and comprehensive statement of any form of Judaism or any expression of Christianity, let alone Islam. The generative and definitive documents will be those distinctive to the particular form of Judaism or Christianity subject to study. It must follow that, when we search for a full and comprehensive account of "Judaism," that is, of the form of Judaism that refers to the critical symbol of torah, the authority of the rabbi, and the dual Torah of Moses, our rabbi, we have to find the goal of our inquiry elsewhere than in Scripture.

But if we eliminate the Hebrew Scriptures, we have also to remove from consideration all documents that, without presenting a complete and comprehensive account, merely refer to, or participate in, the larger symbolic structure. Let me give one self-evident example. We cannot point to the Mishnah as the central and definitive document of the form of Judaism under study, however much the later authorities impute to the Mishnah standing as the oral Torah. Why not? A glance at the Mishnah tells us that we cannot find within its pages the required indicators, the definitive evidence, of the form of Judaism at hand. If we do not read into the Mishnah the conception of the oral Torah, we shall not find it there. If we do not take for granted that the Mishnah posits the rule of Israel by the rabbi, qualified through the master-disciple relationship, we shall not discover that leader there. For the Mishnah posits a politics of high priest and king. It knows little of sages' actual government. The Mishnah's holy way of life focuses upon the cult, its consecrated caste is the priesthood, and its central holy action involves sacrifice in the temple. The synagogue, the rabbi, and study of Torah constitute the three pillars of the holy way of life of the kind of Judaism that emerges from the literary canon precipitated by the advent of the Mishnah. But these scarcely appear in the pages of the Mishnah. True, the documents that stand closest to the Mishnah, beginning with tractate Abot and the Tosefta, exhibit some nascent tendencies to read into, or draw out of, the Mishnah the values or indicative symbols or other traits of the later Judaism. But these do not present us with a full statement of that Judaism, whole and complete, and as works of exegesis of a prior document, they cannot have done so. So the question at hand turns our attention to yet another problem. In this one we ask where, in particular, the definitive traits of Judaism as it emerges from late antiquity make their first appearance all together, all at once.

Let me stress that the Mishnah essentially and in its main emphases presents a system distinct from that of the Judaism built upon the Mishnah. The Mishnah speaks about uncleanness and holiness, priests and their rations, holy days and appointed times in the temple, and ordinary, everyday rites at the altar. The Mishnah's picture of Israelite government presents a portrait of a king and a high priest in charge of everything. Its conception of civil law aims at preserving the perfect stability of the status quo, all in the name of the sanctification of Israel. While the Mishnah names sages, called rabbis, it does not present a system of Judaism characterized by those interests of sages definitive, later on, of Judaism. That is, the Mishnah's principal concerns are those of priests, not sages. Its focus of interest is in the temple and its cult, not in the schoolhouse and its ritual learning. Its conception of the civil life rests upon an orderly world in majestic stasis and does not deal with that disorderly detritus of ordinary life to which, later on, the rabbis addressed themselves in their small claims courts. Above all, the Mishnah provides little place in its system for the upheavals of history—public or personal—and the ordering and end to be effected by the Messiah. Judaism, fully exposed, would rest its claim upon its supernatural power to bring the Messiah: do things our way and he will come. So the persona of the Mishnah may be described as a priest, facing the destroyed temple and the now-forbidden city of Jerusalem. The system of the Yerushalmi, circa A.D. 400, to emerge within two centuries after the closure of the Mishnah in A.D. 200, addressed the everyday life of Israel in the towns and villages of the Holy Land. Its persona is a rabbi, walking with his disciples through the streets and marketplaces of the country as well as abroad. The contrast therefore is between the Mishnah's priestly system of an Israelite world laid out in lines of structure focused upon and emanating from the temple, and the Talmud's striking reshaping of that system through the grafting of a separate value system.

That is why the Mishnah cannot be described as at heart a typically rabbinic document. From the perspective of the third and fourth centuries, the Mishnah speaks about the wrong things, on behalf of the wrong group of people, turned toward the wrong time and located in the wrong place: sanctification, temple, and cult, for the priests, in the evermore distant past, of the forbidden city of Jerusalem. The Talmuds, viewed whole and complete, testify to a different vision for Israel. They speak of learning, on behalf of sages, living in the present, and are located everywhere that Israel now is found. The Mishnah scarcely speaks of *a* messiah. Whoever is anointed bears, at best, a particular status, not a general power over Israel's history. The Talmuds, at the end, tie themselves tightly to the messianic fervor of Israel, promising that when Israel does what sages teach, *the* Messiah will come. The Mishnah scarcely alludes to the end of time or the world to come. The Talmuds will present a road map of how to get there.

Our inquiry now turns to the penultimate question in this exercise in the definition of the Bavli. Just as in the prior parts of this study, so now, first, we have to see how the two Talmuds stand in relationship to the Mishnah, as well

as to other compositions of their time. Second, we have to ask how the two
Talmuds stand in relationship to one another. Thus the same procedures that
have guided us in the earlier parts of the study tell us how to proceed now.
How shall we deal with Judaism? In my view, the best way to parse the canon
of the system as a whole, an ideologically complete statement, is to introduce
yet anther constant. Against that constant we can discern the variables in respect to a systemically indicative idea. So we shall trace a single idea from its
earliest expression to its fullest formulation. What is to be done is to take that
single theme, to list everything—every fact, every detail—that is ultimately
said about that theme in the entirety of the rabbinic canon viewed whole.
Then, once again, we shall ask what each document, in succession, contributes to the formation of the large picture of the theme yielded by canonical
Judaism all together in its complete expression. When we see where and in
what sequence each document stands in the unfolding of details on the topic
and hand, examined in a small and suggestive setting, we may gain perspective on the literary evidence of the ideational structure as a whole. In this way
we parse the system and discover the Talmuds' place in it.

Messiah

The topic of the Messiah will serve as the constant, and things said about the
Messiah in the several components of the canon of Judaism will define the
variables. The importance of the topic is self-evident and demands no consid-
erable amplification. For the theme of the Messiah supplies the teleology to
the fully worked-out Judaism that flourished from talmudic times to our own
day. To be sure the Messiah defines a theme, common to a number of systems,
worked out in ways distinctive to each. The shape of the messianic theme
moreover expresses the larger points of insistence of the system by which the
theme was adopted. Scripture to begin with provided a sizable repertoire of
information—facts about the Messiah, when he would come, what he would
do, and the like. In the diverse writings collected as the Old Testament Apoc-
rypha and Pseudipigrapha, we find many more facts. But if we turn to the
writings of particular social groups or individuals, we discover not a random
repertoire of information but carefully selected and purposefully used facts.
So these points of reference to the Messiah form part of a larger worldview
brought to expression in the composite theological literature of a given social
group. That was the case for the Israelite religious commune of Essenes at
Qumran. Everyone knows that it was the case for the Israelite religious com-
munes organized in the name of Christ. What each group did with the messianic theme tells us about the larger, distinctive perspective of the group
rather than about the "Messianic idea of Judaism," in general.

When we come to the writing by rabbis, from the end of the second century
to the end of the seventh, which, all together, constitutes the canon of the Judaism normative from late antiquity to the present day (talmudic, rabbinic,

normative, classical), we find a still more suggestive fact. The messianic theme is carefully shaped in the foundation document of the rabbinic canon, the Mishnah, and serves the larger purposes of that document. When, many centuries later, the Bavli reached closure, a great many more facts about the Messiah were swept up and drawn in. These facts, used also in other Judaic systems of late antiquity, served to make a point distinctive to the ultimate rabbinic system.

How shall we proceed? To make matters simple, I shall now list the bulk of statements made about the Messiah in the documents of the rabbinic canon, from the Mishnah through the Bavli. I shall indicate in a simple way in which document a given statement first made its appearance. Then I shall point to the distinctions exhibited in the facts about the Messiah stated in the diverse documents and propose to explain the differences. In this way, it will soon be clear, the two Talmuds will be shown to relate to the antecedent literature, on the topic at hand, in a clear and identifiable way. The character of that relationship then will allow us to describe the documents as a whole. That is the point of the procedure at hand.

The summary tables in this section thus show the provenance of diverse assertions concerning the Messiah, on the one side, and Israel's history and destiny, on the other, that add up to the canonical corpus on formative Judaism's eschatological teleology. I list the topics in the rough order of the rabbinic documents in which they occur. The important point, however, is not documentary sequence. We must not confuse the evident precedence of one rabbinic compilation over another with the historical order by which a given fact appeared before some other. That claim is undemonstrable, and, further, it is quite beside the point I wish to make in this exercise. Our concern is only with the traits of documents.

Let me briefly explain the order and division of documents. The Mishnah is assumed to have reached closure at circa A.D. 200, so it comes first. The next group, Tosefta, Abot, and Abot de R. Nathan, came to closure sometime after the formation of the Mishnah; Abot serves as the Mishnah's first apologetic. The Tosefta constitutes a corpus of secondary amplification of the Mishnah. It is cited, normally verbatim, in the Yerushalmi and therefore presumably reached a conclusion prior to the formation of the latter document, which follows next in sequence (ca A.D. 400). As I said earlier, the group beyond, the four compilations of exegeses of the Pentateuchal books of Exodus, Leviticus, Numbers, and Deuteronomy, bear the names only of authorities who appear, also, in the Mishnah and so are regarded as Tannaitic, for one title was accorded to the Mishnah's authorities. But the Mishnah itself turns out to be cited in the documents that deal with Leviticus, Numbers, and Deuteronomy, so these compositions also follow in time. We do not know when they were composed; setting them after the Yerushalmi is only a guess. Genesis and Leviticus Rabbah, compilations of exegeses of the named biblical books, construct their units of disclosure along the lines of exactly the same logoi as we find in the Yerushalmi and are located in the same period, circa A.D. 400. The next groups—Lamentations Rabbah, Esther Rabbi I, Song of Songs Rabbah, Ruth Rabbah, and Pesiqta de R. Kahana—are assumed to have been composed in roughly the two hundred years after the Yerushalmi. In the canon of rabbinical writings, the Bavli then comes at the end. So before us is only the canonical order of the ideas at hand. By that I mean the ideas concerning the Messiah, that are found in various rabbinical compositions of late antiquity, are laid out in the rough and approximate order in which they appear in the documents that preserve them. Further discussion of the items at hand is found in my *Messiah in Context: Israel's History and Destiny in Formative Judaism* (Philadelphia: Fortress Press, 1984).

I. The Messiah	
1. Messiah = anointed priest	a, b, c, d, e
2. Messiah = son of David (Ruth, Boaz)	a, d, e, f, h
3. This age versus age of the Messiah	a, b, d, e, h
4. Tribulations before Messiah	a, d, f, g, h
5. Sages suffer before the end	a, f, h
6. David's dominion is eternal	c, h
7. David's son restores horn of Israel	c, h
8. Messiah's coming and resurrection of dead	c, h
9. David as a rabbi	c, h
10. Messiah's name: Menahem	c
11. Messiah from Bethlehem	c
12. Messiah born when temple destroyed	c
13. Aqiba said Bar Kokhba was a messiah	c
14. When Israel repents, they will be saved (no messianic reference)	c, h
15. Israel must be humble to bring Messiah. Bar Kokhba was arrogant and no messiah, so he lost.	c, h
16. Israel punished for neglect of Torah	c
17. If Israel would do . . . , the Messiah would come	c, d, h
18. Because Israel does . . . , the Messiah has not come	h
19. Messiah: David-Hillel	e
20. Messiah will gather exiles	e, h
21. Israel will not require the Messiah as teacher	e
22. Messiah records peoples' good deeds	e, h
23. Unusual incidents prior to Messiah	f, h
24. Messiah comes to worst generation	f, g, h
25. Messiah will come when God chooses, do nothing in advance	f, h
26. Reckoning the end	f, h
27. Gentiles convert when Messiah comes	g
28. Gentile rule ends	g, h
29. God clothes Messiah	g

I. The Messiah

30. Description of person of the Messiah	g, h
31. God restores Jerusalem, Zion, temple cult, through the Messiah	g, h
32. 6,000 years, Messiah's age the middle 2,000	g, h
33. Messiah came in Hezekiah's time (denied).	h
34. Messiah's name was Shiloh, etc.	h
35. Length of Messiah's rule	h
36. Messiah in Nisan	g, h
37. Messiah in seventh year	h
38. Messiah not coming on a Sabbath	h
39. Prayer may bring the Messiah	h
40. Messiah comes in A.D. 468	h
41. Messiah will only replace pagan rulers	h
42. Sinners punished by Messiah	h
43. Israel will be served by gentiles; Messiah will rule gentiles	h
44. Messiah comes when souls are all born	h
45. Messiah comes when patriarch + exilarch go	h
46. Messiah of House of Joseph killed	h
47. Messiah called Holy One	h
48. Messiah created before creation	h
49. Messiah comes only after Rome rules the whole world	h
50. King-Messiah is a captive in Rome, etc.	l

II. Israel's History and Destiny

1. Destruction in A.D. 70 marked decline in supernatural world and in life of the sages	a, b, h
2. Legal changes after A.D. 70	a, b, h
3. Periods of history marked by location of cult	a, b, c
4. This world/world to come, life/death	b, h
5. Why was Jerusalem destroyed	b, c, h
6. Tales about sages	b, c, h
7. Tales about priests, cult and supernatural events in cult	b, h
8. Rome's history is the counterpart to Israel's	c, h
9. Rome's deeds explicable in terms of Israel's logic	c, h
10. Age of idolatry versus God's reign	c, h
11. Days distinguished by secular events, not only by natural one	c, h
12. When Israel learns lessons of its history, it commands its destiny	c, h
13. Israel saved by submission to God, not arrogance of its own deeds	c, h
14. Four kingdoms, four periods (four animals)	e, f, h
15. Just as punishment has come, so redemption will surely follow	f, g, h
16. Israel must accept pagan rule, pagans must not oppress Israel too much. Israel must not act on its own.	, h

II. Israel's History and Destiny	
17. Iran (Persia) parallel to Rome	h
18. Various empires' history governed by their relationship to Israel	h
19. Nations wise to treat Israel well	h
20. Israelites are own worst enemy but control own destiny	h
21. Decline in merit of generations	h
22. God shares Israel's fate	h
23. Empires' history governed by study of Torah	h
24. Exile of Israel is so that proselytes might join them	h
25. Nations hate Israel because of the Torah	h
26. God loves Israel because it is humble (cf. no. 13)	h

Note: a = Mishnah; b = Tosefta, Abot, and Abot de R. Nathan; c = Talmud of the Land of Israel; d = Mekhilta, Sifra, Sifre Num., Sifre Dt.; e = Gen. Rabbah and Lev. Rabbah; f = Lam. R., Est. R. I, Song R., Ruth R.; g = Pesiqta de R. Kahana; h = Talmud of Babylonia.

Tracing the principal expressions of the Messiah myth across the canon of rabbinical writings tells us more about the canon than about the history of the Messiah myth. We see which documents tend to group themselves around a given set of ideas and which stand essentially distinct from the other. The Mishnah and its close associates, Abot, the Tosefta, and Abot de R. Nathan, fall together on the one end of the spectrum, the Yerushalmi and the Bavli, on the other. Closer to the former pole are the exegetical compilations serving the Pentateuch, specifically, Mekhilta, Sifra, Sifre Numbers, and Sifre Deuteronomy. The Rabbah collections of the pre-Islamic period—Genesis Rabbah, Leviticus Rabbah, Lamentations, Song of Songs, Ruth, and Esther Rabbah I—fit somewhere closer to the Pentateuchal-exegetical compilations than they do to either of the two Talmuds, and Pesiqta de R. Kahana stands close to the Bavli. Overall, therefore, we may group the rabbinical canon in two parts: first, the Mishnah and its circle, on the one side; second, the two Talmuds and their associates, at the other. There can be no doubt about what is the most comprehensive document. The Bavli covers everything found in all the other writings. It is the great vacuum cleaner of ancient Judaism, sucking up the entire antecedent corpus. The achievement of its compilers was to create encyclopaedic summaries of all the data at their disposal, then to attempt to harmonize the mass of contradiction and conflict that resulted.

What we now see clearly is how the Mishnah and its associated compositions relate to the Talmuds and their literary fellows. The two components of the great rabbinical canon—the Mishnah, the Talmuds—stand essentially separate from one another, though related in important ways. They are separate in that the Mishnah's circle covers a limited number of topics and does so in a distinctive way. The Talmuds' circle covers the Mishnaic material, but encompasses a much larger territory of its own as well. The Mishnah's circle exhibits its own traits of mind and method, presenting a system unto itself. The two Talmuds fully cover the Mishnah's range, in their own way absorbing the Mishnah's entire repertoire of ideas, one by one, but making of those ideas, taken up discretely, something quite other than what they had been when viewed in the Mishnah's system.

So the principal result of this survey is to uncover, for the subject at hand, two concentric circles. These contain two "Judaisms," so to speak—one small, the other huge; one quite compact and internally coherent, the other, while not totally formless, yet not entirely self-consistent. The Mishnah presents us with a complete system. The two Talmuds offer us a huge repertoire of facts, a fair number of which serve as major elements in the system but some that remain unintegrated and discrete. The Mishnah integrates everything that comes its way or that it selects. The Bavli uses to its own advantage some of the components of the larger Messiah myth, while preserving but essentially neglecting others.

If I had to specify the systemically characteristic, even definitive, elements of the catalogs of facts at hand, I should have no difficulty pointing to what the Mishnah finds critical, namely, the few topics appearing in the Mishnah column of the catalog (nos. 1–5 on the Messiah list). Indeed, what the Mishnah does not utilize is more interesting than what it does. The Mishnah's framers choose for their system five facts, three of them commonplaces and (once the subject comes up) unavoidable. These are, first, that the Messiah comes from the House of David; second, that there is a difference between the present age and the age of the Messiah; and, third, that there will be tribulations before the coming of the Messiah, for the people in general but especially for sages.

These commonplaces, deriving from Scripture and well known to virtually every writer on the subject of the Messiah, are joined by another. There is no such thing as *the* Messiah; there is only the taxonomic classification *messiah*. Into that classification fall two kinds of messiahs, both cultic: that is, priests anointed for office as specified in Mosaic law and another kind, the Messiah not as a type of priest but as a historical-eschatological figure. The former appear extensively and play a significant part in specified tractates. *The* Messiah in the other guise, the one familiar to everyone else in ancient Israel, appears only as part of the undifferentiated background of accepted, but systemically neutral, facts. *The* Messiah receives no close attention; no problems take shape around which a tractate, an intermediate unit of discourse, or even a single pericope might take shape. Obviously, the Mishnah's framers wished to reshape the issue into terms they found interesting, hence their special concern for the classification, Messiah-priest, on the one side, and their special pleading about the special suffering of sages in the awful times prior to the Messiah's coming, on the other. These facts about the use and neglect of the Messiah myth point to a single conclusion. The philosophers of the Mishnah chose to talk about other things. Hence they were addressing people other than those eager to learn about the eschatological Messiah, when he would come, and what he would do.

We now need hardly belabor the fact that the rest of the rabbinical canon saw matters otherwise. Our tables require no substantial amplification. What we do not find in the Mishnah, we find everywhere else. Distinctive to rabbis are two sorts of views about the Messiah. First, the rabbis express in their particular way what were generally held convictions. Second, some of their formulations constitute doctrines in fact distinctive to their own estate. In the present context, we may point to the notion that Israel can hope for just government only when God rules. That belief, though stated in a way peculiar to rabbis, in fact expresses what must have been a widespread yearning. But the doctrines that, to prove worthy of God's rule, Israel must accept the dominion of gentiles and demonstrate its humility in order to make itself worthy, and that rabbis provide the model for the way in which Israel at large must live— these and parallel points derive from, and express, the larger system of the rabbinical canon. They mark the rabbinical canon as distinctive.

We therefore see two clearly differentiated sectors within the rabbinical canon. One, the Mishnah's, is well defined in its interest. We can offer a plausible explanation of the way in which, consonant with those larger systemic points of insistence, the Messiah myth makes its modest contribution. The other, the Talmud's more encompassing sector of the canon, also yields a coherent viewpoint. In accordance with that larger viewpoint, we can discern the systemic usefulness of parts of the larger representation of facts about the Messiah. But a number of facts referred to in the second (the talmudic) sector of the canon do not clearly relate to the systemic interests of that sector as a whole. If, then, we take seriously the differentiation of the larger canon into two separate, though related, sectors, as our parsing shows we should, we may tell the story of the Messiah in the present context in just a few words.

1. The Mishnah's framers formulated a worldview and a way of life for the Jewish nation in which historical events played little part. The framers insisted on uncovering the ongoing patterns of life, eternal laws of nature and supernature. To these points of insistence, the concept of the Messiah and of the meaning and destiny of Israel among the nations proved irrelevant. The framers of the Mishnah spoke of other things. We do not know to whom they wished to address their vision.

2. The continuators of the Mishnah in the Talmuds constructed their exegetical essays through, but also around, the Mishnah. They explained and expanded upon the Mishnah's points. But they also made provision for expressing their own views, as distinct from those stated in the Mishnah. So some ideas are particular and early, and some are general and late. The governing criterion is special to the canon at hand. What is distinctive to the Mishnah, namely its malign neglect of the Messiah myth, reaches expression early in the canon at hand. What is expressive of the rabbinical perception of the Mes-

siah reaches its present condition later in the formation of the canon, even though some of the facts that are reshaped are of ancient origin.

The rabbinic system took over the fundamental convictions of the Mishnaic worldview about the importance of Israel's constructing for itself a life beyond time. The rabbinic system then transformed the Messiah myth, in its totality, into an essentially ahistorical force. If people wanted to reach the end of time, they had to rise above time, that is, history, and stand off at the side of great movements of political and military character. That is the message of the Messiah myth as it reaches full exposure in the rabbinic system of the two Talmuds. It therefore is at its foundation *precisely* the message of teleology without eschatology expressed by the Mishnah and its associated documents. In the Talmuds and their associated documents we see the restatement of the ontological convictions that informed the minds of the second-century philosophers of the Mishnah: Israel must turn away from time and change, submit to whatever happens, so as to win for itself the only government worth having, that is, God's rule, accomplished through God's anointed agent, the Messiah.

To state matters in simple terms, salvation depended upon sanctification, which therefore took precedence as the governing principle of the worldview and way of life commanded by the rabbis' Torah. It follows, of course, that the rabbis who stand behind the principles of messianic eschatology worked out in the Talmuds in fact continued on an absolutely straight line the fundamental convictions of the Mishnah. That document they claimed to continue and complete. Superficially, that claim is without justification, but at a deeper level it is quite proper.

So if the Mishnah was forced by the Talmuds into that very grid of history and eschatology that it had been formulated to reject, the Mishnah's ontology in turn drastically modified the Messiah myth as the Talmuds would portray it. For the Messiah theme was recast into the philosophical mode of thought and stated as the teleology of an eternally present sanctification attained by obedience to patterns of holiness laid out in the Torah. This grid is precisely the one that the framers of the Mishnah had defined. By no means may we conclude that what changed, in the end, was the Mishnah's system. Its modes of thought intact, its fundamental points of insistence about Israel's social policy reaffirmed, the Mishnah's system ended up wholly definitive for Judaism as it emerged in the canon at the end of its formative centuries, the "one whole Torah of Moses, our rabbi."

How so? The version of the Messiah myth incorporated into the rabbinic system through the Talmuds simply restates the obvious: Israel's sanctification is what governs. So if Israel will keep a single Sabbath (or two in succession), the Messiah will come. If Israel stops violating the Torah, the Messiah will come. If Israel acts with arrogance in rejecting its divinely assigned condition, the Messiah will not come. Everything depends, then, upon the here-and-now of everyday life. The operative category is not eschatology, salvation through what Israel does, but ontology, sanctification of what Israel is. The fundamental convictions of the Mishnah's framers, flowing from the reaction against the apocalyptic and messianic wars of the later first and early second centuries, here absorbed and redirected precisely those explosive energies that, to begin with, had made the critical concern Israel's salvation through history. So while the Talmuds introduced a formerly neglected myth, in fact in their version the Messiah became precisely what the sages of the Mishnah and their continuators in the Talmud most needed: a sage-Messiah who would save an Israel sanctified through Torah. Salvation then depended upon sanctification and so was subordinated to it.

The upshot for the purpose of the present study may now be briefly stated. The two Talmuds assuredly take up a position distinct from, but in relationship to, the Mishnah. They further may be distinguished from the other documents of the larger canon, though, as we have seen, the relationships between and among the Talmuds and those other documents prove diverse and not readily characterized.

The Yerushalmi and Judaism

Now that we find the two Talmuds both closely aligned with one another and a distinct component of the canon of Judaism, we want specifically to know whether we find in the Yerushalmi in particular that full and complete statement of the symbolic system and structure of the Judaism that emerged from the masters and disciples of late antiquity. If the first complete statement of Judaism emerges in the Yerushalmi, then the Bavli will have to be relegated to second place. It will constitute a mere restatement of what had already been completely said. If the Yerushalmi proves partial, then the Bavli's task, at least in theory, receives full definition, so we shall be able to ask how the Bavli accomplished that task. The character of the Yerushalmi once more must inform us about how to proceed to the definition of the Bavli. To answer the question at hand, we briefly review the relationship between the Yerushalmi and the Mishnah for we have at hand a two-stage problem: (1) how the Yerushalmi relates to the Mishnah, then (2) how the Bavli relates to the Yerushalmi (if also to the Mishnah, a separate matter).

The exercise—the Yerushalmi on the Mishnah—encompasses two issues. First, how does the Yerushalmi approach the work of Mishnah exegesis? Second, how much of the Yerushalmi serves the work of Mishnah exegesis, and how much of the document provides a forum for the expression of values and concerns essentially distinct from those of the Mishnah? At issue in the analysis of the Yerushalmi's approach to Mishnah exegesis is a deeper question than one of mere quantity. The Yerushalmi's hermeneutics requires definition. Does the document read the Mishnah in terms of values distinct from the Mishnah, in the way in which the bulk of the canon reads Scripture in terms of values we recognize as distinct from those of Scripture? Or does the Yerushalmi read the

Mishnah essentially along lines dictated by the Mishnah's character, its doctrines, wording, rules, and logic? This set of questions yields a simple answer. First, most of the Yerushalmi is devoted to Mishnah exegesis, 90% of the probe I made in *Talmud of the Land of Israel, volume 35, Introduction: Taxonomy*. That figure of course is subject to variation. But it must be regarded as fact that the bulk of the Yerushalmi addresses questions of the meanings of words and phrases in the Mishnah and, in a secondary way, the implications of laws of the Mishnah for the interpretation of other laws of the Mishnah. When the authors of the units of discourse devoted to Mishnah exegesis approached the Mishnah, they proposed to say what the Mishnah meant in pretty much its own terms. Let me explain.

What was the exegetical repertoire of the Yerushalmi's rabbis? The roughly 335 individual pericopes of the Mishnah surveyed in my earlier probe of the Yerushalmi are susceptible to categorization into just four classifications. That is to say, the Yerushalmi invariably does to the Mishnah one of these four things: (1) text criticism; (2) exegesis of the meaning of the Mishnah, including glosses and amplifications; (3) addition of scriptural proof texts of the Mishnah's central propositions; and (4) harmonization of one Mishnah passage with another such passage or with a statement of Tosefta. The first two of these four procedures remain wholly within the narrow frame of the Mishnah passage subject to discussion. The second pair take an essentially independent stance vis-à-vis the Mishnah pericope at hand. In the main, when people read a passage of the Mishnah, they wanted to know mainly what that passage meant in its own terms and setting. Approaching a given rule of the Mishnah, a sage represented in a unit of discourse of the Yerushalmi would do one of two things: (1) explain the meaning of the passage, or (2) extend and expand the meaning of the passage. Of the two sorts, the work of straightforward explanation of the plain meaning of a law of the Mishnah by far predominates. If we may state the outcome very simply: what the framers of the Talmud want to say—whatever else their purpose or aspiration—is what they think the Mishnah means in any given passage.

The facts of the Mishnaic law remain facts in the Yerushalmi. They rarely were revised or drastically reshaped into something different from what, to the naked eye, their plain meaning appears to be. I cannot point to a single passage in which, as the goal of their exegetical work, the Yerushalmi's sages seemed to wish to set aside a statement of the Mishnah or otherwise drastically twist it out of its original form and meaning. True, we must concede the possibility that among the many thousand passages of interpretation of the Mishnah in the Yerushalmi, some people may have intended to rewrite the Mishnah's law and may have done so. But the overall impression is the reverse. And that impression is so strong and self-evident (though it may be a flaw in my vision or learning) that I cannot see the need to prove it.

Let us now turn to the other half of our problem, the sorts of things the framers of units of discourse in the Yerushalmi accomplished when they turned to discourse not involving Mishnah exegesis. What is striking is that once again we are able to take much data—335 pericopes of the Mishnah probed in my earlier study—and discover no more than four taxa into which they may be divided. Here by no means do we have a mass of random sayings, collected we know not how, for a purpose we cannot imagine—a mere anthology. Rather, when we collect all units of discourse, or larger parts of such units, in which exegesis of the Mishnah or expansion upon the law of the Mishnah is absent, we find at most four types, which in fact are only two.

1. Theoretical questions of law not associated with a particular passage of the Mishnah. There is some tendency to move beyond the legal boundaries set by the Mishnah's rules themselves. More general inquiries are taken up. These of course remain within the framework of the topic of one tractate or another, although there are some larger modes of thought characteristic of more than a single tractate. To explain what I mean, I point to the mode of thought in which the scriptural basis of the law of the Mishnah will be investigated, without regard to a given tractate. Along these same lines, I point to a general inquiry into the count under which one may be liable for a given act, comments on the law governing teaching and judging cases, and the like. But these items tend not to leave the Mishnah far behind.

2. Exegesis of Scripture separate from the Mishnah. It is under this rubric that we find the most important instances in which the Yerushalmi presents materials essentially independent of the Mishnah. Virtually all of the items in this category stand totally separate from the Mishnah. They pursue problems or themes through what is said about a biblical figure, expressing ideas and values simply unknown to the Mishnah. This matter occupied chapter 4.

3. Historical statements. The Yerushalmi contains a fair number of statements that something happened or narratives about how something happened. While many of these are replete with biblical quotations, in general they do not provide exegesis of Scripture, which serves merely as illustration or reference point. This matter was covered in chapter 5.

4. Stories about, and rules for, sages and disciples, separate from discussion of a passage of the Mishnah. The Mishnah contains a tiny number of tales about rabbis. These serve principally as precedents for, or illustrations of, rules. The Yerushalmi, by contrast, contains stories about sages and their relationships to other people. Like the items in the second and third lists, these too may be adduced as evidence of the values of the people who stand behind the Talmud, the things they thought important. The main, though not the only, characteristic theme is the power of the rabbi, the honor due to the rabbi, and the tension between the rabbi and others, whether the patriarch, the heretic, or the gentile.

The first thing we learn when we ask about those units of discourse (or large segments of such units) independent of the interests of the Mishnah is that they are not numerous. Varying in bulk from one tractate to the next, they are not apt to add up to much more than 10% of the whole. We dealt with this matter in chapter 5.

The second thing, complementary to the first, is that, where we do find extensive passages in which the Mishnah is left far behind, they normally are of two kinds: (1) exegesis of narrative or theological passages of Scripture, and (2) fables about heroes. These latter divide into tales about rabbis and historical accounts. But there is no important distinction between the two, except that the former speaks of what rabbis said and did while the latter tells about events on a more generous scale.

Accordingly, when the Yerushalmi presents us with ideas or expressions of a world related to, but fundamentally separate from, that of the Mishnah, that is, when the Yerushalmi wishes to say something other than what the Mishnah says and means, it will take up one of two modes of discourse. Either we find exegesis of biblical passages, with the value system of the rabbis read into the scriptural tales, or we are told stories about holy men and paradigmatic events, once again through tales told in such a way that a didactic and paranaetic purpose is served. This fact is critical to the next stage in my argument.

Partial Evidence of a Complete System

When we revert to the question with which we began, we find that the Yerushalmi takes for granted a context—a Judaism at large—that it does not fully document. The bulk of the document focuses upon the Mishnah. Only a small portion of the whole speaks of those matters at once not characteristic of the Mishnah but profoundly definitive of the Judaism that emerges from the rabbinic canon at the end of its formation. When we ask what, in the sense just now expressed, is truly Judaic about the Yerushalmi—Judaic, not Mishnaic—the answers are clear.

First, we see that, in sheer volume, my probe of five Yerushalmi tractates in *Introduction: Taxonomy* yielded very little. The Yerushalmi centers mainly upon the Mishnah. Second, if we remove the component constituted by the Mishnah, the Yerushalmi cannot be said to present us with a sustained, coherent, and cogent statement of a world view. That is partly because the Yerushalmi is organized around the Mishnah and in accord with the Mishnah's categories. But it is mainly because the Yerushalmi simply does not present a systematic and well-articulated account of anything else.

Elements of a talmudic system, distinct from that of the Mishnah, thus appear as fragments. It is as if a whole world of reference lay outside, about which, to be sure, everyone within the document was well informed. Clearly, it was important to people to organize and transmit units of discourse on the meaning of Scripture and on the character of the rabbi as much as on the message of the Mishnah and its secondary amplification. On the other hand, once these units of discourse had come into being, no effort was made to group them and make of them something comparable to the sustained and systematic discussions of the Mishnah's rules and principles.

A simple example shows what might have been done. A glance at Y. Meg. 1:9 shows that the Yerushalmi's framers were entirely able to develop a whole chapter on writing Torah scrolls. Y. Yeb. 8:1, similarly, gives us a vast amount of material on circumcision, systematically analyzed and not required for the exegesis of the Mishnah's rule. Equivalent chapters, or even larger units, can be constructed out of materials on still other themes, such as mourning. So the Yerushalmi could have been augmented by tractates on the laws of scribes, circumcision, and mourning. Later on such tractates as would indeed deal with scribes, mourning, and other important topics would be compiled. But for the moment represented by the Yerushalmi's two hundred years, tractates on such characteristically rabbinic concerns as Talmud study and discipleship, so far as we know, were not brought into being. The materials of which they would be constituted later on came to full expression and closure. What follows for our inquiry is that the Yerushalmi, viewed as an organized whole, stands for one system only, that of the Mishnah.

At the same time the very character of materials of which the Yerushalmi is made up proves that the Mishnaic system as such was in process of expansion, augmentation, and revision in terms of another one, the one we call the way of the Torah, or Judaism. If that is the fact for the formation of new legal categories and constructions, for instance, mourning, circumcision, and scribal rules, it also was still more true for the formation of new theological and mythic categories and constructions, such as are represented by the supernatural categories shaped around the figure of the rabbi himself. The same fact pertains to new social and institutional constructions, such as are represented by the units of discourse devoted to the rabbi in relationship to other social types, on the one side, and the rabbi in the court school, on the other. But all of this nascent system is yet secondary to, and structurally unimportant in, the Yerushalmi. There was no provision in the fundamental structure of the Yerushalmi for what, in fact, defined the very matrix and context of the Yerushalmi: the rabbinic world, successor and heir to the world portrayed by the Mishnah. It would therefore appear that the entire legal program and value system of the Yerushalmi is defined by that of the Mishnah. The framers of the Yerushalmi added bits and pieces of that other, rabbinic value system. But these scarcely attained a significant position in the main literary and redactional components of the Yerushalmi. They were peripheral, negligible in volume, and undeveloped in composition and expression: stories about sages, observations on verses of Scripture. We have now to distinguish the Bavli from the Yerushalmi and to ask how and where it differs in its composition and expression of that larger systemic matrix, the system of the Torah, to which, as we see, the Yerushalmi testifies only partially.

10

The Bavli
Judaism in Conclusion

Context in Quest of Text

The Yerushalmi points outward, beyond its pages and toward a nurturing context of symbol and myth. We do not discover full expression of that context in the Yerushalmi. The task then is to find a text fully expressive of context. Let me explain. Even as it speaks of its most intimate and particular concerns in exegesis of small passages of the Mishnah, the Yerushalmi testifies to a world beyond itself. The Yerushalmi's sages spoke of the Mishnah and how to find certainty in its uncertain phrasing and mooted principles. But in doing so they testified vividly about themselves and what they had to do. The Yerushalmi's text therefore directs us to its matrix: Why these particular points of stress? As we just saw, discourse on the Mishnah, so peculiar to the Talmuds, in some measure carries us to a world altogether beyond the narrow province of the Mishnah and its exegesis.

The reason is clear. If we proposed to describe the kind of Judaism revealed in the pages of the Yerushalmi solely out of what is in those pages, as we can and do describe the Judaism of the Mishnah upon the basis of the resources of the Mishnah alone, we should find ourselves at an impasse. Everything we learn, beyond the simple and trivial facts about what some people thought the Mishnah's rules said and meant, points to a system of Judaism. Of that world view and way of life, expressed within a distinct social group of which the Yerushalmi provides a partial expression, however, we do not receive the entire account. To it the Yerushalmi devotes approximately 10% of its units of discourse.

What about the Bavli and its system of Judaism? We begin once more with the Yerushalmi, the only valid approach to the Bavli. Let me explain. What we want to know is whether and how the Bavli brings to conclusion and full expression what in the Yerushalmi appears partially and through adumbration. We noted, for example, that the Yerushalmi's corpus of materials pertinent to values and symbols external to the Mishnah forms a thin layer indeed. Approximately 90% of the Yerushalmi's units of discourse in my sample probe of five tractates dealt with the Mishnah, doing so in the Mishnah's terms and framework. So while in the Yerushalmi we find important expressions of fundamental aspects of Judaism, these scarcely constitute in volume the principal message and address of the Yerushalmi. We turn to the Bavli, in relation to the Yerushalmi, to see how the final document compares.

It surely will not do to allege, and I do not allege, that the Bavli contains elements of the final system of Judaism absent in the Yerushalmi. Such a claim seems to me beyond proof or even clear amplification. Nor can we suppose without clear criteria of falsification and verification that the Bavli provides a full and complete picture of that system to which the Yerushalmi bears only partial testimony. What, after all, would constitute a full and complete picture? How should we know that we have it, short of the claim that, since the Bavli presents everything, it therefore gives us the final and full picture of the system. That glorious blunder in logic would flow from approaching the Bavli essentially on its own. That is why we approach the Bavli only in the context of comparison with the Yerushalmi. The Yerushalmi then forms the base against which the Bavli defines itself. All of our statements about the Bavli rest upon the perspective supplied by the Yerushalmi. When, therefore, we approach these final issues—the locus of the Bavli's testimony about Judaism, the reason internal to the Bavli's character for the Bavli's remarkable authority in the entire history of Judaism from its time to ours—we have to follow the familiar path. We have to move not from nowhere to the Bavli, but solely—in a small step indeed—from the Yerushalmi to the Bavli.

The comparison of the Bavli to the Yerushalmi, we know, presents the one important and demonstrable difference between them. While the Yerushalmi rarely makes intensive use of Scripture as the framework for the composition of units of discourse and the organization of several such units of discourse into a large-scale and sustained statement, the Bavli often does. To use rough figures yielded by our earlier inquiry, the Bavli does so from four to six times more frequently than does the Yerushalmi. In the Bavli's tractates (varying to be sure by reason of subject matter) we may discern that as much as a third of the units of discourse focus not upon the Mishnah but upon Scripture. The Yerushalmi's equivalent proportions in no way correspond.

We shall return to this matter by a circuitous route. For that fact, by itself, raises possibilities but settles no questions. Rather, we shall take the same route we did in the preceding chapter. We begin by tracing the appearance of an important symbol as it makes its way across the canon of Judaism, beginning to end. Just as with the theme of the Messiah, so here what we want to know specifically is whether and how the Bavli differs from the Yerushalmi in its portrayal and use of a symbol and its associated myth.

That is how we compare the Bavli's system of Judaism to the Yerushalmi's. We take the definitive systemic symbol, the one that stands at the heart and center of Judaism as defined in the rabbinic canon, namely, the symbol of torah. We treat only a single aspect of the protean intellectual construct associated with that symbol, the mythic detail absolutely characteristic of, and totally distinctive to, the Judaism of the rabbis' canon. It is the symbol of the dual Torah, the story of the dual media of God's revelation of the Torah to Moses, our rabbi, at Sinai. Where and how do we find that very particular detail of myth in the successive components of the canon? We want to know what in particular the sages of the Bavli say, and how what they say differs from, or relates to, what the sages of the Yerushalmi had already said on the same topic. The answers to these questions will lead us to the final exercises and the end of our inquiry.

The Definitive Symbol: The Dual Torah

We now proceed to the substance of the question—the unfolding aspect of the myth associated with the symbol of torah in the canon at hand. Let me begin with a clear statement of what is at stake in the symbol and the myth of torah. Judaism as we know it at the end of late antiquity reached its now-familiar definition when *the Torah* lost its capital letter and definite article and ultimately became *torah,* the definitive taxon—Judaism. What for nearly a millennium had been a particular scroll or book came to serve as a symbol of an entire system. When a rabbi spoke of torah, he no longer meant only a particular object, a scroll and its contents. Now he used the word to encompass a distinctive and well-defined worldview and way of life. Torah now stood for something one does. Knowledge of the Torah promised not merely information about what people were supposed to do but ultimate redemption or salvation. The shift in the use of the word, accomplished in a particular set of writings out of Judaism in late antiquity, appears dramatically in the following tale drawn from the Bavli:

R. Kahana [a disciple] went and hid under Rab's [his master's] bed. Hearing Rab "discoursing" and joking with his wife . . . , [Kahana] said to [Rab], "You would think that Abba's [Rab's] mouth had never before tasted the dish." [Rab] said to [Kahana], "Kahana, are you here? Get out! This is disgraceful!" [Kahana] replied, "My lord, it is a matter of torah, and I have the need to learn" (B. Ber. 62A).

As soon as we ask ourselves what the word torah means in such a context, we recognize the shift captured by the story. For—to state the obvious—to study the Torah, meaning the Scriptures, one need not practice cultic voyeurism.

The framers of the Talmuds regarded Torah as the source and guarantor of salvation. But what they understood by the word *Torah* took on meanings particular to rabbis. They took to heart as salvific acts what others, standing outside of sages' social and mythic framework, would have regarded as merely routine, on the one side, or hocus pocus, on the other. For to the rabbis the principal salvific deed was to study Torah, by which they meant memorizing

Torah sayings by constant repetition and, as the Talmud itself amply testifies, (for some sages) profound analytic inquiry into the meaning of those sayings. This act of study of Torah imparted supernatural power. For example, by repeating words of Torah, the sage could ward off the angel of death and accomplish other miracles as well. So Torah formulas served as incantations. Mastery of Torah transformed the man who engaged in Torah learning into a supernatural figure, able to do things ordinary folk could not do. In the nature of things, the category of Torah was vastly expanded so that the symbol of Torah, a Torah scroll, could be compared to a man of Torah, namely, a sage or rabbi. Once it was established that salvation would come from keeping God's will in general, as Israelite holy men had insisted for so many years, it was a small step for rabbis to identify their particular corpus of learning, namely, the Mishnah and associated sayings, with God's will expressed in Scripture, the universally acknowledged revelation. In consequence Torah would include pretty much whatever rabbis knew (inclusive of Scripture) and did—that alone.

Since Heaven was conceived in the model of earth so that the analysis of traditions on earth corresponded to the discovery of the principles of creation, the full realization of the teachings of Torah in the life of Israel would transform Israel on earth into a replica of heaven. We deal, therefore, with a doctrine of salvation in which the operative symbol, namely, Torah, and the determinative deed, namely, Torah learning, defined not only how to reach salvation but also the very nature of the salvation to be attained. The system was whole and cogent. Entering it at any point, we find ourselves at once before the structure as a whole. It is important, then, to recognize, as we do, that the profound issues confronting Israelite existence, national and individual alike, were framed in terms of Torah and resolved through the medium of Torah. Stated simply: Salvation was to come from Torah; the nature of salvation was defined in Torah.

As is clear, therefore, the word *torah* bears a number of meanings in the rabbinic canon. Let me set forth the classifications that encompass all of those meanings. The definition of these categories requires only brief explanation.

1. When the Torah refers to a particular thing, it is to a scroll containing divinely revealed words.

2. The Torah may further refer to revelation, not as an object but as a corpus of doctrine.

3. When one "does Torah," the disciple studies or learns and the master teaches or exemplifies Torah. Hence while the word *Torah* never appears as a verb, it does refer to an act.

4. The word also bears a quite separate sense, *torah* as category or classification or corpus of rules, for example, "the torah of driving a car" is a usage entirely acceptable to some documents. This generic usage of the word does occur.

5. The word *Torah* very commonly refers to a status, distinct from and

above another status, as teachings of Torah against teachings of scribes. For the Mishnah in some measure, and for the two Talmuds overall, that distinction is critical to the entire hermeneutic enterprise.

6. Obviously, no account of the meaning of the word *Torah* can ignore the distinction between the two Torahs, written and oral, even though, as we shall now see, it is important only in the Talmuds' stage of the formation of the literature.

7. Finally, as I have already explained, the word *Torah* refers to a source of salvation, often fully worked out in stories about how the individual and the nation will be saved through Torah.

Among the seven classifications within which meanings of the word *torah* may be sorted out, I select as important the one characteristic of the rabbinic system at the end of its development. It is the sixth, the theory of the two Torahs. I ask where, when in the canonical sequence, and how the word *Torah* stands for the "one whole Torah—oral and written—of Moses, our rabbi." We accomplish the survey in two parts. First, we survey all of the components of the canon except for the two Talmuds. Then we deal with the two Talmuds by themselves. The reason for this procedure derives from the results of the survey of references to the Messiah presented in the preceding chapter. Just as we found there that the two Talmuds closely related to one another and stood separate, because of their comprehensive character, from the rest of the canon, so here too we shall come up with the same result. The reader will find a full account of the matter at hand in my *Torah: From Scroll to Symbol in Formative Judaism* (Philadelphia, 1985).

From the Mishnah to the Yerushalmi

Mishnah. The distinction between the oral Torah and the written Torah does not occur in the Mishnah, nor do the formulations *torah she-bikhtab* and *torah she-be͑al peh*. No passage demands the meaning "not-written-down-Torah." None makes clear reference to a corpus of doctrine external to the written Torah, yet bearing correlative authority, and thus oral Torah. Quite to the contrary, the contrast between the status of Torah (words of Torah) and the status of authoritative-but-not-Torah (teachings of scribes) precludes the conception of two Torahs of *equal* standing and authority, both deriving from God's revelation to Moses at Mount Sinai. Let me restate a simple, probative fact. Every Mishnah passage in which the Torah speaks or in which people refer to Torah in either a denotative way or connotative setting, alludes to what is in the written Torah, either in general—as a status—or in particular, as a source of the given fact adduced in evidence. Accordingly, not only does the Torah or Torah in the Mishnah not denote the myth of the dual Torah, it also in no way even connotes it. Indeed, it forbids it. All the evidence of the Mishnah points to a single conclusion, in two parts. First, no one in the Mishnah has heard of any Torah revealed by God to Moses at Sinai except for the one in writing. Second, no one in the Mishnah imagines that the Mishnah, in particular, is either derived from revelation at Sinai or even related to it. Whatever its authors thought the Mishnah was supposed to be, they never indicate that it enjoyed the status of Torah.

Abot. Abot does not know this distinction in its mythic formulation.

Tosefta. The counterpart of Scripture is Mishnah (T. Ber. 2:12). But that usage does not demand reference to the mythic language to encompass both within the Torah. The framers of the Tosefta never refer to the myth of the dual Torah, nor do they know the Mishnah in particular as either Torah or oral Torah.

Mekhilta. This distinction between the written word and oral Torahs does not appear. Mekhilta makes no unambiguous reference to the myth of the two Torahs of Sinai.

Sifra. The use of the plural *Torot* refers to two Torahs, one in writing, the other oral, so Behuqotai 8:12. But Israel was given not two but many Torahs (Torot), so Aqiba at the same passage.

Sifre Numbers. No passage alludes to the myth of the two Torahs.

Sifre Deuteronomy. Sifre Deut. 351 states that two Torahs were given to Israel—one in writing, one transmitted through memorization. This reference is unambiguous.

Genesis Rabbah. I find no relevant passages.

Leviticus Rabbah. One should study Torah, prophets, writings, oral law, Midrash, and so forth (Lev. R. 3:7). Teachers of Scripture and of the oral law "set right the way" (Lev. R. 9:2). Words of Torah were given in clear divisions—Scripture, Mishnah, Talmud, law, and lore (Lev. R. 15:2). This statement seems to me decisive evidence of the notion that Torah encompasses more than Scripture. There are specialists of equal merit in Scripture, Mishnah, Talmud, and lore (Lev. R. 36:2). But the myth of the two Torahs in particular is not attested here.

The upshot of this rapid survey is that the myth of the two Torahs is not told in any of the documents reviewed just now. The distinction between the Torah's rules and the rules promulgated on the authority of the scribes is a commonplace. But, by itself, that distinction does not bear the myth of the dual Torah and, as I said, it contradicts it. I find no allusion to the myth at hand in Mekhilta, Sifra, or Sifre Numbers. I find an ambiguous allusion to it in Sifre Deuteronomy and in Leviticus Rabbah. We now contrast this handful of allusions, attesting that the myth at hand can have circulated, if not in its specific form involving the dual Torah only, and proved useful in some settings, to what we find in the Yerushalmi, then the Bavli.

The Yerushalmi and the Bavli: From Implicit to Explicit

When we compared the Bavli's versions of stories to those of the Yerushalmi, we saw time and again that the Bavli's authors as rhetoricians liked to make explicit many details that the Yerushalmi's writers treated as implicit, or as not present at all. If we now translate into the realm of ideas the result of parsing stories in the two Talmuds, we find a parallel result. The authors of the Bavli's materials bring to full and explicit expression what—I think I may fairly claim—is implicit but assuredly present in the Yerushalmi's treatment of the same symbol.

In the Yerushalmi the Mishnah is held equivalent to Scripture (Y. Hor. 3:5). But the Mishnah is not called Torah. Still, once the Mishnah has entered the status of Scripture, it is but a short step to a theory of the Mishnah as part of the revelation at Sinai—hence, oral Torah. But sages recorded in this Talmud do not appear explicitly and clearly to have taken that step. In the Yerushalmi we find the first glimmerings of an effort to theorize in general, not merely in detail, about how specific teachings of Mishnah relate to specific teachings of Scripture. The citing of scriptural proof texts for Mishnaic propositions, after all, would not have caused much surprise to the framers of the Mishnah; they themselves included such passages, though not often. But what conception of the Torah underlies such initiatives, and how do the Yerushalmi's sages propose to explain the phenomenon of the Mishnah as a whole? The following passage gives us one statement. It refers to the assertion at M. Hag. 1:8D that the laws on cultic cleanness presented in the Mishnah rest on deep and solid foundations in the Scripture.

Y. Hag. 1:7.V

    A.   *The laws of the Sabbath [M. 1:8B]:* R. Jonah said R. Hama bar Uqba raised the question [in reference to M. Hag. 1:8D's view that there are many verses of Scripture on cleanness], "And lo, it is written only, 'Nevertheless a spring or a cistern holding water shall be clean; but whatever touches their carcass shall be unclean' (Lev. 11:36). And from this verse you derive many laws. [So how can M. 1:8D say what it does about many verses for laws of cultic cleanness?]"

    B.   R. Zeira in the name of R. Yohanan: "If a law comes to hand and you do not know its nature, do not discard it for another one, for lo, many laws were stated to Moses at Sinai, and all of them have been embedded in the Mishnah."

The truly striking assertion appears in B. The Mishnah now is claimed to contain statements made by God to Moses. Just how these statements found their way into the Mishnah, and which passages of the Mishnah contain them, we do not know. That is hardly important, given the fundamental assertion at hand. The passage proceeds to a further, and far more consequential, proposition. It asserts that part of the Torah was written down and part was preserved in memory and transmitted orally. In context, moreover, that distinction must encompass the Mishnah, thus explaining its origin as part of the Torah. Here is a clear and unmistakable expression of the distinction between two forms in which a single Torah was revealed and handed on at Mount Sinai, part in writing, part orally.

While the passage below does not make use of the language, Torah-in-writing and Torah-by-memory, it does refer to the "written" and the "oral." I believe I am fully justified in supplying the word *Torah* in square brackets. The reader will note, however, that the word *Torah* likewise does not occur at K and L. Only when the passage reaches its climax, at M, does it break down into a number of categories—Scripture, Mishnah, Talmud, laws, lore. It there makes the additional point that everything comes from Moses at Sinai. So the fully articulated theory of two Torahs (not merely one Torah in two forms) does not reach final expression in this passage. But short of explicit allusion to Torah-in-writing and Torah-by-memory, which (so far as I am able to discern) we find mainly in the Talmud of Babylonia, the ultimate theory of Torah of formative Judaism is at hand in what follows.

Y. Hag. 1 :7.V

D. R. Zeirah in the name of R. Eleazar: " 'Were I to write for him my laws by ten thousands, they would be regarded as a strange thing' (Hos. 8 : 12). Now is the greater part of the Torah written down? [Surely not. The oral part is much greater.] But more abundant are the matters that are derived by exegesis from the written [Torah] than those derived by exegesis from the oral [Torah]."

E. And is that so?

F. But more cherished are those matters that rest upon the written [Torah] than those that rest upon the oral [Torah].

J. R. Haggai in the name of R. Samuel bar Nahman, "Some teachings were handed on orally, and some things were handed on in writing, and we do not know which of them is the more precious. But on the basis of that which is written, 'And the Lord said to Moses, Write these words; in accordance with these words I have made a covenant with you and with Israel' (Exod. 34:27), [we conclude] that the ones that are handed on orally are the more precious."

K. R. Yohanan and R. Yudan b. R. Simeon—one said, "If you have kept what is preserved orally and also kept what is in writing, I shall make a covenant with you, and if not, I shall not make a covenant with you."

L. The other said, "If you have kept what is preserved orally and you have kept what is preserved in writing, you shall receive a reward, and if not, you shall not receive a reward."

M. [With reference to Deut. 9: 10: "And on them was written according to all the words that the Lord spoke with you in the mount,"] said R. Joshua b. Levi, "He could have written, 'On them,' but wrote, 'And on them.' He could have written, 'All,' but wrote,

'According to all.' He could have written, 'Words,' but wrote, 'The words.' [These then serve as three encompassing clauses, serving to include] Scripture, Mishnah, Talmud, laws, and lore. Even what an experienced student in the future is going to teach before his master already has been stated to Moses at Sinai."

N.   What is the scriptural basis for this view?

O.   "There is no remembrance of former things, nor will there be any remembrance of later things yet to happen among those who come after" (Qoh. 1:11).

P.   If someone says, "See, this is a new thing," his fellow will answer him, saying to him, "This has been around before us for a long time."

Here we have absolutely explicit evidence that people believed part of the Torah had been preserved not in writing but orally. Linking that part to the Mishnah remains a matter of implication. But it surely comes fairly close to the surface when we are told that the Mishnah contains Torah traditions revealed at Sinai. From that view it requires only a small step to the allegation that the Mishnah is part of the Torah, the oral part.

At the risk of repetitiousness, let us consider yet another example in which the same notion occurs. The following passage moves from the matter of translating from the written Torah into Aramaic, so that the congregation may understand the passage, to a distinction between two forms of the Torah. The same discourse then goes over the ground we have just reviewed. The importance of the issue to the larger argument of this book justifies our reviewing the whole.

Y. Megillah 4:1.II

G.   R. Samuel bar R. Isaac went to a synagogue. He saw someone standing and serving as translator, leaning on a post. He said to him, "It is forbidden to you [to lean while standing]. For just as the Torah was given, originally, in fear and trembling, so we have to treat it with fear and trembling."

H.   R. Haggai said R. Samuel bar R. Isaac went to a synagogue. He saw Hunah standing and serving as translator, and he had not set up anyone else in his stead [so he was both reading and translating himself]. He said to him, "It is forbidden to you, for just as it was given through an intermediary [namely, Moses], so we have to follow the custom of having an intermediary [so that the same person may not both read from the Torah and translate]."

I.   R. Judah bar Pazzi went in and treated the matter as a question: "'The Lord spoke with you face to face at the mountain . . . while I stood between the Lord and you at that time, to declare to you the word of the Lord'" (Deut. 5:4–5).

J.   R. Haggai said R. Samuel bar R. Isaac went into a synagogue. He saw a teacher [reading from] a translation spread out, presenting the materials from the book. He said to him, "It is forbidden to do it that way. Things which were stated orally must be presented orally. Things which were stated in writing must be presented in writing."

K.   R. Haggai in the name of R. Samuel bar Nahman: "Some teachings were stated orally, and some teachings were stated in writing, and we do not know which of the two is more precious.

L.   "But on the basis of that which is written, 'And the Lord said to Moses, Write these words; in accordance with these words I have made a covenant with you and with Israel' (Exod. 34:27), that is to say the ones that are handed on orally are more precious."

M.   R. Yohanan and R. Judah b. R. Simeon—one said, "[The meaning of the verse is this:] 'If you have kept what is handed on orally and if you have kept what is handed on in writing, then I shall make a covenant with you, and if not, I shall not make a covenant with you.'"

N.   The other one said, "'If you have kept what is handed on orally, and if you have kept what is handed on in writing, then you will receive a reward, and if not, you will not receive a reward.'"

O.   [With reference to the following verse: "And the Lord gave me the two tablets of stone written with the finger of God; and on them were all the words that the Lord had spoken with you on the mountain in the midst of the fire on the day of the assembly" (Deut. 9:10),] said R. Joshua b. Levi, "[It is written,] 'on them,' *and* on them,' 'words,' '*the* words,' '*all*,' '*with* all.' [These additional usages serve what purpose?]

P.   "The reference is to Scripture, Mishnah, Talmud, and lore—and even what an experienced disciple is destined to teach in the future before his master has already been stated to Moses at Sinai."

Q.   That is in line with the following verse of Scripture: "Is there a thing of which it is said, 'See, this is new'? He and his fellow will reply to him, 'It has been already in the ages before us'" (Qoh. 1:10).

Here again, the penultimate statement of the theory of the Torah of formative Judaism lies at hand. The final step is not taken here, but it is a short step indeed.

The first point is that when the Torah (the written Scripture) is read in the synagogue, the original revelation is reenacted. God used Moses as intermediary. So the one who proclaims the Torah (in the place of God) must not be the one who then repeats Torah to the congregation (in the place of Moses). This further leads, at J, to the explicit statement that parts of the Torah were stated orally and parts in writing. Here, however, the part that is oral clearly means the Aramaic translation (Targum). In context, we need not invoke the conception of two kinds of one Torah, let alone of two Torahs constituting the one whole Torah of Moses our rabbi. That does not appear. Then (Kff.) comes the familiar discussion about two modes of one Torah. This passage then precipitates a statement of what constitutes that whole Torah, written and oral. Here, as before, Mishnah, Talmud, and lore join Scripture. The main point again is the assertion that whatever a sage teaches falls into the category of the Torahs of Sinai. That point, of course, is familiar and conventional. First, what the sage says is Torah. Second, the sage cites Mishnah. Third, the Mishnah (too) is Torah. But I do not yet see a statement that there were *two* Torahs in particular. There seem to have been many. The myth of the dual Torah is not yet at hand.

When we come to the Bavli, we need not repeat the numerous times in which the Yerushalmi's points are repeated. Let us turn directly to what is new and important. That is what will answer our question of whether, and how, the Bavli differed from the Yerushalmi in its treatment of the component of the Torah myth under consideration. *Torah* refers specifically to Scripture as written Torah at b. Ber. 5a and b. Qid. 30a. The greater part of the Torah was given in writing, the lesser part orally (b. Git. 60b). The distinction between written and oral Torah, with stress on revelation of two Torahs at Sinai, appears at the following passages: b. Shab. 31a, b. Yoma 28b, and b. Qid. 66a. All three references occur in stories about conflicts or heresy. This myth certainly is distinctive to the sages' circles. The "complete Torah" that is "ours," that is, sages', at b. Men. 65b and b. B.B. 116a, contains a possible allusion to the myth of the dual Torah, also in the setting of controversy, now between Pharisees and Sadducees. Apart from these we find no reference to the conception of a written and an oral Torah revealed at Sinai. We find no passage in which the Mishnah as such is described as oral Torah or in which the teachings of scribes or rabbis are called oral Torah. Such teachings are called torah, that is, part of revelation, in the generic sense alone. The claim that Jews believed in the myth of the two Torahs is generally accompanied by citation of the following story.

Our Rabbis taught: A certain heathen once came before Shammai and asked him, "How many Torahs have you?"

"Two," he replied: "the Written Torah and the Oral Torah."

"I believe you with respect to the Written, but not with respect to the Oral Torah; make me a proselyte on condition that you teach me the Written Torah [only]." [But] he scolded and repulsed him in anger.

When he went before Hillel, he accepted him as a proselyte. On the first day he taught him, *"Alef, beth, gimmel, daleth"*; the following day he reversed [them] to him.

"But yesterday you did not teach them to me thus," he protested. "Must you then not rely upon me? Then rely upon me with respect to the Oral [Torah] too."

—B. Shabbat 31a; translated by H. Freedman, pp. 139–140

The foregoing passage is most commonly cited as evidence of belief "from very early times" in the doctrine of the two Torahs. Since it speaks of Hillel, it is conventionally assumed that people in the time of Hillel held such beliefs. But, as we observe, the story occurs for the first time only in the final composition of the entire rabbinic canon. Standing by itself, it demonstrates that at circa A.D. 500–600, people not only believed in the myth of the two Torahs but ascribed that conviction to Hillel. The Bavli took that short step that the Yerushalmi had charted. Now we have the story of the two Torahs revealed at Sinai. The Bavli's allusions to the "one whole Torah of Moses, our rabbi," complete the picture, most details of which the Yerushalmi had already laid forth. So, in a word, here the Bavli has made explicit what the Yerushalmi had earlier implied. As with rhetoric, so with myth, the authors of the Bavli draw matters into a full expression in conclusion.

The Yerushalmi and the Bavli: The Literary and Redactional Distinction

Since we know that the Bavli differs from the Yerushalmi in a fundamental literary-redactional policy, let us return to that important starting point of the argument at hand. We seek the literary and redactional counterpart to the fact just now adduced, that the Bavli completed what the Yerushalmi had started. The Bavli's writers and redactors made up Scripture units of discourse on a large scale. They built out of such units of discourse enormous and sustained constructions. The Yerushalmi's writers and redactors less commonly did the former and never did the latter, so what is distinctive to the Bavli has now to return to the center stage. What we have to do is reconsider those fully exposed Scripture units of discourse. At issue is not whether the Bavli presents whole and complete what the Yerushalmi portrays only partially. As I have explained, that is scarcely a question one can answer at all. All I wish to do is review this question: Is the principal difference between the Yerushalmi and the Bavli that the Bavli makes more extensive use than the Yerushalmi of Scripture in its literary-redactional structure? If I can do so, then I can point to parallel relationships between the two documents: one in the Bavli's expressing explicitly what the other states by implication; a second in the Bavli's adding details omitted in the Yerushalmi's version of stories; and a third in the Bavli's joining for redactional purposes the two media of the Torah, one of which the Yerushalmi's authors had neglected. Since, in quantity and redactional character, we find such a distinction, we shall want to know how the distinction takes form. Then we may turn, in the discussion to follow, to what difference the distinction makes. Let me now spell out what I think is at issue.

We have seen that the one substantial literary-redactional difference between the Bavli and the Yerushalmi lies in the Bavli framers' inclusion of sizable sequences and proportionately substantial compositions of Scripture units of discourse. These the Yerushalmi presents in only limited volume and

in significantly modest proportion. If we wish to compare the two compositions as to the picture of the larger system of Judaism supplied by each, we
had best revert to the simple fact at hand. If the Bavli devotes a sizable proportion of the whole (30–40%) to Scripture units of discourse, then are we able,
in those units, to identify important statements of the larger system of Judaism
to which each constituent of the canon of Judaism testifies?

That simple question lies at the end of our inquiry. Let me unpack it. If the
Bavli's Scripture units of discourse turn out to comprise the principal bearers
of its account of the larger system at hand, then we may account for what
seems to be the full and more complete picture of that system supplied by the
Bavli than that presented by the Yerushalmi. How so? We may claim that, in
taking within the framework of redaction what is supplied not only by the
Mishnah but also by Scripture, the authors of the Bavli found the way to sur-
pass all that had gone before. That is to say, by extensive resort to units of
discourse providing an exegesis of Scripture, the Bavli's framers made provision for ample expression of the system, through the reading of its values into
the texts of Scripture. In omitting such units of discourse, the Yerushalmi's
authors lost the opportunity to spell out in a whole and complete way the
larger system of Judaism that both Talmuds portray. The key to the success of
the Bavli, by this theory, lies in the very foundations of its literary structure,
in the redactional-literary decision to lay the basis of the main beams of the
Bavli's composition upon not only the Mishnah but also upon passages of
Scripture.

It remains to recall that both documents in approximately equal proportion
present stories about sages, commonly told to convey some characteristic and
definitive aspect of the value system of the sages' group. Since those stories
nearly always serve as vehicles for the expression of what is not Mishnaic but
distinctively rabbinic or talmudic in both of the Talmuds at hand, they serve as
potential indicators as much as do Scripture units of discourse. But on the
basis of proportions of such stories we cannot distinguish one Talmud from
the other. To be sure, when we took up the ways in which stories about sages
serve the larger redactional structure, we noted a slight tendency for the
Yerushalmi's stories to stand on their own, outside of the larger redactional
purpose served by including them. The Bavli tended—in our modest sample—
to revise pretty much everything for its larger purpose. In any event distinguishing the documents on the basis of provenance and use of stories exemplary of sages' values led nowhere. So, as is clear, we revert to the matter at
hand, as the sole point of differentiation.

What the charts that follow tell us, specifically, are the simple facts of
where, in the Scripture units of tradition, the Yerushalmi's and the Bavli's authors and compositors make clear reference to a conception distinctive to the
rabbinic system, and where they do not. What we want to know is whether the
Scripture units of tradition in particular serve as the principal vehicle for bearing the distinctive message of Judaism of the form attested in the rabbinic

canon as a whole. In comparing the Scripture units of discourse in the two Talmuds, we wish to see whether there is any substantial and measurable difference in the purpose and definition of what we find in the one document as against what is presented by the other. That comparison will tell us whether the difference is merely in volume as is already established or also, and especially, in the essential character of the Scripture units of discourse of the one document as against that of the ones in the other.

1. Scripture units of discourse that contain an important expression of the Torah myth of the rabbinic canon and the trait deemed definitive or even distinctive, such as arrogance or Torah study, respectively.

Sotah		Yerushalmi	Sotah		Bavli
1:8	II.	Samson's parents warned against intermarriage.	1:1–2	XVII–XXIX.	Arrogance.
	III.	Holy Spirit rested on Samson.	1:8–9	XV–XVI.	Divine justice on how punishment is meted out.
	V.	This world, to come.			
	VIII.	Concern for proper order, for forgiveness.		XX.	Bless God after eating.
	IX.	Forgiveness a principal virtue.		XXI.	Modesty.
				XXII.	Rabbinization of tale.
1:10	I.	Merit.		XXIII.	Avoid embarrassing another.
	II.	Merit of righteous protects Israel.		XXV.	As above.
	V.	Merit of righteous.		XXVIII.	God's plan.
	VI.	Fair exchange of merit.		XXXV.	God has his own plans.
5:4	II.	Redemption.		XLIX.	Messiah.
5:5	III.	Impulse to do evil/good.		LXVI.	Angels argue with God.
5:6	III.	Forgiveness.			
7:1	II.	God spoke to Sarah directly.		LXXVII.	Joseph failed to protect father's honor.
7:3	III.	Rabbinic mode of Scripture exegesis.		LXXXIII.	Torah study read into Scripture.
7:5	I.	Nations want to study Torah.		LXXXVI.	Imitate God's traits.
				LXXXVII.	Carry out religious duties.
			2:3	II.	Merit.
			3:3–4	VI.	Merit, Torah study.
			7:1–5	XV.	Words of Torah to be treated as holy.
				XXI.	Merit.
				XXII.	Merit.
			7:6	XIV–XVI.	Importance of generosity.
			7:8	VI.	Flattery is a sin.
				VII.	As above.
			9:5–6	XIII.	Torah study.
				XX.	Merit.
				XXIV.	Rabbinization of story.
			9:11–13	XI.	David's prayers. Discipleship.
				XII.	As above.
				XIII.	As above.

Sukkah	Yerushalmi	Sukkah		Bavli
5:1	IV. Holy spirit favors happy person.	4:9–10	XII.	Merit of Abraham.
			XIII.	Torah study.
			XV.	Charity.
		5:1D–4	IV.	Messiah sayings.
			V.	Inclination to do evil.
			VI.	Messiah sayings.
			VII.	Evil inclination.
			VIII.	As above.
			IX.	As above.
			X.	As above.
			XI.	As above.
			XII.	As above.
			XIII.	As above.
			XIV.	As above.
			XV.	As above.
			XVI.	As above.
			XVII.	Messiah sayings.
			XVIII.	Messiah sayings.

Sanhedrin	Yerushalmi	Sanhedrin		Bavli
1:2	II. Rabbinization of biblical hero or event.	1:1–6	XVIII.	Torah verses prove truth of popular sayings.
1:3	III. As above.		XXI.	David as rabbi.
2:3	V. As above.		XXX.	Rabbinization of verses of Scripture.
2:5	III. As above.			
	IV. As above.		LXXXVI.	God rewarded humility.
2:6	II. Solomon sinned against a letter of the Torah.	2:1–2	XI.	David and Saul on halakhah.
4:9	II. God does not rejoice at downfall even of the wicked.		XIII.	God intervened to prevent sin.
6:7	II. Israelites are characterized by mercy.	2:4E–I	III.	Rereading of story.
		2:5	IV.	Reasons a wife dies.
10:1	VI. Merit of patriarchs protects Israel.		V.	Making marriages.
		3:1	XI.	Rabbinization of verse
	VII. Korach treated as heretic in rejecting rabbis' authority.	3:3	XI.	As above.
		3:6–7	III.	As above.
10:2	IV. Ahaz was enemy of synagogues and school houses.		IV.	As above.
		4:3–4	I.	Rabbinization of a verse.
	V. Merit.		II.	As above.
	VII. Power of repentance.		III.	As above.
			IV.	As above.
		4:5	IV.	Exile atones.
			VI.	God is righteous in dealings with Israel.
			IX.	Man naturally sins.
			X.	Angels opposed creating man.
			XI.	Rabbinic reading of verses on creation of man.
			XI.	Rabbinic reading of verses on creation of man.

Sanhedrin	Yerushalmi	Sanhedrin	Bavli
		XII.	As above.
		XIII.	As above.
		XV.	Polemic against heretics read into Scripture.
		XVI.	As above.
		XVII.	As above.
		XVIII.	As above.
		XX.	As above.
		XXI.	As above.
		XXV.	As above.
		XXVI.	As above.
		XXVII.	As above.
		XXVIII.	As above.
		XXXIII.	God favors one who resists evil.
	5:1–5	XVII.	Rabbinization of a verse of Scripture.
	6:1H–J	II–III.	Verses used in polemic against Jesus.
	6:2	II.	Punishment of hidden sins.
		III.	Achan violated all five books of Torah.
		IV.	As above.
		V.	As above.
		IX.	Contrast of Moses' humility, Joshua's insolence.
		X.	Joshua's error.
		XI.	Rabbinic reading of verse.
		XII.	As above.
	6:4–6	VI.	Where in Torah is proof one has to bury dead.
		VIII.	Who benefits from eulogy.
		XVI.	Halakhic standards applied to biblical colloquy.
	7:2	III.	Korach's rebellion against Moses; leadership punished by God.
	7:5	XIX.	First man was a vegetarian.
	8:1	VI.	Early generations more favored than later ones.
	8:2	IV.	Wine is for the bereaved.
		VII.	Wine causes woe, God tells Noah.
		VIII.	Rabbinization of biblical heroine.
	9:6	VII.	Priority of Moses.
	10:5–6	X	Testing of Abraham; merit.
	11:1–2	V.	Resurrection based on prooftexts of Scripture.
		VI.	As above.
		VII.	As above.
		VIII.	As above.
		IX.	As above.
		X.	As above.
		XV.	Dispute over meaning of verses, defense of Israel.

Sanhedrin	Yerushalmi	Sanhedrin	Bavli
		XVI.	As above.
		XVII.	As above.
		XXII.	Resurrection verses.
		XXIII.	As above.
		XXIV.	As above.
		XXV.	As above.
		XXVI.	As above.
		XXVII.	As above.
		XXVII.	As above.
		XXVIII.	As above.
		XXX.	Study of Torah saying.
		XXXI.	Study of Torah saying re world to come.
		XXXII–XXXVI.	Proofs from Scripture of resurrection of the dead.
		XXXVII.	Miracles for Daniel's friends in furnace.
		XL.	As above.
		XLII.	As above.
		XLIII.	Where did the rabbis, Hananah, Mishtel, Azariah, go?
		XLIV–XLV.	Further expansions.
		XLVI.	Nebuchadnezzar and Israel.
		XLVII.	Messiah theme written into verses.
		L.	Why Ezra's book is not given Nehemiah's name.
		LI.	Messiah theme written into verses.
		LIII.	Miracle.
		LVII.	Divine punishment is exact.
		LXII.	Torah theme introduced.
		LXIV.	As above.
		LXVIII.	As above.
		LXXI.	Messiah theme introduced.
		LXXIII.	Discourse of God and angel made up.
		LXXV.	God takes human form to punish Sennacherib.
		LXXVII.	Concern with proper form.
		LXXIX.	Destruction due to sins.
		LXXX.	Torah sayings.
		LXXXI.	Merit.
		LXXXII.	Messiah sayings and verses of Scripture.
		LXXXIII.	As above.
		LXXXIV.	As above.
		LXXXVII.	As above.
		LXXIX.	As above.
		XC.	As above.
		XCIV.	As above.
		XCV.	Rabbis as the righteous.
		XCVI.	Repentance.
		XCVII.	Disciples of sages.

Sanhedrin	Yerushalmi	Sanhedrin	Bavli
		XCVIII.	Messiah theme read into verses.
		XCIX.	As above.
		C.	As above.
		CI.	As above.
		CV.	As above.
		CVII.	As above.
		CIX.	As above.
		CX.	As above.
		CXII.	As above.
		CXIII.	As above.
		CXIV.	As above.
		CXV.	As above.
		CXX.	Torah theme introduced into verses.
		CXXI.	As above.
		CXXII.	As above.
		CXXIII.	As above.
		CXXIV.	As above.
		CXXVII.	Good form of discipleship.
		CXXIX.	Torah theme introduced into verses
		CXXXIII.	As above.
		CXLIV.	Self-serving pleas rejected.
		CXLVIII.	Errors of prophets not favored by God.
		CXLIX.	World to come.
		CL.	Merit.
		CLI.	Arrogance rejected.
		CLV.	Torah theme read into verse.
		CLX.	Repentance.
		CLXVI.	World to come.
		CLXVII.	Merit.
		CLXXV.	Repentance.
		CLXXVII.	Measure for measure.
		CLXVIII.	Manasseh as rabbi.
		CLXXIX.	Absalom and world to come.
		CLXXX.	As above.
		CLXXXIV.	As above.
		CLXXXIX.	Measure for measure.
		CXC.	As above.
		CXCVIII.	Whoever persecutes Israel becomes head.
		CCV.	Merit protects descendant.
		CCVII.	Repentance.
		CCVIII.	Redemption.
		CCIX.	Repentance.
		CCXIII.	Balaam and world to come.
		CCXVIII.	God shows forgiveness to Israel.
		CCXXVIII.	Redemption.
		CCXXXIX.	Torah theme read into verses.
		CCXL.	As above.
		CCXLII.	As above.
		CCXLIII.	As above.
		CCXLIV.	As above.

Sanhedrin	Yerushalmi	Sanhedrin	Bavli
		CCXLV.	As above.
		CCXLVI.	God tests the righteous.
		CCXLVII.	God and David.
		CCXLVIII.	David wanted to worship idols.
		CCXLIX.	David forgiven.
		CCL.	As above.
		CCLI.	David punished.
		CCLII.	Repentance.
		CCLVI.	Favor shown to patriarchs.
	11:3		
	A-CC	XI.	Repentance.
		XX.	Measure for measure.
		XXXVIII.	Rabbinic activity read into verse.
		XXXIX.	As above.
		XL.	Avoid contention.
		XLI.	Do not contend with David's heirs.
	11:3		
	DD-FF	III.	Must observe all details of law.
		IV.	Messiah theme introduced.
		V.	Merits of ancestors.
		VI.	Divine patience.
		VIII.	World to come.

2. Scripture units of discourse to which the Torah myth and other rabbinic values in all its forms are irrelevant. Focus is defined by facts of Scripture alone.

Sotah	Yerushalmi	Sotah	Bavli
1:4-5	III.	1:8-9	III-XIV, XVII-XIX,
1:8	I, IV, VI, VII		XXIV, XXVI, XXXIX,
1:10	II, IV, VIII		XXXI, XXXII, XXXIII
5:6	I, II		XXXIV, XXXVI, XXXVII
7:2	III		XXXVIII, XXXIX, XL,
7:3	IV		XLI, XLII, XLIII,
7:4	V		XLIV, XLV, XLVI,
8:3	I, III, IV, VI-VII, IX		XLVII, XLVIII, L, LI, LII, LIII, LIV, LV, LVI, LVII, LVIII, LIX, LX, LXI, LXII, LXIII, LXIV, LXV, LXVI, LXVII, LXVIII, LXIX, LXX, LXXI, LXXIII, LXXIV, LXXVI, LXXVIII, LXXIX, LXXX, LXXXI, LXXXII, LXXXV
		7:1-5	XIII, XIX
		8:1	VI, VII, VIII, IX, X, XI, XIV
		9:5-6	X, XI, XVII, XVIII, XIX, XXI, XXII, XXIII

Sukkah	Yerushalmi	Sukkah	Bavli
5:1	VI	4:9-10	II, III
5:4	V		
5:5	III		

Sanhedrin	Yerushalmi	Sanhedrin	Bavli
1:4	V, VI	1:1-6	LXXXV, XCIII
2:4	III	2:1-2	XII
6:3	I	2:3	III
10:2	VI	2:4A-D	IV
11:5	III	2:4J-N	III
		2:5	II
		4:5	XXX, XXI, XXXII, XXXIV, XXXV
		6:2	VI, VII, VIII
		6:4-6	XVI
		7:6	XIII, XIV
		7:11	X
		8:2	VI
		9:6	VIII, IX, X
		10:5-6	II, III
		11:1-2	XXXVIII, XXXIX, XLI, XLVIII, XLIX, LII, LIV, LV, LVI, LVIII, LIX, LX, LXI, LXIII, LXV, LXVI, LXVII, LXIX, LXX, LXXII, LXXIV, LXXVI, LXXVIII, CXXVIII, CXXX, CXLI, CXLVII, CLIII, CLIV, CLVI, CLVIII, CLIX, CLXIII, CLXIV, CLXV, CLXVII, CLXIX, CLXX, CLXXII, CLXXXVI, CLXXX, CLXXXII, CLXXXIII, CXCI, CXCII, CXCIII, CXCIV, CXCVI, CXCVII, CC, CCI, CCII, CCIII, CCIV, CCVI, CCXI, CCXII, CCXIV, CCXV, CCXVI, CCXVII, CCXXI, CCXXIII, CCXXIV, CCXXV, CCXXVI, CCXXVII, CCXXIX, CCXXXI, CCXXXII, CCXXXIII, CCXXXIV, CCXXXV, CCXXXVI, CCXXXVIII, CCXLI, CCLV
		11:3A-CC	III, IV, V, VI, VII, VIII, IX, X, XII, XIII, IV, XVI, XVII, XVIII, XIX, XXI, XXII, XXIII, XXIV, XXVI, XXVII, XXVIII, XXX, XXXII, XXXIII, XXXIV, XXXVI, XXXVII, XLII, XLIII, XLIV, XLV, XLVI
		11:4-6	XX, XXI,

Summary

	1. "Rabbinic" Scripture Units of Discourse				2. "Other" Scripture Units of Discourse		
	Y.	%	B.	%	Y.	%	B.	%
Sotah	15/34	44.9	43/126	34.1	19/34	55.8	83/126	65.8
Sukkah	1/4	25	18/20	90	3/4	75	2/20	10
Sanhedrin	13/19	68	182/319	57	6/19	31.5	137/319	43

I see no pattern at all in the charts at hand. The distinction that forms the premise of the classification, a distinction imposed from without to begin with, yields no interesting points of difference between the two Talmuds. The pattern proves to be random. In one tractate the majority of Scripture units of discourse in both Talmuds attend to considerations intrinsic to the verses that are under analysis. In another tractate the preponderance of Scripture units of discourse in both Talmuds bears the hermeneutic extrinsic to the verses and distinctive to and definitive of sages' themselves. Thus while the Scripture units of discourse in tractate Sotah, for both Talmuds, seem to focus on what we should now call the "plain meaning" or intrinsic topic of Scripture and its exegesis, the parallel types of units of discourse in Sanhedrin turn out markedly different. In Sanhedrin, the majority, again in both Talmuds, turns upon the reading into Scripture of extrinsic values—those we regard as characteristic of sages' system and viewpoint, e.g., David as rabbi, Torah study as a principal dimension of hermeneutics, and the like. What conclusions may we draw from the probe at hand?

First, we may form the hypothesis (of no particular interest to the present study) that the character of a given tractate, the subject matter to which it is devoted, and the corpus of verses of Scripture upon which it draws will dictate the hermeneutical possibilities at hand. A tractate that rests fairly firmly upon verses of Scripture of the written Torah will tend to read those verses in intrinsic terms, that is, guided by what they actually say. Hence Sotah collects a large number of Scripture units of discourse that spell out or amplify the obvious and intrinsic sense of verses of Scripture. A tractate that takes its own measure and finds in Scripture little interest (or few relevant verses) for its large theme and subject matter will do otherwise. Such a tractate will find ample place for more particularly extrinsic and hence distinctively "rabbinic" readings of biblical verses. Less tightly bound to the factual assertions of Scripture on the topic of such a tractate, the framers will have read Scripture more freely than otherwise. The hypothesis at hand may prove an interesting exercise in classification of Scripture and analysis of biblical hermeneutics in the Talmuds. It does not materially advance our inquiry.

The second conclusion does contribute to our concern. When it comes to types of Scripture units of discourse I see no difference, yielded by our small probe, between the preferences of framers of the Bavli and those of the authors of the Yerushalmi. Whether or not they drew upon a common corpus of already-completed materials, whether or not they shared or differed in the types of materials they wished to use, whether or not one Talmud's authors chose to interpret Scripture more "rabbinically" than the other—the answers to none of these questions is before us. What we do have is a clear indication that the authors of the two tractates did not differ about the types of materials they wanted to use. The framers of the Bavli, in particular, assuredly gave no evidence of reading Scripture more "rabbinically" than did the authors of the Yerushalmi.

I should find it difficult to make distinctions among the materials in the corpus of Scripture units of discourse from which the two groups made their selections. It would not be hard to concede that further study may yield such differences in the character of already-available materials. But that, too, would not make much difference to us, for the finished product is what we seek to describe, analyze, and interpret.

The description and analysis now complete, we must conclude that the facts point in one direction only. Specifically, we have now to dismiss the possibility with which we began.

First, the Bavli differs from the Yerushalmi, but not because in the materials more commonly found in the Bavli than in the Yerushalmi viewpoints and methods distinctive to the sages came to more lucid expression. That has not been demonstrated. The contrary appears to be the case. When the Bavli's authors turned to Scripture, they found lessons in accord with the larger worldview and way of life of the sages. But so did the Yerushalmi's authors, with equal perspicacity.

Second, it follows that it is simply not true that, in that demonstrably thicker layer of Scripture units of discourse in the Bavli, the Bavli carried the burden of rabbinic Judaism, a freight of messages and meanings represented in less proportion and in diminished clarity in the Yerushalmi's layer of equivalent materials. That second proposition, like the first, not only cannot be demonstrated but, on the basis of the probe at hand, surely has been proven false.

So the distinction between the Bavli and the Yerushalmi lies not in the contents of Scripture exegesis any more than it lies in the provenance of sage units of discourse. The upshot demands emphasis: *The distinction lies solely in the redactional character of the Bavli. The difference between the Bavli and the Yerushalmi is the Bavli's far more ample use of Scripture not only for proof, nor even only for truth, but solely the Bavli's resort to Scripture for the redaction and organization of large-scale discourse.* In the Bavli the Scripture serves alongside the Mishnah and in volume is not enormously less than it. Scripture and the Mishnah in the Bavli together define structure and impart proportion and organization. In the Yerushalmi, by contrast, Scripture forms an important component of the canon. But it does not dictate lines of order and main beams of structure. So that is the distinction, the only distinction I am able to find fundamental and generative, between the Bavli and the Yerushalmi. What difference does it make?

And That Has Made All the Difference

On the basis of the simple fact before us, I may now propose an answer to the simple question of why the Bavli, and not the Yerushalmi, enjoyed the definitive status that it did. I dismiss at the outset the notion that the Bavli presents doctrines or conceptions essentially different from those in the Yerushalmi. While, in some minor detail, differences do exist, overall, we now realize, they do not. When we examine two central and generative symbols—Torah and Messiah—we cannot materially distinguish the conceptions of the Bavli from those of the Yerushalmi. Nor can we claim that in the matter of the Torah the Bavli vastly improves upon what the Yerushalmi lays down. The topical programs of the two Talmuds exhibit a rough but ample correspondence. The Bavli's systematic addition of details to tales and sayings received from the earlier tradents and redactors constitutes marginal improvements at best.

What distinguishes the one document from the other is one thing, which has made all the difference: the Bavli's complete union in its redactional substrate of the Mishnah and Scripture. In presenting a summa of Judaism, the Bavli joined the two streams that, like the Missouri and the Mississippi at St. Louis, had until its time flowed separate and distinct within the same banks. The one stream, coursing from the source of the Mishnah, and the other stream, emanating from the source of Scripture, had mingled only in eddies, at the edges. But the banks of the mighty river had been set from Sinai, and (in the mythic dimension) the two streams had been meant to flow together as one river. In the Yerushalmi, Scripture found a place along the sides. The Mishnah formed the main stream. In the collections of scriptural exegesis (midrashim), Scripture had flowed all by itself down the center, wholly apart from the Mishnah. In the Bavli, for the first time, the waters not only flowed together but mingled in the middle and in the depths, in common and sustained discourse. So the Bavli for the first time from Sinai (to speak within the Torah myth) joined together in a whole and complete way, in both literary form and doctrinal substance, the one whole Torah of Moses, our rabbi.

That is why the Bavli became the Torah par excellence, the Torah through which Israel would read both Scripture and Mishnah, the Torah all together, the Torah all at once, as God at Sinai had revealed it to Moses, our rabbi. It was because the Bavli's writers accomplished the nearly perfect union of Scripture and Mishnah in a single document that the Bavli became Israel's fullest Torah. That is why when the people of the Torah, Israel, the Jewish people, for the next fifteen hundred years, wished to approach the Mishnah, it was through the reading of the Bavli. That is why when that same people wished to address Scripture, it was through the reading of the Bavli. All the other components of the canon, while authentic and authoritative too, stood in line, from second place backward, behind the primary reading of the Bavli. It is no accident that authentic avatars of the classical literature of Judaism even today learn Scripture through the Bavli's citations of verses of Scripture just as much as, commonly, they learn the Mishnah and assuredly interpret it exactly as the Bavli presents it.

Judaism in Conclusion: The Crisis Precipitated by the Mishnah, the Resolution Accomplished by the Bavli

The advent of the Mishnah circa A.D. 200 demanded that people explain the status and authority of the new document. The lines of structure emanating from the Mishnah led to the formation of a vast and unprecedented literature of Judaism. The explosive force of the return to Zion, in the time of Ezra, had produced the formation of the Torah book and much else. The extraordinary impact of the person and message of Jesus (among other things) had led to the creation of an unprecedented kind of writing in yet another sector of Israel's life. So too would be the case with the Mishnah, Israel's response to the disaster wrought by Bar Kokhba's calamity.

The reason the Mishnah, a philosophical essay rich in theoretical initiatives, which also serves as a law code, presented a stunning challenge to its age and heirs, is simple. It was because of the Mishnah's sponsorship in Israel's politics. To begin with, the Mishnah enjoyed the sponsorship of the autonomous ruler of the Jewish nation in the Land of Israel, namely, Judah the Patriarch. The result was that the Mishnah served for purposes other than simple learning and speculative thought. Whatever had been intended for it, at its very beginnings the Mishnah was turned into an authoritative law code, the constitution, along with Scripture, of Israel in its Land. Accordingly, when completed, the Mishnah emerged from the schoolhouse and forthwith made its move into the politics, courts, and bureaus of the Jewish government of the Land of Israel. Men (never women, until our own day) who mastered the Mishnah thereby qualified themselves as judges and administrators in the government of Judah the Patriarch as well as in the government of the Jewish community of Babylonia. As we know, over the next three hundred years, the Mishnah served as the foundation for the Talmuds' formation of the system of law and theology we now know as Judaism. Exegesis of the Mishnah furthermore defined the taxonomy for hermeneutics of Scripture.

The vast collection constituted by the Mishnah therefore demanded explanation. What is this book? How does it relate to the (written) Torah revealed to Moses at Mount Sinai? Under whose auspices, and by what authority, does the law of the Mishnah govern the life of Israel? These questions, we realize, bear political as well as theological implications. But, to begin with, the answers emerge out of an enterprise of exegesis, of literature. The reception of the Mishnah followed several distinct lines, each of them symbolized by a particular sort of book. Each book, in turn, offered its theory of the origin, character, and authority of the Mishnah. For the next three centuries these theories would occupy the attention of the best minds of Israel, the authorities of the two Talmuds, and the numerous other works of the age of the seed time of Judaism.

One line from the Mishnah stretched through the Tosefta—a supplement to the Mishnah—and the two Talmuds, one formed in the Land of Israel, the other in Babylonia, both serving as exegesis and amplification of the Mishnah.

The second line stretched from the Mishnah to compilations of biblical exegesis of three different sorts. First, there were exegetical collections framed partly in relation to the Mishnah and the Tosefta, in particular Sifra, on Leviticus, Sifre on Numbers, and Sifre on Deuteronomy. Second, exegetical collections were organized mainly in relation to Scripture, with special reference to Genesis Rabbah and Leviticus Rabbah. Third, exegetical collections focused on constructing abstract discourse out of diverse verses of Scripture but on a single theme or problem, represented by Pesikta de Rab Kahana.

This simple catalog of the types, range, and volume of creative writing over the three hundred years from the closure of the Mishnah indicates an obvious fact. The Mishnah stands at the beginning of a new and stunningly original epoch in the formation of Judaism. Like such generative crises as the return to Zion for the nation as a whole and the advent of Jesus for his family and followers, the Mishnah ignited in Israel a great burst of energy. The extraordinary power of the Mishnah, moreover, is seen in its very lonely position in Israelite holy literature of its time and afterward. The subsequent literature, for centuries to come, would refer back to the Mishnah or stand in some clearcut hermeneutical relationship to it. But for its part, the Mishnah referred to nothing prior to itself—except (and then, mostly implicitly and by indirection) to Scripture. So from the Mishnah back to the revelation of God to Moses at Sinai—in the view of the Mishnah—lies a vast desert. But from the Mishnah forward stretches a fertile plain.

The crisis precipitated by the Mishnah therefore stimulated wide-ranging speculation, inventive experiments of a literary and (in the nature of things) therefore also of a political, theological, and religious character. As I showed in *Midrash in Context,* for example, the Yerushalmi's work of defining and explaining the Mishnah in relation to the (written) Torah, interpreting the meaning of the Mishnah, expanding upon and applying its laws, ultimately precipitated the making, also, of compilations of exegeses of Scripture. The formation of the Talmuds and scriptural-exegetical collections thus made necessary—indeed, urgent—extraordinary and original reflection on the definition of the Torah, through inquiry into the nature of canon and scriptural authority, the range and possibilities of revelation. The results of that work all together would then define Judaism from that time to this. So the crisis presented opportunity. And Israel's sages took full advantage of the occasion. What then was this crisis? Let me begin the tale by returning to the Mishnah itself. I must first of all explain why and how the Mishnah presented such an unprecedented problem to the patriarch's sages who received the Mishnah. It is easy to do so in a way accessible to people to whom all of these events and writings have been, up to now, entirely unknown or, if known, alien and incomprehensible. To phrase the theological question so that anyone in the West may grasp it, I need simply point out one fact. So far as Judaism was concerned, revelation had been contained in the Hebrew Scriptures later on called the written Torah. True, God may have spoken in diverse ways. The last of the biblical books had been completed—so far as Jews then knew—many centuries before. How then could a new book now claim standing as holy and revealed by God? What validated the authority of the people who knew and applied that holy book to Israel's life? These questions would define the critical issue of formative Judaism, from 200 to 600. The resolution of the problem defines Judaism today. Accordingly, the crisis precipitated by the Mishnah came about because of the urgent requirement of explaining, first, just what the Mishnah was in relation to the Torah of Moses; second, why the sages who claimed to interpret and apply the law of the Mishnah to the life of Israel had the authority to do so; and, third, how Israel, in adhering to the rules of the Mishnah, kept the will of God and lived the holy life God wanted them to live.

But why should the Mishnah in particular have presented these critical problems of a social and theological order? After all, it was hardly the first piece of new writing to confront Israel from the closure of Scripture to the end of the second century. Other books had found a capacious place in the canon of the groups of Israelites that received them and deemed them holy. The canon of some groups, after all, had made room for those writings of apocryphal and pseudepigraphic provenance so framed as to be deemed holy. The Essene library at Qumran encompassed a diverse group of writings, surely received as authoritative and holy, that other Jews did not know within their canon. So, as is clear, we have to stand back and ask why, to the sages who received and realized the Mishnah, that book should have presented special, particularly stimulating, problems. Why should the issue of the relation of the Mishnah to Scripture have proved so pressing in the circles of talmudic rabbis of the third, fourth, and fifth centuries? After all, we have no evidence that the relation to the canon of Scripture of the Manual of Discipline, the Hymns, the War Scroll, or the Damascus Covenant perplexed the teacher of righteousness and the other holy priests of the Essene community. To the contrary, those documents at Qumran appear side by side with the ones we now know as canonical Scripture. The high probability is that, to the Essenes, the sectarian books were no less holy and authoritative than Leviticus, Deuteronomy,

Nahum, Habakkuk, Isaiah, and the other books of the biblical canon that they, among all Israelites, revered.

The issue had to be raised because of the peculiar traits of the Mishnah itself. But the dilemma proved acute, not merely chronic, because of the particular purpose the Mishnah was meant to serve and because of the political sponsorship behind the document. As I said above, the Mishnah was to provide Israel's constitution. It was promulgated by the patriarch—the ethnic ruler—of the Jewish nation in the Land of Israel, Judah the Patriarch, who ruled with Roman support as the fully recognized Jewish authority in the Holy Land. So the Mishnah was public, not sectarian, nor merely idle speculation of a handful of Galilean rabbinical philosophers, though in structure and content that is precisely what it was.

The Mishnah emerged as a political document. It demanded assent and conformity to its rules, where they were relevant to the government and court system of the Jewish people in its land. So the Mishnah could not be ignored and therefore had to be explained in universally accessible terms. Furthermore, the Mishnah demanded explanation not merely in relation to the established canon of Scripture and apology as the constitution of the Jew's government, the patriarchate of second-century Land of Israel. The nature of Israelite life, lacking all capacity to distinguish as secular any detail of the common culture, made it natural to wonder about a deeper issue. Israel understood its collective life and the fate of each individual under the aspect of God's loving concern, as expressed in the Torah. Accordingly, laws issued to define what people were supposed to do could not stand by themselves; they had to receive the imprimatur of Heaven, that is, they had to be given the status of revelation. Accordingly, to make its way in Israelite life, the Mishnah as a constitution and code demanded for itself a theory of beginnings at (or in relation to) Sinai, with Moses, from God. As was pointed out above, other new writings for a long time had proved able to win credence as part of the Torah, hence as revealed by God and so enjoying legitimacy. But they did so in ways not taken by the Mishnah's framers. How did the Mishnah differ?

It was in the medium of writing that, in the view of all of Israel until about A.D. 200, God had been understood to reveal the divine word and will. The Torah was a written book. People who claimed to receive further messages from God usually wrote them down. They had three choices in securing acceptance of their account. All three involved linking the new to the old. In claiming to hand on revelation, they could, first, sign their books with the names of biblical heroes. Second, they could imitate the style of biblical Hebrew. Third, they could present an exegesis of existing written verses, validating their ideas by supplying proof texts for them. From the closure of the Torah literature in the time of Ezra, circa 450 B.C. to the time of the Mishnah, nearly seven hundred years later, we do not have a single book alleged to be holy and at the same time standing wholly out of relationship to the Holy

Scriptures of ancient Israel. The pseudepigraphic writings fall into the first
category, the Essene writings at Qumran into the second and third. We may
point also to the Gospels, which take as a principal problem demonstrating
how Jesus had fulfilled the prophetic promises of the Old Testament and in
other ways carried forward and even embodied Israel's Scripture.

Insofar as a piece of Jewish writing did not find a place in relationship to
Scripture, its author laid no claim to present a holy book. The contrast between Jubilees and the Testaments of the Patriarchs, with their constant and
close harping on biblical matters, and the several books of Maccabees, shows
the differences. The former claim to present God's revealed truth, the latter,
history. So a book was holy because in style, in authorship, or in (alleged)
origin it continued Scripture, finding a place therefore (at least in the author's
mind) within the canon, or because it provided an exposition on Scripture's
meaning.

But the Mishnah made no such claim. It entirely ignored the style of biblical Hebrew, speaking in a quite different kind of Hebrew altogether. It is silent
on its authorship through sixty-two of the sixty-three tractates (the claims of
Abot pose a special problem). In any event, nowhere does the Mishnah contain the claim that God had inspired the authors of the document. These are
not given biblical names and certainly are not alleged to have been biblical
saints. Most of the book's named authorities flourished within the same century as its anonymous arrangers and redactors, not in remote antiquity. Above
all, the Mishnah contains scarcely a handful of exegeses of Scripture. These,
where they occur, play a trivial and tangential role. So here is the problem of
the Mishnah: different from Scripture in language and style, indifferent to the
claim of authorship by a biblical hero or divine inspiration, stunningly aloof
from allusion to verses of Scripture for nearly the whole of its discourse—yet
authoritative for Israel.

So the Mishnah was not a statement of theory alone, telling only how things
will be in the eschaton. Nor was it a wholly sectarian document, reporting the
view of a group without standing or influence in the larger life of Israel. True,
in some measure it bears both of these traits of eschatology and sectarian
provenance. But the Mishnah was (and is) law for Israel. It entered the government and courts of the Jewish people, both in the motherland and also
overseas, as the authoritative constitution of the courts of Judaism. The
advent of the Mishnah therefore marked a turning in the life of the nation-
religion. The document demanded explanation and apology.

The one thing one could not do, as a Jew in third-century Tiberias, Sep-
phoris, Caesarea, or Both Shearim, in Galilee, was ignore the thing. True,
one might refer solely to ancient Scripture and tradition and live life out
within the inherited patterns of the familiar Israelite religion-culture. But as
soon as one dealt with the Jewish government in charge of everyday life—
went to court over the damages done to a crop by a neighbor's ox, for in-

stance—one came up against a law in addition to the law of Scripture, a document the principles of which governed and settled all matters. So the Mishnah rapidly came to confront the life of Israel. The people who knew the Mishnah, the rabbis or sages, came to dominate that life. And their claim, in accord with the Mishnah, to exercise authority and the right to impose heavenly sanction came to perplex. Now the crisis is fully exposed.

The Mishnah therefore made necessary the formation of the Talmuds, its exegetical companions. Within the processes of exegesis of the Mishnah came the labor of collecting and arranging these exegeses, in correlation with the Mishnah, read line by line and paragraph by paragraph. The sorts of things the sages who framed the Talmuds did to the Mishnah, they then went and did to Scripture. Within the work of exegesis of Scripture was the correlative labor of organizing what had been said verse by verse, following the structure of a book of the Hebrew Bible. The type of discourse and the mode of organizing the literary result of discourse suitable for the one document served the other as well. The same people did both for the same reasons. So to the Tosefta, Sifra, and the Yerushalmi alike, the paramount issue was Scripture, not merely its authority but especially its sheer mass of information. The decisive importance of the advent of the Mishnah in precipitating the vast exegetical enterprise represented by the books at hand emerges from a simple fact. The documents all focus attention on the Mishnah in particular. Two of them, the Tosefta and the Yerushalmi, organize everything at hand around the redactional structure supplied by the Mishnah itself.

The importance of the Bavli's distinctive contribution now becomes entirely clear. The Bavli carried forward a long-established enterprise, namely, the forging of links between the Mishnah and Scripture. But the organizers and redactors of the materials compiled in the Bavli did something unprecedented. They allowed sustained passages of Scripture to serve, as much as sustained and not merely episodic passages of the Mishnah served, as main beams in the composition of structure and order. In a single document, the Mishnah and Scripture functioned together and for the first time in much the same way. The original thesis, that the Mishnah depended upon the written Torah, thus all of its statements were linked to proof texts of Scripture, now gave way to its natural and complete fulfillment. Once sets of verses of Scripture could be isolated and made, in all of their continuity, to provide a focus of discourse just as the Mishnah did, Scripture would join the Mishnah in a single statement, cut down and reshaped to conform to the model of the Mishnah. So Scripture now joined the Mishnah in a new union, in mythic language, one whole Torah, or in my language, the Bavli at the end. In so revising Scripture as to recast it into that same discursive and rhetorical framework that defined how and where the Mishnah would serve, the authors—framers of larger-scale units of discourse, ultimate redactors alike—made their unique contribution. Imposing a literary and redactional unity upon documents so remarkably disparate in every respect as the Mishnah and Scripture, the Bavli's authors created something both entirely their own and in no way original to them: Judaism in its final and complete statement, Judaism in conclusion.

It was for good reason that the Bavli has formed the definitive statement of Judaism from the time of its closure to the present day. The excellence of its composition, the mastery and authority of those who everywhere studied it and advocated its law, the sharpness of its exegesis and discussion, the harmonious and proportionate presentation of all details, these virtues of taste and intellect may well have secured for the document its paramount position. The Babylonian Talmud moreover incorporated a far broader selection of antecedent materials than any other document that reaches us out of Judaism in late antiquity, far more, for instance, than the Yerushalmi. This vast selection, moreover, was so organized and put together that systematic accounts of numerous important problems of biblical exegesis, law and theology alike, emerged. Consequently, the Bavli would serve from its closure as both an encyclopedia of knowledge and a summa of the theology and law of Judaism. But what to begin with gained for the Bavli the priority it would enjoy was the comprehensive character, in form and in substance, of its statement, based as it was both on the Scripture's and the Mishnah's redactional framework. No one had done that before; no one had to do it again.

Abbreviations

Af.: Arakhin

ARN.: Abopt deRabbi Nathan

A.Z.: Abodah Zarah

B.: Bavli, Babylonian Talmud

Ber.: Berakhot

Chron.: Chronicles

Deut.: Deuteronomy

Est.: Esther

Est.R.: Esther Rabah

Ex.: Exodus

Ez.: Ezekiel

Gen.: Genesis

Git.: Gittin

Hab.: Habakkuk

Hag.: Hagigah

Hos.: Hosea

Is.: Isaiah

Jer.: Jeremiah

Josh.: Joshua

Ju.: Judges

Ket.: Ketubot

Kgs.: Kings

Lam.R.: Lamentations Rabbati

Lev.: Leviticus

M.: Mishnah

Meg.: Megillah

Num.: Numbers

Prov.: Proverbs

Ps.: Psalms

Qid.: Qiddushin

Qoh.: Qohelet/Ecclesiastes

R.: Rabbah

Sam.: Samuel

San.: Sanhedrin

Shab.: Shabbat

Song R.: Song of Songs Rabbah

Sot.: Sotah

Suk.: Sukkah

T.: Tosefta

Y.: Yerushalmi, Palestinian Talmud

Bibliography

Joseph M. Davis

Introduction

This bibliography presents a list of books and articles that compare the Talmud Bavli and the Talmud Yerushalmi.

Three categories of works, however, have been excluded from the list.
First, commentaries and novellas written within the traditional modes of interpretation are not listed. Second, comparisons of the *Mishnah sheba-Bavli*
and the *Mishnah sheba-Yerushalmi,* the Mishnah texts printed with the Bavli
and Yerushalmi, have likewise been excluded. Third, the bibliography does
not include comparisons of the Aramaic dialects used in the Bavli and
Yerushalmi.

The last three sections of the bibliography include works that do not compare the Bavli and the Yerushalmi per se. Rather, these works provide a context of cultural differences and antagonisms within which the differences between the Bavli and the Yerushalmi can be understood.

Other lacunae in the bibliography are unintentional. The list is not a complete one. It is limited to the holdings of the J.T.S. library, the Brown University library, and the Brandeis University library; it is further limited by my
ignorance of languages.

The sections into which the bibliography is divided are not hard and fast
divisions. For example, studies of the development of the sugya shade off im-
perceptibly into studies of particular passages; studies of history are not always readily distinguished from studies of aggadah, on the one hand, or from
studies of legal history, on the other; the same is true, more or less, of the
other categories. Many items could have been placed equally well in any one
of several categories. I chose the single category that seemed the most
suitable.

Articles published in *Bar Ilan Annual, Cathedra, Dine Israel,* and *Tarbiz*
are written in Hebrew, unless otherwise noted. Their titles, however, are given
in English.

Abbreviations

Bar Ilan	*Annual of Bar Ilan University*
De Vries, *Mehkarim*	B. De Vries, *Mehkarim ba-Sifrut ha-Talmudit,* no. 72
DI	*Dine Israel*
Dor, *Torat*	Z. M. Dor, *Torat Eretz Yisra'el be-Vavel*, no. 102
HUCA	*Hebrew Union College Annual*
JQR	*Jewish Quarterly Review*, new series
MGWJ	*Monatsschrift für Geschichte und Wissenschaft des Judenthums*
PAAJR	*Proceedings of the American Academy for Jewish Research*
TzLY	*Ha-Tzofeh le-Hokhmat Yisra'el*
Weiss, *Mehkarim*	A. Weiss, *Mehkarim ba-Talmud*, no. 88

Bibliography

1. Bokser, Baruch, and David Goodblatt. *The Study of Ancient Judaism: The Palestinian and Babylonian Talmuds.* New York, 1981. Also in *Aufstieg und Niedergang der Römischen Welt* II.19.2 (1979), ed. Wolfgang Haase, pp. 139–336.

Cross-References

2. Ettinger, Mordechai Ze'ev, and Joseph Saul ha-Levi Natansohn. *Mesoret ha-Shas.* Printed in the Vilna; 1922 edition of the Talmud Yerushalmi.
3. Jellin, Aryeh Loeb, *Yefeh 'Einaim.* Printed in the standard (Vilna, 1880–86) edition of the Talmud Bavli.
4. Levin, Joshua Heschel. *Mesoret ha-Shas 'al kol Talmud Bavli mi-Talmud Yerushalmi.* Vilna, 1869. Reprinted in Jerusalem, 1970.

Introductions and General Comparisons

5. Bacher, Wilhelm. "Talmud." In *Jewish Encyclopedia*, 12:pp. 1–26.
6. De Vries, Benjamin. *Mavo Kelali la-Sifrut ha-Talmudit.* Tel Aviv, 1966.
7. Elon, Menahem. *Ha-Mishpat ha-'Ivri: Toledotav, Mekorotav, Ekronotav*, 3:pp. 892–902. Tel Aviv, 1973.
8. Epstein, Jacob Nahum. *Mevo'ot le-Sifrut ha-'Amora'im, Bavli vi-Yrushalmi*, ed. E. Z. Melamed. Jerusalem, 1962.
9. Frankel, Zechariah. *Mavo ha-Yerushalmi.* Breslau, 1870.
10. Gafni, Isaiah. "Ha-Yetzirah ha-Ruhanit-Sifrutit." In *Eretz Yisra'el me-*

Hurban Bayit Sheni ve-'ad ha-Kibush ha-Muslami, ed. Zvi Baras et al., 1:pp. 486–90. Jerusalem, 1982.

11. Ginzberg, Louis. *Perushim ve-Hidushim bi-Yrushalmi: Meyusadim 'al mehkarim be-hishtalshelut ha-halakhah veha-hagadah be-Eretz Yisra'el u-Vavel.* 4 vols. New York, 1941–61. Reprinted in New York, 1971. "Introductory Essay" (in English) is also published in *Jewish Law and Lore* (Philadelphia, 1955), pp. 3–57.

12. Halevy, Isaak. *Dorot ha-Rishonim,* 2:esp. pp. 522–36. Frankfurt am Main, 1901–18. Reprinted in Jerusalem 1967.

13. Krochmal, Abraham. *Yerushalayim ha-Benuyah,* pp. 6–10. Lemberg, 1867.

14. Melamed, Ezra Zion. *Pirkei Mavo la-Sifrut ha-Talmudit.* Jerusalem, 1973.

15. Mielziner, Moses. *Introduction to the Talmud.* 4th ed. New York, 1968.

16. Neusner, Jacob. *Invitation to the Talmud.* New York, 1973.

17. Rabinowitz, Ze'ev Wolf. *Sha'arei Torat Eretz Yisra'el.* Jerusalem, 1940.

18. Rodkinson, Michael. *The History of the Talmud.* New York, 1903.

19. Stern, Tibor. *The Composition of the Talmud: A Complete Analysis of the Relationship between the Babylonian and the Talmud Yerushalmi.* New York, 1959.

20. Tabiov, I. H. "Talmudah shel Bavel ve-Talmudah shel Eretz Yisra'el." *Ha-Tekufah* 1 (1918):pp. 546–61.

21. Weiss, Isaac Hirsch. *Dor Dor ve-Dorshav,* 3:esp. pp. 233–38. Berlin, 1924.

22. Wiesner, Jonas. *Giv'at Yerushalayim.* Vienna, 1871.

Relation of the Talmudim to the Tosefta and Other Tannaitic Literature

23. Albeck, Hanokh. "Die Herkunft des Toseftamaterials." *MGWJ* 69 (1925):pp. 311–28.

24. ———. *Mavo la-Talmudim.* Tel Aviv, 1969.

25. ———. *Mehkarim ba-Beraita ve-Tosefta ve-Yahasan la-Talmud.* Jerusalem, 1944.

26. Avramski, Menahem Ezra. "Ha-Tosefta bi-Dfus." *Kirjath Sepher* 29 (1953–54):pp. 149–61. Bibliography of works on the Tosefta.

27. Cohen, Boaz. *Mishnah and Tosefta: A Comparative Study. Part I: Shabbat.* New York, 1935.

28. De Vries, Benjamin. "The Problem of the Relationship of the Two Talmuds to the Tosefta." *Tarbiz* 28 (1958–59), pp. 158–70. Also in De Vries, *Mehkarim,* pp. 148–60.

29. Dünner, Joseph Hirsch. *Die Theorien ueber Wesen und Ursprung der Tosephtha.* Amsterdam, 1874.

30. Epstein, Jacob Nahum. *Mavo le-Nusah ha-Mishnah*. 2 vols. 2d. ed. Tel Aviv, 1964.

31. ———. *Mevo'ot le-Sifrut ha-Tanna'im: Mishnah, Tosefta, u-Midreshei Halakhah*. Tel Aviv, 1957.

32. Goldberg, Abraham. "The Use of the Tosefta and the *Baraitha* of the School of Samuel by the Babylonian Amora Rava for the Interpretation of the Mishnah." *Tarbiz* 40 (1970–71):pp. 144–57.

33. Levine, Chaim. "Exegesis of the Mishna in the Mechilta de Rashbi and its Relation to Amoraic Teaching." *Bar Ilan* 16–17 (1979):pp. 59–69.

34. Lieberman, Saul. *Tosefta ki-fshutah: A Comprehensive Commentary on the Tosefta*. 8 vols. to date. New York, 1955-.

35. Schwartz, Adolf. *Die Tosifta des Traktates Nesikin: Baba Kamma*. Frankfurt am Main, 1912.

36. Spanier, Arthur. *Die Toseftaperiode in der Tannaitischen Literatur*. Berlin, 1936.

37. Zuckermandel, Moses Samuel. *Tosefta, Mischna, und Boraitha in ihrem Verhältnis zu einander oder paläštinensische und babylonische Halacha: Ein Beitrag zur Kritik und Geschichte der Halacha*. 2 vols. Frankfurt am Main, 1908–9. See also review by Henry Malter, "A Talmudic Problem and Proposed Solutions," *JQR* 2 (1911–2):pp. 75–95.

Interpretation of Particular Passages

38. Burstein, Abraham. "Yoshevei Keranot ve-Yoshevei Keranot ba-Shuk." *Sinai* 42 (1957–58):pp. 243–48.

39. Florsheim, Joel. "Tum'at 'Avodah Zarah u-Meshamshehah." *Sinai* 63 (1968):pp. 219–228.

40. Francus, Israel. "Berurim u-Ve'urim be-Masekhet Ketuvot." *Sinai* 73 (1973):pp. 24–49.

41. ———. "Berurim u-Ve'urim ba-Talmud." *Sinai* 71 (1972):pp. 32–45.

42. ———. "Be'urim u-Verurim ba-Talmud." In *Mehkarim u-Mekorot: Me'asef le-Mada'ei ha-Yehadut*, ed. H. Z. Dimitrovsky, pp. 123–66. New York, 1978.

43. ———. "Be'urim u-Verurim le-Sugyat 'Ahat be-Hayav ve-Ahat be-Moto.'" *Sinai* 89 (1981):pp. 248–55.

44. ———. "Ha-Re'ayon 'Ein lo Shi'ur." *Sinai* 65 (1969):pp. 244–50.

45. ———. "Hora'at ha-Po'al P-R-T bi-Lshon Hakhamim." *Sinai* 74 (1973–74):pp. 178–82.

46. ———. "Mehkarim ba-Harkavah shel Masekhet Betzah shebe-Talmud ha-Bavli uve-Darkhei 'Arikhatah." Ph.D. thesis, Hebrew University, 1961.

47. ———. "The Original Location of Three Talmudic Discussions." *Tarbiz* 38 (1968–69):pp. 338–53.

48. ———. "Mavo." In *Talmud Yerushalmi: Masekhet Betzah 'im perush . . . R. El'azar 'Azkari*, pp. 15–31. New York, 1967.

49. ———. "Textual Reading and Explanation of the Sugya in TB Yoma 82a." *Tarbiz* 43 (1973–74):pp. 34–45.
50. Frankel, Zechariah. *Talmud Yerushalmi: Seder Zera'im 'im Sefer 'Ahavat Tziyon.* Vienna, 1874–75.
51. Friedman, Shamma. "Kidushin be-Milvah." *Sinai* 76 (1974–75):pp. 47–76.
52. ———. "Perek 'Ha-'Ishah Rabah' ba-Bavli." In *Mehkarim u-Mekorot: Me'asef le-Mada'ei ha-Yehadut,* ed. H. Z. Dimitrovsky, pp. 275–441. New York, 1978.
53. Guttmann, Alexander. "Akiba, 'Rescuer of the Torah.'" *HUCA* 17 (1942–3):pp. 395–421.
54. Heinemann, Isaac. "Hekera le-Tinokot." *TzLY* 10 (1926):pp. 129–32.
55. Sperber, Daniel. "Sugya 'Ahat be-Masekhet Horayot." *Sinai* 70 (1971–72):pp. 157–62.
56. Weiss, Abraham. *Diyunim u-Verurim be-Vava Kama.* Jerusalem, 1967.
57. ———. "Ha-Pelugta be-Ferush Milat 'Mav'eh' ba-Mishnah, ba-Bavli, uva-Yerushalmi." *TzLY* 10 (1926):pp. 144–58.
58. ———. "Hatza'at ha-Homer be-Masekhet Kidushin, Mishnah ve-Tosefta, u-Verur ha-Be'ayot ha-Kerukhot be-Ferek 'Ha-Kinyanim." *Horeb* 12 (1956):pp. 70–149.
59. ———. "He'arot 'al Masekhet Shabat Perek Gimel." *Beit Shemu'el* 3 (1939):pp. 146–53.
60. ———. "He'arot la-Bavli vi-Yrushalmi." In *Sefer ha-Yovel li-Khvod Dr. Mordechai Ze'ev Braude,* pp. 123–35. Warsaw, 1931.
61. ———. "He'arot le-Masekhet Berakhot." *Beit Shemu'el* 2 (1938):pp. 97–104.
62. ———. "He'arot le-Masekhet Shevu'ot va-'Avodah Zarah." *Beit Shemu'el* 1 (1937):pp. 25–32.
63. ———. "Kol Kinuyei Nedarim." In *Sefer ha-Zikaron le-Veit ha-Midrash le-Rabanim be-Vienna,* pp. 125–38. Jerusalem, 1946.
64. ———. "Perushim ve-He'arot ba-Mishnah uva-Talmud (He'arot li-Verakhot Perek Vav)." *Horeb* 10 (1948):pp. 1–26; 11 (1951):pp. 83–122; 13 (1958):pp. 122–47; 14–15 (1960):pp. 127–56.
65. ———. "Sugyat ha-Bavli veha-Yerushalmi shele-Mishnat Bava Metzi'a Rosh Perek Vav." In *Essays Presented to Chief Rabbi Israel Brodie on the Occasion of His Seventieth Birthday,* 2:pp. 137–49, Heb. sec. London, 1967.
66. Weiss-Halivni, David. "Be-Karonah shel Tzipori." *Sinai* 55 (1964):pp. 121–26. See also note by Saul Lieberman, pp. 277–78.
67. ———. *Mekorot u-Mesorot.* 4 vols. to date. Tel Aviv, 1968-.

Development of the Sugya

68. Atlas, Samuel. "Ha'ada'at 'Edim ve-Heilakh." In *Abraham Weiss Jubilee Volume*, pp. 73–90, Heb. sec. New York, 1964.

69. ——. "Le-Hitpathut ha-Sugya veha-Halakhah." *HUCA* 17 (1942–43):pp. 1–12, Heb. sec.

70. Bokser, Baruch. "A Minor for Zimmun (Y. Ber. 7:2 11c) and Recensions of Yerushalmi." *AJS Review* 4 (1979):pp. 1–26.

71. Burgansky, Israel. "The Babylonian Talmud Tractate of Sukkah: Its Sources and Methods of Compilation" (in Hebrew). 2 vols. Ph.D. thesis, Bar Ilan University, 1979.

72. De Vries, Benjamin. *Mehkarim ba-Sifrut ha-Talmudit.* Jerusalem, 1968. See nos. 28, 73, 74, 95, 127, 128, 129.

73. ——. "Ve-Havinan Bah." *Tarbiz* 35 (1965–66):pp. 254–68. Also in De Vries, *Mehkarim,* pp. 200–15.

74. ——. "Tzuratan ha-Mekoriyot shel Sugyot Bavliot 'Ahadot." In *Mazkeret: Kovetz Torani le-Zekher . . . ha-Rav Yitzhak Isaac ha-Levi Herzog,* pp. 483–92. Jerusalem, 1962. Also in De Vries, *Mehkarim,* pp. 249–58.

75. Feldblum, Meyer. "The Impact of the 'Anonymous Sugyah' on Halakic Concepts." *PAAJR* 37 (1969):pp. 19–28, Eng. sec.

76. ——. "Professor Abraham Weiss: His Approach and Contribution to Talmudic Scholarship." In *Abraham Weiss Jubilee Volume,* pp. 7–80, Eng. sec. New York, 1964.

77. ——. *Talmudic Law and Literature: Tractate Gittin, a Comparative Study of Mishnah, Tosephta, Babylonian and Palestinian Talmuds, with a general introduction on their composition and evolvement* (in Hebrew). New York, 1969.

78. Fraenkel, Johan. "Ha Gufa Kashya: Internal Contradictions in Talmudic Literature." *Tarbiz* 42 (1973):pp. 266–301.

79. Goldberg, Abraham. "Hitpathut ha-Sugya be-Talmud Bavli u-Mekoroteha." *Tarbiz* 32 (1962–63):pp. 143–52.

80. ——. "Le-Hitpathut ha-Sugya ba-Talmud ha-Bavli." In *Sefer ha-Yovel le-Rabi Hanokh Albeck,* pp. 101–13. Jerusalem, 1963.

81. Hauptman, Judith. "The Evolution of the Talmudic Sugya: A Comprehensive Source-Critical Analysis of Sugyot Containing Braitot Introduced by Tanya Nami Hakhi." Ph.D. thesis, Jewish Theological Seminary, 1982.

82. Klein, Hyman. "Some General Results of the Separation of Gemara from Sebara in the Babylonian Talmud." *Journal of Semitic Studies* 3 (1958):pp. 363–72.

83. Rosenthal, David. *"Pirqa de 'Abbaye* (TB *Rosh Hashana* II)." *Tarbiz* 46 (1976–77):pp. 97–109.

84. Weiss, Abraham. "The Dispute between R. Yehuda and the Tana Kama

in the Mishna B. Kama III:1, Its Parallel in the Tosephta, and the Talmudic Material Relating to It." *Bar Ilan* 9 (1972):pp. 102–25.

85. ———. *Hithavut ha-Talmud bi-Shlemuto.* New York, 1943.

86. ———. *Le-Heker ha-Talmud.* New York, 1956.

87. ———. "Li-Sh'elat Mekorot ha-Sugya." *TzLY* 9 (1925):pp. 177–203. Also in Weiss, *Mehkarim,* pp. 28–55.

88. ———. *Mehkarim ba-Talmud.* Jerusalem, 1975. See nos. 87, 89, 90.

89. ———. "Studien zur Redaktion des babylonischen Talmuds." *MGWJ* 73 (1929):pp. 131–43, 184–211. Also in Weiss, *Mehkarim,* pp. 86–123.

90. ———. "Sugyot shel Keta'im." *TzLY* 9 (1925):pp. 97–116. Also in Weiss, *Mehkarim,* pp. 6–27.

Traditions and the Sources of the Talmudim

91. Aminoah, Noah. *The Redaction of the Tractate Qiddushin in the Babylonian Talmud* (in Hebrew). Tel Aviv, 1977.

92. Bacher, Wilhelm. *Tradition und tradenten in den schulen Palästinas und Babyloniens.* Leipzig, 1914. Reprinted in Berlin, 1966.

93. Bokser, Baruch. "Two Traditions of Samuel: Evaluating Alternative Versions." In *Christianity, Judaism, and Other Greco-Roman Cults: Studies for Morton Smith at Sixty,* ed. J. Neusner, 4:pp. 46–55. Leiden, 1975.

94. De Vries, Benjamin. "Literary Transfer as a Factor in the Development of Talmudic Law." *Bar Ilan* 1 (1963):pp. 156–64.

95. ———. "The Tractate *Me'ila* in the Babylonian Talmud." *Tarbiz* 30 (1960–61):pp. 370–78. Also in De Vries, *Mehkarim,* pp. 230–38.

96. Dor, Zvi Moshe. "Ha-Mekorot ha-Eretz-Yisra'eliyim be-Veit Midrasho shel Rava." *Sinai* 52 (1963):pp. 128–44; 53 (1963):pp. 31–49; 55 (1964) pp. 306–16.

97. ———. "On the Sources of Gittin in the Babylonian Talmud." *Bar Ilan* 4–5 (1967):pp. 89–103.

98. ———. " 'Onshei Mamon u-Malkot bi-Msorot Eretz Yisra'el u-Vavel." *Sinai* 54 (1964):pp. 120–39. Also in Dor, *Torat,* pp. 178–202.

99. ———. "The Original Forms of Some Statements of the First Palestinian Amoraim." *Tarbiz* 26 (1956–57):pp. 357–69. Also in Dor, *Torat,* pp. 116–40.

100. ———. "The Palestinian Sources Appearing in the Tractate Gittin of the Babylonian Talmud." *Bar Ilan* 1 (1963):pp. 120–42. Also in Dor, *Torat* pp. 211–38.

101. ———. "The Palestinian Tradition and the Halakhic Teaching of Rabbi Pappa." In *Fourth World Congress of Jewish Studies,* 1:pp. 157–62, Heb. sec. Jerusalem, 1965.

102. ———. *Torat Eretz Yisra'el be-Vavel.* Tel Aviv, 1971. See nos. 98, 99, 100, 130, 131.
103. Epstein, Abraham. "Ha-Sifra veha-Talmud ha-Bavli, ha-Sifrei veha-Talmud ha-Yerushalmi." In *Mi-Kadmoniot ha-Yehudim,* ed. A. M. Haberman (= *Kit Kitvei Abraham Epstein,* 2), pp. 47–53. Jerusalem, 1957.
104. Goldberg, Abraham. "Palestinian Sources in Babylonian Tradition, as Revealed in a Study of *Perek 'Arvei Pesahim* (Trac. Pesahim Chap. X)." *Tarbiz* 33 (1963–64):pp. 337–48. See also comment by Z.M. Dor, *Tarbiz* 34:p. 98.
105. ———. "Rabbi Ze'ira and Babylonian Custom in Palestine." *Tarbiz* 34 (1966–67):pp. 319–41.
106. Guggenheimer, Hayyim. "Ha-Yerushalmi ke-Vasis la-Bavli." *Sinai* 83 (1978):pp. 191–92.
107. Hanschke, David. "Abbaye and Rava: Two Approaches to the Mishna of the Tannaim." *Tarbiz* 49 (1979–80):pp. 187–93.
108. Segal, Eliezer Lorne. "The Terminology of Case-Citation in the Babylonian Talmud: A Study in the Limitations of Form Criticism." *Journal for the Study of Judaism* 9 (1978):pp. 205–11.

Redaction and Transmission of the Talmudim

109. Albeck, Hanokh. "Studies in the (Babylonian) Talmud." *Tarbiz* 3 (1931–32):pp. 1–14; 9 (1939):pp. 163–78.
110. Aminoah, Noah. "An Inquiry into the Talmudic Tradition of R. Jose Be R. Bun." In *Proceedings of the Eighth World Congress of Jewish Studies* 3:pp. 13–18, Heb. sec. Jerusalem, 1981.
111. ———. "Kit'ei Talmud mi-Sidur Kadum be-Masekhet Rosh Ha-Shanah." In *'Iyunim be-Sifrut Hazal, be-Mikra, uve-Toledot Yisra'el,* ed. Y. D. Gilat et al., pp. 185–97. Ramat Gan, 1982.
112. Arzi, Abraham. "Two Types of Transcription Errors in our Talmudim: *'Ashgara de-Lishna u-Gerara de-Lishna.*" *Bar Ilan* 6 (1968):pp. 117–26.
113. Florsheim, Joel. "La-ʿArikhat ha-Talmud ha-Yerushalmi." *Sinai* 79 (1976):pp. 30–43.
114. Greenwald, Leopold [Yekuti'el]. *Ha-ra'u mesadrei ha-Bavli et ha-Yerushalmi?* New York, 1954.
115. Jacobs, Louis. "Are There Fictitious Baraitot in the Babylonian Talmud?" *HUCA* 42 (1971):pp. 185–96.
116. ———. "The Talmudic Sugya as a Literary Unit: An Analysis of Baba Kamma 2a-3b." *Journal of Jewish Studies* 24 (1973):pp. 119–26.
117. Lieberman, Saul. "Talmudah shel Kisrin, Yerushalmi Masekhet Nezikin." Supplement to *Tarbiz* 2 (1930–31). Reprinted in New York, 1968.
118. Neusner, Jacob, ed. *The Formation of the Babylonian Talmud: Studies*

in the Achievements of Late Nineteenth and Twentieth Century Historical and Literary-Critical Research. Leiden, 1970.

119. Regensberg, Chaim David. " 'Al 'Arikhat ha-Talmudim." In *Gibeath Saul: Essays Contributed in Honor of Rabbi Saul Silver,* pp. 124–38, Chicago, 1935.

120. Rosenthal, David. "On 'Foreign Bodies' in the Babli." *Bar Ilan* 18–19 (1981):pp. 150–69.

121. Tenenblatt, Mordechai. *Ha-Talmud ha-Bavli be-Hithavuto ha-Histori.* Tel Aviv, 1972.

122. Weiss-Halivni, David. "Doubtful Attributions in the Talmud." *PAAJR* 46–47 (1979–80):pp. 67–84, Heb. sec.

Law and Legal History

123. Albeck, Shalom. "The Development of the Concept of Transfer of Debts in the Talmud." *Tarbiz* 26 (1956–57):pp. 262–86.

124. Blidstein, Gerald. "The Sale of Animals to Gentiles in Talmudic Law." *JQR* 61 (1970–71):pp. 188–98.

125. Cohen, Yedidiah. "The Husband's Liability for the Medical Treatment of His Wife according to Jewish Family Law." *DI* 7 (1976):pp. 67–78.

126. ———. "Some Rights and Duties Created by the Death of a Widow: According to Rabbinic Law." *DI* 8 (1977):pp. 171–86.

127. De Vries, Benjamin. "Partial Admission." *Tarbiz* 36 (1966–67):pp. 229–38. Also in De Vries, *Mehkarim,* pp. 275–83.

128. ———. "Kinyan Sudar." *Sinai* 50 (1962):pp. 138–43. Also in De Vries, *Mehkarim,* pp. 165–71.

129. ———. "The Testimony of Witnesses and the Instantaneous Delivery of the Confessed Amount *(heilakh).*" *Tarbiz* 34 (1964–65):pp. 346–50. Also in De Vries, *Mehkarim,* pp. 270–74.

130. Dor, Zvi Moshe. "Kedei Hayav." In *Sefer ha-Yovel le-Rabi Hanokh Albeck,* pp. 152–59. Jerusalem, 1963. Also in Dor, *Torat* pp. 203–10.

131. ———. "Thou Shalt Not Bear False Witness against thy Neighbour." *Bar Ilan* 2 (1964):pp. 107–124. Also in Dor, *Torat* pp. 157–78.

132. Elinson, Eliakim. "Acquisitions for a Limited Time as Interpreted by the Rishonim." *DI* 3 (1972):pp. 147–58.

133. ———. "Ha-Pilagshot ba-Sifrut ha-Talmudit: Ha-'Im Mistamnot Mesorot be-Eretz Yisra'el uve-Vavel?" *Sinai* 73 (1973):pp. 127–36.

134. ———. "Talmudic Restrictions in Divorce: Their Nature and Validity." *DI* 5 (1974):pp. 37–48.

135. Elon, Menahem. "Freedom of Contract Regarding the Law of Surety." In *Fourth World Congress of Jewish Studies,* 1:pp. 197–208, Heb. sec. Jerusalem, 1965.

136. Francus, Israel. "Shitat ha-Bavli veha-Yerushalmi bi-Tfisat Metaltelin li-Gvi'at Ketuvah." *Sinai* 86 (1980):pp. 136–48.

137. Friedman, Shamma. "Hana'ah and Acquisitions in Talmud." *DI* 3 (1972):pp. 115–46.

138. ———. "Lost Objects in the Public Domain according to Talmudic Law." *DI* 6 (1975):pp. 169–76.

139. Gamoran, Hillel. "Talmudic Controls on the Purchase of Futures." *JQR* 54 (1973–74):pp. 50–66.

140. Gartner, Jacob. "Hag Tu be-'Av ba-Talmud ha-Yerushalmi uva-Talmud ha-Bavli." *Sinai* 84 (1978–79):pp. 22–32.

141. Gilat, Yitzhak D. "If You Are Taken Captive, I Will Ransom You and Take You Back as My Wife." *Bar Ilan* 13 (1976):pp. 58–72.

142. ———. "A Rabbinical Court May Decree the Abrogation of a Law of the Torah." *Bar Ilan* 7–8 (1970):pp. 117–32.

143. Goldberg, Abraham. "Shevut ude-Oraita bi-Mlekhet Shabat." *Sinai* 46 (1959–60):pp. 181–89.

144. Goldenberg, Robert. *The Sabbath-Law of Rabbi Meir.* Missoula, Mont., 1978.

145. Gulak, Asher. "Deed of Betrothal and Oral Stipulations in Talmudic Law." *Tarbiz* 3 (1931–32):pp. 361–76.

146. ———. *Le-Heker Toledot ha-Mishpat ha-'Ivri bi-Tkufat ha-Talmud: Dinei Karka'ot.* Jerusalem, 1929.

147. ———. "*Tzon Barzel* in Talmudic Law." *Tarbiz* 3 (1931–32):pp. 134–46.

148. Hakohen, Aviad. "Hilufei Minhagim be-Virkat ha-Geshamim." *Sinai* 92 (1983):pp. 247–54.

149. Heinemann, Joseph. "On the Meaning of Some Mishnayot." *Bar Ilan* 3 (1965):pp. 9–24.

150. Levine, Chaim. "The Development of the Concept of Fire as a Damage of Human Agency." *Bar Ilan* 11 (1973):pp. 26–48.

151. Melamed, Ezra Zion. "Hitpathut Dinei ha-'Ona'ah bi-Mkorot ha-Mishnah veha-Talmud." *Yavneh* 3 (1942):pp. 35–56.

152. Potolsky, Moshe. "The Rabbinic Rule: 'No Laws Are Derived from before Sinai.'" *DI* 6 (1975):pp. 195–230.

153. Shtruzman, Uri. "The Significance of the Overt Market Enactment in Jewish Law." *DI* 9 (1978–80):pp. 7–26.

154. Sperber, Daniel. "*Anachoresis* and *Usucapio.*" *Bar Ilan* 9 (1972):pp. 290–96.

155. Urbach, Ephraim Elimelech. *The Laws Regarding Slavery as a Source for Social History in the Period of the Second Temple, the Mishnah, and the Talmud.* New York, 1979. Also in *Zion* 25 (1960):pp. 141–89; and *Papers of the Institute of Jewish Studies, London* 1 (1964):pp. 1–94.

156. Weinberg, Jehiel Jakob. "Hakirat ha-Mekorot le-Hilkhat 'Idit." In *Sefer ha-Yovel li-Khvod ha-Rav Jakob Freimann,* pp. 171–96, Heb. sec. Berlin, 1937.

157. Weiss, Abraham. "Kinuyin, Yadot, ve-Yadayim she-'ein Mokhihot." In *Sefer ha-Yovel le-Rabi Hanokh Albeck*, pp. 211–37. Jerusalem, 1963.
158. ———. *Sefer ha-Diyun: Mehkarim be-Mishpat ha-Talmud*. New York, 1958.
159. Weiss, Moshe. "On R. Yossi's System of 'The Responsibility of a Man towards Neighbor's Property.'" *Bar Ilan* 12 (1974):pp. 64–107.
160. Zeitlin, Solomon. "*Derelictio* in Tannaitic Jurisprudence." In *Louis Ginzberg Jubilee Volume*, pp. 365–80, Heb. sec. New York, 1945.
161. ———. "Foreword." In Leo Landman, *Jewish Law in the Diaspora: Confrontation and Accommodation*, pp. 11–13. Philadelphia, 1968.
162. ———. "Slavery during the Second Commonwealth and the Tannaitic Period." *JQR* 53 (1962–63):pp. 185–213.
163. Zuckermandel, Moses Samuel. *Zur Halachakritik Aufsätze*. 2 vols. Frankfurt am Main, 1911–13.
164. Zuri [Szezak], Jacob Samuel. *Annulment in Law (Avoidance of Contracts)* (in Hebrew). London, 1935.

History

165. Burstein, Abraham. "Le-Minuyav shel Rabi Natan ha-Bavli le-'Av Beit Din ha-Sanhedrin be-Eretz Yisra'el." *Sinai* 36 (1954):pp. 479–96.
166. Goldberger, Israel. "Ha-Mekorot bi-Dvar 'Aliyat Hillel la-Nesiyut." *TzLY* 10 (1926):pp. 68–76.
167. Goldenberg, Robert. "The Deposition of Rabban Gamaliel II: An Examination of the Sources." *Journal of Jewish Studies* 23 (1972):pp. 167–90. Also in *Persons and Institutions in Early Rabbinic Judaism*, ed. William Scott Green, pp. 9–47 (Missoula, Mont., 1977).
168. Guttmann, Alexander. "Foundations of Rabbinic Judaism." *HUCA* 23 (1950–51) part 1, pp. 453–73.
169. ———. "The Patriarch Judah I: His Birth and His Death." *HUCA* 25 (1954):pp. 239–61.
170. Karlin, A. "Sipurim Historiyim ba-Talmud." *Sinai* 15 (1944):pp. 217–25.
171. Levine, Lee I. *Caesarea under Roman Rule*. Leiden, 1975.
172. ———. "Rabi Simeon bar Yohai, Bones of the Dead, and the Purification of Tiberias: History and Tradition." *Cathedra* 22 (1982):pp. 9–42.
173. Neuhausen, H. Sh. "Tzava'at Rabi." *TzLY* 12 (1928):pp. 324–30.
174. Neusner, Jacob. *Development of a Legend: Studies on the Traditions concerning Yohanan ben Zakkai*. Leiden, 1970.
175. ———. "The Development of the *Merkavah* Tradition." *Journal for the Study of Judaism* 2 (1971):pp. 149–60.
176. ———. *The Rabbinic Traditions about the Pharisees before 70*. 3 vols. Leiden, 1971.

177. Porton, Gary. *The Traditions of Rabbi Ishmael.* 4 vols. Leiden, 1976–82.
178. Safrai, Shmuel. "Ha-Hakhra'ah ke-Veit Hillel be-Yavneh." In *Proceedings of the Seventh World Congress of Jewish Studies* 3:pp. 21–44. Jerusalem, 1977.
179. Sperber, Daniel. "Flight and the Talmudic Law of Usucaption: A Study in the Social History of Third Century Palestine." *Revue internationale des droits de l'antiquité* 19 (1972):pp. 29–42.
180. ———. "On the Transfer of Property from Jew to Non-Jew in Amoraic Palestine (200–400)." *DI* 4 (1973):pp. xvii–xxxiv, Eng. sec.
181. ———. *Roman Palestine 200–400: Money and Prices.* Ramat Gan, 1974.
182. ———. *Roman Palestine 200–400, The Land: Crisis and Change in Agrarian Society as Reflected in Rabbinic Sources.* Ramat Gan, 1978.
183. Vermes, Geza. "Hanina ben Dosa." *Journal of Jewish Studies* 23 (1972):pp. 28–50; 24 (1973):pp. 51–64.
184. Weiss, Abraham. "Li-Sh'elat Tiv ha-Beit Din shel Shiv'im ve-Ehad." In *Louis Ginzberg Jubilee Volume,* pp. 189–216, Heb. sec. New York, 1945.
185. Zahavy, Tzvee. *The Traditions of Eleazar ben Azariah.* Missoula, Mont., 1977.

Aggadah

186. Amir, Abraham. "Gilguleihem shel Sipur u-Vitui." *Sinai* 90 (1982): pp. 260–68.
187. Bacher, Wilhelm. *Die Agada der Palästinensischen Amoräer.* 3 vols. Strassburg, 1892–99.
188. ———. *Die Agada der Babylonischen Amoräer,* Strassburg, 1902.
189. Bokser, Baruch. "Hanina ben Dosa and the Lizard: The Treatment of Charismatic Figures in Rabbinic Literature." In *Proceedings of the Eighth World Congress of Jewish Studies* 3:pp. 1–6., Eng. sec. Jerusalem, 1981.
190. Fraenkel, Jonah. "Kavim Boletim be-Toledot Mesoret ha-Tekst shel Sipurei ha-'Agadah." In *Proceedings of the Seventh World Congress of Jewish Studies* 3:pp.45–69, Heb. sec. Jerusalem, 1977.
191. Greenstone, Julius. "Popular Proverbs in the Jerusalem Talmud." In *Essays in Honour of the Very Rev. Dr. J. H. Hertz,* pp. 187–202. London, 1944.
192. Guttmann, Alexander. "The Significance of Miracles for Talmudic Judaism." *HUCA* 20 (1947):pp. 363–406.
193. Meir, Ofra. "The Acting Characters in the Stories of the Talmud and the Midrash (A Sample)" (in Hebrew). Ph.D. thesis, Hebrew University, 1977.

194. Neusner, Jacob. *Messiah in Context: Israel's History and Destiny in Formative Judaism.* Philadelphia, 1984.
195. Safrai, Shmuel. "Tales of the Sages in the Palestinian Tradition and the Babylonian Talmud." *Scripta Hierosolymitana* 22 (1971):pp. 209–32.
196. Sperber, Daniel. "On Sealing the Abysses." *Journal of Semitic Studies* 11 (1966):pp. 168–74.

Relations of the Palestinian and Babylonian Amoraim

197. Davidowicz, Michael David. "Ha-Nigudim bein Hakhmei Eretz Yisra'el ve-Hakhmei Bavel." *Ha-Soker* 5 (1937–38):pp. 101–9.
198. Gottlieb, Ze'ev Wolf. "Mitzvat Yishuv Eretz Yisra'el be-Aspeklarya shel Rabi Yohanan u-Veit Midrasho bi-Tveria." In *Essays Presented to Chief Rabbi Israel Brodie on the Occasion of his Seventieth Birthday,* 2:pp. 79–106, Heb. sec. London, 1967.
199. Greenwald, Leopold [Yekuti'el]. *Talmud Bavli vi-Yrushalmi.* New York, 1936.
200. Kimelman, Ronald Reuben. "Rabbi Yohanan of Tiberias: Aspects of the Social and Religious History of Third Century Palestine." Ph.D. thesis, Yale University, 1977.
201. Lieberman, Saul. " 'That Is How It Was and That Is How It Shall Be': The Jews of Eretz Israel and World Jewry during Mishnah and Talmud Times." *Cathedra* 17 (1980):pp. 3–10.
202. Rabinovitz, Alexander Siskind. "Ha-Yahas she-bein Hakhmei Eretz Yisra'el u-vein Hakhmei Bavel." *Yerushalayim* 13 (1919):pp. 286–92.
203. Schwartz, Joshua. "Babylonian Commoners in Amoraic Palestine." *Journal of the American Oriental Society* 101 (1981):pp. 317–22.
204. ———. "Tension between Palestinian Scholars and Babylonian Olim in Amoraic Palestine." *Journal of the Study of Judaism* 11 (1980):pp. 78–94.
205. Sperber, Daniel. "The Social and Economic Conditions in Third Century Palestine." *Archiv Orientální* 38 (1970):pp. 1–25.
206. Steinsalz, Adin. "Ha-Kesharim bein Bavel le-Eretz Yisra'el." *Talpiot* 9 (1964):pp. 294–306.

Comparisons of Other Aspects of Palestinian and Babylonian Rabbinic Culture

207. Beer, Moshe. "Kavod u-Vikoret ('al Yahaseihem shel Hazal le-Roshei ha-Golah vela-Nesi'im)." *PAAJR* 38–39 (1972):pp. 47–57, Heb. sec.
208. ———. "Regarding the Sources of the Number of the 36 Zaddiqim." *Bar Ilan* 1 (1963):pp. 172–76.
209. ———. *Roshut ha-Golah be-Vavel bi-Ymei ha-Mishnah veha-Talmud.* Tel Aviv, 1970.

210. Heinemann, Joseph. "The Work of My Hands Is Being Drowned in the Sea . . ." *Bar Ilan* 7–8 (1970):pp. 80–84.
211. ———. "Yahasam shel Hakhmei Bavel la-'Agada." *Agadot ve-Toledoteihen,* pp. 163–80. Jerusalem, 1974.
212. Heschel, Abraham. "Mavo." In *Torah min ha-Shamayim be-'Aspeklaryah shel ha-Dorot,* 1:pp. xvi–xx. New York, 1962.
213. Jacobs, Louis. "The Economic Conditions of the Jews in Babylon in Talmudic Times Compared with Palestine." *Journal of Semitic Studies* 2 (1958):pp. 349–59.
214. Schwartz, Joshua. "Southern Judaea and Babylonia." *JQR* 72 (1982): pp. 188–97.
215. Tenenblatt, Mordechai. *Perakim Hadashim le-Toledot Eretz Yisra'el u-Vavel bi-Tkufat ha-Talmud.* Tel Aviv, 1966.
216. Zuri [Szezak], Jacob Samuel. *Toledot Darkhei ha-Limud bi-Yshivot Darom, Galil, Sura, ve-Neherde'a.* Jerusalem, 1914.

Sefer ha-Hilukim she-bein 'Anshei Mizrah u-Venei Eretz Yisra'el

217. Ephrati, Jacob Eliahu. *Tekufat ha-Savora'im ve-Sifrutah be-Vavel uve-Eretz Yisra'el.* Petah Tikvah, 1973.
218. Finkelstein, Louis. "The Persistence of Rejected Customs in Palestine." *JQR* 29 (1938–39):pp. 179–86.
219. Lewin, Benjamin Manasseh. *'Otzar Hiluf Minhagim bein Benei Eretz Yisra'el u-vein Benei Bavel.* Jerusalem, 1942. Also in *Sinai* 1 (1937): pp. 116–31, 249–59, 351–60, 489–97; 2 (1938):pp. 109–15, 251–56, 423–29; 3 (1939):pp. 47–54, 193–200, 432–39; 4 (1939):pp. 140–45, 259–64, 386–91; 10 (1942):pp. 161–68; 11 (1942):pp. 1–8. Partially reprinted in 1947, with additional notes by Saul Lieberman.
220. Margulies [Margaliot], Mordechai. *Ha-Hilukim she-bein 'Anshei Mizrah u-Venei Eretz Yisra'el.* Jerusalem, 1937.
221. ———. *Hilkhot Eretz Yisra'el min ha-Genizah,* ed. Israel Ta-Shema and Jehuda Feliks. Jerusalem, 1973.
222. ———. "'Mo'adim ve-Tzomot be-Eretz Yisra'el uve-Vavel bi-Tkufat ha-Ge'onim." *Areset* 1 (1944):pp. 204–16.
223. Müller, Joel ha-Kohen. *Hiluf Minhagim bein Benei Bavel li-Vnei Eretz Yisra'el.* Vienna, 1878.
224. Revel, Bernard [Dov]. "Ha-Hilufim bein Benei Bavel u-vein Benei Eretz Yisra'el u-Mekorot ha-Halakhah shel ha-Kara'im." *Horeb* 1 (1934):pp. 1–20.

Index of Biblical and Talmudic References

Arthur W. Woodman

Bible

1 Chronicles
5:1, 32

2 Chronicles
17:9, 35

Daniel
9:17, 31

Deuteronomy
5:4–5, 219
9:10, 218, 220
33:6, 40
76:13, 60–61, 63, 65

Ecclesiastes
1:10, 220
1:11, 219
12:13, 39

Esther
2:2, 113

Exodus
9:20, 112
15:17, 117
19:16, 39
19:19, 39
24:12, 27
33:14, 32
34:27, 218, 220

Genesis
2:6, 60, 63
15:8, 31
19:27, 36
22:20–21, 112
25:33, 32

27:12, 118
27:36, 32
27:41, 32
29:35, 32
34:7, 112
37:21, 32

Habakkuk
1:13, 34
3:9, 118

Hosea
5:13, 117
6:3, 36
8:12, 218
9:1, 112
11:10, 37

Isaiah
3:14, 39
5:13, 118
27:11, 117
49:10, 117
50:2, 36
65:11, 118

Jeremiah
10:15, 118
31:27, 107
33:11, 38–39

Job
1:1, 109
1:8, 112
1:15, 113
1:17, 113
1:20, 113
2:10, 112

15:17–18, 112
16:11, 112
20:21, 118
20:26, 118
27:12, 112
42:15, 113

Joel
3:5, 118

Judges
13:24, 108
13:25, 108
14:4, 107
16:28, 108
16:31, 108

1 Kings
18:36–37, 38

2 Kings
3:11, 35

Leviticus
11:36, 217
23:40, 62
23:43, 61

Nehemiah
8:15, 62

Numbers
16:33, 40

Proverbs
3:34, 108
12:21, 34

General Index

Arthur W. Woodman